Apple Pro Training Series

Logic Pro 9 and Logic Express 9

David Nahmani

Apple
Certified

Apple Pro Training Series: Logic Pro 9 and Logic Express 9
David Nahmani
Copyright © 2010 by David Nahmani

Published by Peachpit Press. For information on Peachpit Press books, contact:

Peachpit Press
1249 Eighth Street
Berkeley, CA 94710
(510) 524-2178
Fax: (510) 524-2221
www.peachpit.com
To report errors, please send a note to errata@peachpit.com.
Peachpit Press is a division of Pearson Education.

Apple Series Editor: Serena Herr
Editor: Bob Lindstrom
Production Coordinator: Kim Wimpsett, Happenstance Type-O-Rama
Technical Editor: Robert Brock
Copy Editor: Elissa Rabellino
Technical Reviewers: Josh Hinden, Chris Colatos
Compositor: Craig Johnson, Happenstance Type-O-Rama
Indexer: Jack Lewis
Media Producer: Eric Geoffroy
Cover Illustration: Kent Oberheu
Cover Production: Happenstance Type-O-Rama

Acknowledgments My deepest gratitude to the artists and producers who agreed to provide their Logic sessions for this book: Blumpy and Joe Hedges for the song "Mitral Valve Prolapse," Klayton from Celldweller for his remix "LVL-Home," Myron for his song "Darkside," and Alessandro Cortini from Modwheelmood for their song "Sunday Morning."

Contents at a Glance

Table of Contents

Getting Started

Welcome to the official Apple Pro Training Series course for Logic Pro 9 and Logic Express 9. This book is a comprehensive introduction to professional audio production with Logic Studio. It uses real-world music and hands-on exercises to teach you how to record, arrange, mix, produce, and polish audio and MIDI files in a professional workflow. So let's get started!

The Methodology

This book takes a hands-on approach to learning the software, so you'll be working through the project files and media on the accompanying DVD. It's divided into projects that methodically introduce the interface elements and ways of working with them, building progressively until you can comfortably grasp the entire application and its standard workflows.

Each lesson in this book is self-contained, so you can jump to any lesson at any time. However, each lesson is designed to support the concepts learned in the preceding lesson, and newcomers to audio production should go through the book from start to finish. The first seven lessons, in particular, teach basic concepts and are best completed in order.

Course Structure

The book is designed to guide you through the music production process as it teaches Logic. The lessons are organized into two sections:

Building a Song: Lessons 1–7

In this section, you'll learn the fundamentals of building a song. Lesson 1 starts you out with an overview of the entire process. You'll get familiar with the interface and the various ways to navigate a project while building a song from scratch using Apple Loops, and then arranging, mixing, and exporting the song to an MP3 file.

In each of the following lessons, you'll focus on a single topic in detail. You'll start by learning how to come up with the building blocks of your musical project: recording, editing, and programming both audio and MIDI files. Finally, you'll manipulate the project tempo, stretch audio files, and apply time and pitch effects.

Arranging and Mixing: Lessons 8–11

In Lessons 8–10, you'll arrange and mix audio and MIDI files into a final project: adding and deleting sections, muting elements, eliminating noise, adjusting levels, panning, EQing, adding reverb, and automating the mix. You'll also learn how to use hardware control surfaces to manipulate various parameters.

Lesson 11 concludes your exploration of Logic by describing useful troubleshooting techniques that can improve your Logic system's reliability and efficiency. You'll learn effective backup procedures, how to resolve audio and MIDI routing problems, and ways to optimize your hardware. Appendix A covers how to use external MIDI devices, and Appendix B lists a wealth of useful keyboard shortcuts.

Using the DVD Book Files

The *Apple Pro Training Series: Logic Pro 9 and Logic Express 9* DVD (included with the book) contains the project files you will use for each lesson, as well as media files that contain the audio and video content you will need for each exercise. After you transfer the files to your hard disk, each lesson will instruct you in the use of the project and media files.

Installing Logic

The exercises in this book require that you install Logic Studio or Logic Express along with the default content pre-selected in the installer. To install Logic Studio or Logic Express, insert the first installation DVD in your computer, double-click the installer, and follow the installer's instructions to complete the installation.

> **NOTE ▸** If you have already installed Logic Studio but did not install some of the content, you can run the installer again and choose to install only the Logic Studio Content.

Using Default Preferences and the U.S. Key Command Preset

All the instructions and descriptions in this book assume that you are using the default set of preferences (unless instructed to change them) and the U.S. key command preset. If you have changed some of your preferences or have not selected the factory U.S. key command preset, you may not get the same results described in the exercises. To make sure you can follow along with this book, it's best to revert to the initial set of Logic preferences and choose the U.S. shortcut preset before you start the lessons. Keep in mind that when you initialize your preferences, you will lose your custom settings, and later you may want to reset your favorite preferences manually.

1   From the main menu bar, choose Logic Pro > Preferences > Initialize All Except Key Commands.

A confirmation message pops up.

LOGIC EXPRESS ▶ When instructed to choose an item from the Logic Pro menu, choose the same item from the Logic Express menu.

2   Click Initialize.

Your preferences are initialized. To choose your key commands preset, you need to open the Key Commands window.

3   In the main menu bar, choose Logic Pro > Preferences > Key Commands.

The Key Commands window opens.

4   Click the Options pop-up menu and choose Presets > U.S.

5   Close the Key Commands window.

Screen Resolution

If you are using a small screen resolution, some of the project files may appear different on your screen than they do in the book. When you open a project, if you can't see the whole Arrange window, move the window until you can see the three window controls at the left of the title bar, and click the zoom button (the third button from the left) to make the window fit the screen.

When using a small screen resolution, you may also have to zoom or scroll more often than instructed in the book to perform some of the exercise steps. In some cases, you may have to temporarily resize or close an area of the Arrange window to perform an action in another area.

Installing the Logic Lesson Files

On the DVD, you'll find a folder titled Logic 9 Files, which contains three subfolders: Lessons, Media, and Apple Loops for Logic Express Users. The first two folders contain the lessons and media files for this course. (See the section "Instruction for Logic Express Users" for an explanation of the third folder.) Make sure you keep these two folders together in the Logic 9 Files folder on your hard disk. If you do so, Logic should be able to maintain the original links between the lessons and media files.

1   Insert the *Logic Pro 9 and Logic Express 9* DVD into your DVD drive.

2 Drag the Logic 9 Files folder from the DVD to your desktop to copy it. The Media folder contains about 3 GB of media.

3 Wait for the "Copy" Progress indicator to close, and eject the DVD to make sure that you don't work with the files on the DVD, but with the files you copied on your desktop.

Each lesson will explain which files to open for that lesson's exercises.

Instructions for Logic Express Users

If you're using Logic Express 9, most of the instructions in this book are exactly the same as those for Logic Pro 9. When there are differences, you'll find a note in the exercises addressed specifically to Logic Express users. Keep in mind that Logic Express doesn't come with the same instruments, effects, and sound library as Logic Studio, and sometimes your screen may look different from the pictures in this book (for example, you may see different settings in the Library, different Apple Loops in the Loop Browser, and different names on tracks and channel strips).

To install files from the *Logic Pro 9 and Logic Express 9* DVD, follow the instructions in the previous section and then install the additional Apple Loops as explained in the steps below.

> **LOGIC EXPRESS ▶** The additional Apple Loops for Logic Express Users were taken from the Remix Tools, Rhythm Section, and World Music Jam Packs, which come standard with Logic Studio. The loop Trip Hop Jungle Beat 01 was modified to use a GarageBand instrument available to Logic Express users and sounds different from the original Trip Hop Jungle Beat 01 included in the Remix Tools Jam Pack.

1 Open Logic Express.

The Templates dialog opens (if you have used Logic Express before, and a Logic project automatically opens, skip to step 4).

2 Click the Empty Project template.

An empty template opens, and a New Tracks dialog comes down from the Arrange window's title bar. Don't worry about the settings in that dialog; you just need to create at least one track (of any kind) to continue.

3   In the New Tracks dialog, click Create.

The dialog disappears and a track is created.

4   From the main menu bar, choose Window > Loop Browser.

The Loop Browser opens.

5   Close the main Arrange window underneath, and keep only the Loop Browser open so that you can see your desktop.

You may need to move the Loop Browser aside to see the Logic 9 Files folder on your desktop.

6   Double-click the Logic 9 Files folder on your desktop, and double-click Apple Loops for Logic Express Users.

You should see a folder named "Drag to Loop Browser."

7   Drag the folder "Drag to Loop Browser" onto the Loop Browser window.

A green + (plus) sign appears at the mouse pointer, indicating that you can release the mouse button to install the Apple Loops.

8 In the "Adding Loops to the Loop Browser" dialog, click "Move to Loops Folder" to install the Apple Loops.

System Requirements

Before using *Apple Pro Training Series: Logic Pro 8 and Logic Express 9*, you should have a working knowledge of your Macintosh and the Mac OS X operating system. Make sure that you know how to use the mouse and standard menus and commands, and also how to open, save, and close files. If you need to review these techniques, see the printed or online documentation included with your system.

▸ Mac computer with an Intel processor

  1 GB of RAM (2 GB or more highly recommended)

  Display with 1280 x 800 or higher resolution

  Mac OS X v10.5.7 or later

  QuickTime 7.6 or later

  DVD drive for installation

▸ USB musical keyboard (or suitable MIDI keyboard and interface) to play software instruments

▸ Low-latency multi-I/O audio interface highly recommended for audio recording

About the Apple Pro Training Series

Apple Pro Training Series: Logic Pro 9 and Logic Express 9 is both a self-paced learning tool and the official curriculum of the Apple Pro Training and Certification Program. Developed by experts in the field and certified by Apple, the series is used by Apple Authorized Training Centers worldwide and offers complete training in all Apple Pro products. The lessons are designed to let you learn at your own pace. Each lesson concludes with review questions and answers summarizing what you've learned, which can be used to help you prepare for the Apple Pro Certification Exam.

For a complete list of Apple Pro Training Series books, see the ad at the back of this book or visit www.peachpit.com/apts.

Apple Pro Certification Program

The Apple Pro Training and Certification Program is designed to keep you at the forefront of Apple's digital media technology while giving you a competitive edge in today's ever-changing job market. Whether you're an editor, graphic designer, sound designer, special-effects artist, or teacher, these training tools are meant to help you expand your skills.

Upon completing the course material in this book, you can become a certified Apple Pro by taking the certification exam at an Apple Authorized Training Center. Successful certification as an Apple Pro gives you official recognition of your knowledge of Apple's professional applications while allowing you to market yourself to employers and clients as a skilled, pro-level user of Apple products.

For those who prefer to learn in an instructor-led setting, Apple offers training courses at Apple Authorized Training Centers worldwide. These courses, which use the Apple Pro Training Series books as their curriculum, are taught by Apple Certified Trainers and balance concepts and lectures with hands-on labs and exercises. Apple Authorized Training Centers have been carefully selected and have met Apple's highest standards in all areas, including facilities, instructors, course delivery, and infrastructure. The goal of the program is to offer Apple customers, from beginners to the most seasoned professionals, the highest-quality training experience.

For more information, please see the ad at the back of this book, or to find an Authorized Training Center near you, go to training.apple.com.

Resources

Apple Pro Training Series: Logic Pro 9 and Logic Express 9 is not intended as a comprehensive reference manual, nor does it replace the documentation that comes with the application. For comprehensive information about program features, refer to these resources:

▶ The *Logic Pro 9 User Manual* and the *Logic Express 9 User Manual.* Accessed through the Logic Help menu, the *User Manual* contains a complete description of all features. The other documents available in the Logic Help menu can be valuable resources as well.

▶ Apple's website: www.apple.com.

▶ Logic Pro Help's website, an online community of Logic users moderated by the author of this book, David Nahmani: www.logicprohelp.com.

Building a Song

1

Time	This lesson takes approximately 120 minutes to complete.
Goals	Browse, preview, and use loops
	Edit regions and create an arrangement
	Navigate and zoom in the Arrange area
	Use effect and software instrument plug-ins
	Mix down and export to MP3

Make Music with Logic Now!

Let's get into the heart of the matter and start producing music immediately. In this lesson, you will go straight to the fun part of creating music with Logic 9—producing a grooving trip-hop song using loops—while gaining a global understanding of how you interact with the application and its library of loops, instruments, and effect plug-ins.

You will take an entire Logic project from start to finish. You will open an empty Logic template and build the song from scratch, using the Loop Browser to preview and add loops. Then you'll edit regions to build an arrangement, add effect plug-ins, mix, and export your song.

Opening Logic

You can open Logic by double-clicking the Logic icon in the application folder, double-clicking a Logic project file, or clicking the Logic icon in your Dock. To get started, you will add Logic to the Dock, making it easy to access. You will then open it and open an existing song file.

1   In the Finder, choose Go > Applications (or press Shift-Command-A).

The Applications folder opens in a Finder window.

2   Drag the Logic application icon to your Dock.

TIP You can type the first few letters of an application name to quickly select it, then use the arrows to select adjacent applications. You can then press Command–Down Arrow to open the selected application.

3   In your Dock, click the Logic icon.

Logic starts, you may see a Registration dialog, and after a moment the Templates dialog opens.

NOTE ▶ If you've already used Logic, the last project you worked on automatically opens when you open Logic. In the main menu bar, choose File > Close Project to close that project, and then choose File > New to open the Templates dialog.

The left column displays several folders containing collections of templates. The first three collections—Explore, Compose, and Produce—contain factory templates installed with Logic.

The Empty Project template is available in all the collections, and it is the one you are going to use for this exercise.

4   Click Empty Project.

An empty template opens, and the New Tracks dialog comes down from the Arrange window's title bar. A Logic project always needs to have at least one track. For this exercise, the first track you will need is a software instrument track.

5   Keep Number set to 1, select Software Instrument, and make sure Open Library is selected.

6   Click Create.

A software instrument track is created, and the Media area opens on the right of the Arrange window, displaying the software instrument Library.

Until you manually save the project to a hard disk, it lives only in the computer's RAM, making it vulnerable to a power failure, a computer freeze or crash, or even a loss of notebook battery power. It is extremely important to regularly save your project as you progress.

7   Choose File > Save (or press Command-S).

Since this is the first time you're saving your project, a Save dialog opens. Anytime you save a file on a computer, you have to provide the following:

▶ A filename

▶ A location on the hard disk where you want to save the file

8   In the Save As field, type your project name, *My New Day*. From the Where pop-up menu, choose Desktop (or press Command-D).

9   Click Save (or press Return).

NOTE ▶ If your keyboard has a numeric keypad, you can choose to press Enter instead of Return to confirm a dialog or after entering a value in a parameter field.

Note that the new project name is now on the Arrange window's title bar.

By opening an empty template, creating a software instrument track, and saving the project, you're already on your way with your Logic project.

When you open an empty template, Logic opens the Arrange window, which will be your main work area. In the next section, you will examine the Arrange window and its working areas.

Exploring the Interface

As you work in Logic, you will spend most of your time in the Arrange window. The Arrange window has six areas. Aside from the main Arrange area, each area can be opened and closed, giving you quick access to most of the features you need.

Let's now open the Editing area.

1   Click the Mixer button at the bottom of the Arrange window.

The Mixer is displayed in the Editing area, below the Arrange area.

NOTE ▶ To resize the Editing Area, position the pointer between the Arrange area and the Editing area, and drag the Resize pointer up or down.

Resize pointer

2   Examine the areas of the Logic interface.

The areas of the Arrange window are as follows:

▶   Arrange area

▶   Editing area

▶   Toolbar

▶   Transport bar

▶   Inspector

▶   Media, Lists, or Notes area

Notice that one of the areas has a white frame around it. The white focus frame identifies the area that has key focus. When the same key command can be used in different areas, the area that has key focus responds. You can click the title bar or background of an area to give it key focus.

TIP ▶ You can also press Tab and Shift-Tab to cycle the key focus forward and backward through the Arrange window areas.

Inspector · Toolbar · Arrange area · Media, Lists, or Notes area

White focus frame indicates key focus · Transport bar · Editing area

Arrange Area The Arrange area is where you build a song by arranging audio and MIDI regions on the tracks located below the Bar ruler.

Editing Area The editing area can display the Mixer or various editors that let you edit the contents of MIDI or audio regions.

Toolbar The customizable Toolbar provides quick one-button access to the features and settings you use the most.

Transport Bar The customizable Transport bar displays transport buttons (Play, Record, Forward, Rewind, and others), information displays (indicating the playhead position, tempo, time signature, and so on), and mode buttons (such as Cycle Mode and Metronome).

Inspector The Inspector includes a contextual set of parameters. Its contents automatically update depending on the area in key focus, the selected region, and the selected track.

Media, Lists, or Notes Area The Media, Lists, or Notes area displays media files (such as audio files and plug-in settings), lists of events (such as MIDI events and tempo changes), Project notes, or Track notes.

3   Click the Mixer button to close the Mixer.

Starting a Project with Apple Loops

In a moment, you'll learn more about navigating a project in the Logic interface, but you first need to fill out your project a bit. Using loops can be a great way to start. For the songwriter, loops can quickly provide inspiring rhythmic support, allowing you to focus on the chords and the melody. For the producer, they are a large resource of musical bits that can be layered with your tracks to add texture and interest.

The Apple Loops provided with Logic include professional recordings of top-shelf musicians along with software instrument settings designed by major sound designers. Since they are royalty free, you can use them for professional projects at no charge. In fact, as you become more familiar with Logic's collection of Apple Loops, don't be surprised if you start recognizing some of them in major movies or in platinum-selling hit songs!

LOGIC EXPRESS ▶ If you haven't installed the Apple Loops from this book's DVD, be sure to install them before going further by following the steps in "Getting Started."

Browsing and Previewing Loops

To start building a song, you need to preview loops and decide which ones to use. The Loop Browser is the perfect tool for the job. It allows you to browse loops by instrument, genre, mood, and other attributes.

1   At the top of the Media area, click the Loops tab.

The Loop Browser opens.

2   In the Loop Browser, click the All Drums category button.

3   In the search field, enter *Trip Hop*, and press Return.

The bottom part of the Loop Browser displays the Search Results list: all the drum loops that contain the text *Trip Hop* in their names. The first loop at the top of the Search Results list should be named **Trip Hop 70s Room Beat**.

LOGIC EXPRESS ▶ Only one loop, Trip Hop Jungle Beat 01, will show in the Search Results list.

4   In the Search Results list, click the first loop.

Search Results list

The loop's note icon turns into a speaker, and you can hear the loop. The loop automatically plays at your project's tempo. Logic's default tempo for a new project is 120 bpm (beats per minute), which is way too fast for trip-hop! That explains why that loop's groove doesn't sound quite right. Now is a good time to adjust your song's tempo.

You can adjust any setting in the Transport bar display fields by dragging numbers up and down, or by double-clicking a value and entering a new one.

5   While the loop is playing, look at the Tempo display in the Transport bar. The default tempo is 120 bpm. Drag down the tempo and listen as your loop gets slower.

6   Drag the tempo digits to set your tempo to *70.0000* (bpm). Now it sounds like trip-hop!

Tempo display

TIP ▶ The tempo adjusts by whole increments of the digit you drag. Drag one of the digits on the right of the decimal point when you need more precision.

Now you can try directly entering a new tempo.

7   Double-click the Tempo display.

A text field appears.

8   In the text field, enter *73*, and press Return.

The tempo is set to 73 bpm.

9   In the Loop Browser, click the next loop (or press the Down Arrow).

The Loop Browser starts playing the next loop. You can press the Up Arrow and Down Arrow keys to listen to more loops until you find something you like.

LOGIC EXPRESS ▶ Since your system has only one loop with *Trip Hop* in its name, the Search List's selection won't advance and you won't hear any difference.

10 Click the currently playing loop.

The loop stops playing. Since you're about to drag loops into the Arrange area to build a song, you can close the Mixer to increase your workspace.

11 At the bottom of the Mixer, click the Mixer button.

The Mixer closes.

12 In the Loop Browser, use the scroll bar to scroll down through the alphabetical list of loops and click **Trip Hop Jungle Beat 01.**

That's a nice one! Let's use it for the song.

13 Drag the loop onto the Inst 1 track in the Arrange area, between the bar 1 and bar 2 grid lines.

The Inspector (the left area of the Arrange window) displays two channel strips: the selected Arrange track channel strip on the left and the output channel strip on the right. Logic automatically loads the necessary channel strip setting (the entire configuration of software instrument and effect plug-ins and their settings) to the selected Arrange track channel strip and places the MIDI region containing the drum pattern on the track. The region snaps to the beginning of bar 1.

An abbreviation of the channel strip setting name (2-Step Remix Overdrive) is displayed in the Channel Strip Settings menu. The track header displays the track icon and track name.

LOGIC EXPRESS ▶ The channel strip setting name is *Dance Kit.*

MORE INFO ▶ In the Loop Browser, some loops have a blue waveform icon, while others have a green note icon. Blue loops are audio loops only: They can be used only as audio regions on audio tracks. Green loops are audio loops that also contain the MIDI region and the channel strip settings used to produce them. They can be used as audio regions on audio tracks (like blue loops) or as MIDI regions on software instrument tracks. For more information, see Lesson 7, "Manipulating Tempo and Time Stretching."

Selected Arrange track channel strip

Now you have a drum groove that will be the foundation of your song. Later, you will select more loops that match the feel and style of those drums, so you can keep building the arrangement. Now, let's learn how to find your way around your project.

Navigating the Project

One of the big advantages to producing music with a computer is that the whole song is laid out right before your eyes. This makes it extremely easy to jump to a certain part of the song, start playback, go back to the beginning, or continuously repeat a section.

Logic offers many ways to navigate a song. In the next two exercises, you will learn the Transport buttons and their keyboard commands; and you will learn how to continuously repeat a section of the project, which will allow you to keep the drum loop playing as you preview more loops.

Using Transport Buttons and Key Commands

When producing music, time is of the essence. Many tasks are repetitive, and you will find yourself playing, stopping, and positioning the playhead every few seconds. Minimizing the time it takes you to perform those basic operations will greatly improve your work-flow and save valuable time.

While it may seem easier at first to click buttons with the mouse, using key command shortcuts can really speed up your workflow. Try to memorize at least the basic set of key commands corresponding to the transport buttons in the Transport bar.

> **NOTE** ▶ The key commands used throughout this book are from the U.S. preset. Before you proceed any further, make sure you are using the U.S. preset. Choose Logic Pro > Preferences > Key commands, and in the Key Command window, choose Options > Preset > U.S.

Let's tour the Transport buttons on the left of the Transport bar and learn the basic navigation key commands.

Navigation Key Commands

Function	Key Command
Play or Stop	Spacebar
Rewind	<
Forward	>
Fast Rewind	Shift-<
Fast Forward	Shift->
Go to Beginning or Stop	Return
Play from Selection	Shift-Enter
Record	R

NOTE ▶ If your keyboard does not have an Enter key, you can press the function key (fn) and the Return key at the same time. So, to use the "Play from Selection" key command, press Shift-fn-Return

1   Click the Play button.

The project starts playing, and you can hear the drum loop.

2   Click the Stop button.

The project stops. Before using Key Commands in the Arrange area, you have to make sure the Arrange area has key focus.

3   Click the background of the Arrange area to give it key focus.

4   Press Return.

The playhead returns to the beginning of the project.

5   Press the Spacebar.

The project starts playing.

6   Press the Spacebar again.

The project stops playing.

7   Click the background of the Arrange area.

The Trip Hop Jungle Beat region is deselected. Clicking in the background of the Arrange area deselects all regions.

Desclected region

8   Click the Trip Hop Jungle Beat region.

Selected region

The name of the region is highlighted, displayed in white letters over a black background, indicating that the region is selected. Notice the difference between the way Logic displays the region name when it is deselected and when it is selected.

9   Click the "Play from Selection" button (or press Shift-Enter).

The playhead jumps to the beginning of the selection (the Trip Hop Jungle Beat 01 region) and playback starts.

10   Click the Forward button a few times (or press >, the right angle bracket).

As the project continues to play, the playhead jumps to the next bar each time you click the Forward button or each time you press >.

11   Press the Spacebar.

The project stops playing.

12 Click the Rewind button a few times (or press <, the left angle bracket).

The playhead jumps to the previous bar each time you click the Rewind button or each time you press <.

Continuously Repeating a Section

You may often need to focus on a section of the arrangement and work on the section while it repeats over and over. In this exercise, you will turn on Cycle mode while adjusting the cycle area to match the drums region, and continuously repeat that section as you preview and add more loops.

In the Bar ruler at the top of the Arrange area, you can see a rectangle in a lighter shade of gray, spanning bars 1 through 4. That rectangle indicates the positions of the left and right locators, which are the boundaries of the cycle area when the Cycle mode is on. The cycle area allows you to select a part of the song you want to continuously repeat.

1 Select the Trip Hop Jungle Beat 01 region if it is not already selected.

2 In the Toolbar, click the Set Locators button.

The cycle area turns green, indicating that Cycle mode is on, and it matches the position and length of the selected region.

3 Press the Spacebar to start playback.

Logic starts cycling over the first two bars, allowing you to hear your drums loop as you preview other loops.

4 While Logic is cycling through the drumbeat, at the upper left of the Loop Browser, click the Reset button.

The music-category buttons and search field are reset, and the Search Results list at the bottom is emptied.

5   Click the Bass button, enter *Bright Tone Bass* in the search field, and press Return.

6   Click the first loop in the Search Results list.

You can hear the bass loop while the drums loop is playing. The bass loop plays in time with the drums, at the project's tempo. You can press the Down Arrow to hear the other loops.

7   If necessary, adjust the volume of the loop you are previewing by dragging the volume slider at the bottom of the Loop Browser.

8   Drag **Bright Tone Bass 03** below the drums track, in bar 1.

Logic automatically creates a new audio track, and the blue loop appears as an audio region.

9   Press Command-S to save your project.

To continue the song, use the Loop Browser buttons and search field to find the following loops, and drag each one below the last track in the Arrange area, in bar 1. Remember to click the Reset button before each new search.

▶   **Deep Electric Piano 05** (click the Elec Piano button).

▶   **Orchestra Strings 03** (click both the Orchestral and Strings buttons).

▶   **Wild Slide Distortion** (enter *Wild* in the search field).

10   Click the background of the Arrange area to give it key focus.

11   Press Return to stop playback, and press Return again to go to the beginning.

12   In the Bar ruler, click the Cycle area to turn off Cycle mode.

Your Arrange area now has five tracks: drums, bass, piano, strings, and guitar.

The green regions (drums and piano) are MIDI regions on software instrument tracks, and the blue regions (bass, strings, and guitar) are audio regions on audio tracks.

Now that you have chosen the Apple Loops you will use, you are ready to start building the song.

Building an Arrangement

In Logic, you build projects by arranging regions on tracks, positioned below the Bar ruler. You need to determine where a region starts, how many times it is looped, and where it stops. When editing regions in the Arrange area, the same techniques apply to both MIDI and audio regions.

Before you start building the arrangement, let's make sure you understand two fundamental concepts: saving the project at regular intervals, and being able to undo the most recent actions.

Saving Your Work and Undoing Actions

Accidents do happen. While some of these will turn out to be happy events and improve your composition, at other times they turn out to be outright mistakes. It is therefore a good idea to save your song after every couple of steps. Remember that the key command to save your file is Command-S. Press it often!

On the other hand, don't be afraid to experiment and to make mistakes. It is easy to undo your last action by choosing Edit > Undo Action (or pressing Command-Z). You can press that key command several times to retrace the steps you most recently performed. By default, Logic can undo the previous 30 steps.

Command-S (Save) and Command-Z (Undo) will quickly become your two new best friends, so commit them to memory now!

Looping and Positioning Regions

The first step in building your arrangement is to decide where each instrument should enter. By introducing instruments one after the other, you constantly give something new to the listeners, which keeps them excited and eager to discover what's next.

1   From the Arrange area local menu bar, choose Edit > Select All (or press Command-A).

All five regions are selected and their names appear in white over black.

2   In the Inspector's Region Parameter box, click to select the Loop checkbox (or press L).

Arrange area local menu bar

Region Parameter box

All selected regions are looped until the end of the song. The dimmed sections to the right of each region represent the region looping over and over.

3   Click in the background of the Arrange area (or press Command-Shift-A).

All regions are deselected.

4   Drag the **Bright Tone Bass 03** loop toward the right and drop it on bar 2.

As you perform an operation on a region, a yellow help tag displays the following information:

▶   The operation you are about to perform (in the current step, it is Move Regions)

▶   The number of the track where you are (2 in the current step)

▶   The name of the region you are clicking (Bright Tone Bass 03)

▶   The position of the operation (1 1 1 1 before you drag, 2 1 1 1 after you drag)

▶   The length of the region (1 0 0 0)

Operation

Region name

Track number   Position   Length

The help tag displays positions and lengths in bars (or measures), beats, divisions, and ticks. You will often refer to a position or a length with those four numbers.

▶ The beat is the denominator in the time signature (1/4 note here).

▶ The division is set in the Transport bar, below the time signature (1/16 note here).

▶ A clock tick is 1/960 of a beat. A 1/16 note contains 240 ticks.

So in this case, moving the Bright Tone Bass 03 region to 2 1 1 1 means moving it to bar 2, beat 1, division 1, tick 1: exactly on bar 2.

Playhead position   Time signature

Division

At the left of the Transport bar, the current playhead position is displayed in SMPTE units on the top line, and bars, beats, divisions, and ticks on the bottom line.

MORE INFO ▶ SMPTE timecode is used to synchronize picture and sound in video. SMPTE units are hours, minutes, seconds, frames, and subframes.

5   Drag the piano loop (**Deep Electric Piano 05**) to bar 5.

6   Drag the strings loop (**Orchestra Strings 03**) to bar 9.

7   Drag the guitar loop (**Wild Slide Distortion**) to bar 10.

8   Press the Spacebar to start playback.

You already have the foundation of a simple arrangement, starting with drum and bass patterns that groove together, and you've built on it by layering other elements such as piano and strings as the song progresses.

Your next step is to decide where to eliminate some of the instruments and allow the arrangement to breathe a little.

Copying and Resizing Regions

Let's edit the bass track to make the intro lighter in texture, letting the full bass loop kick in at bar 5 with the electric piano.

1   Option-drag the Bright Tone Bass region to bar 5.

Dragging a region moves it, but Option-dragging makes a copy and lets you place the copy. Now you can manipulate the bass region in the intro; but starting on bar 5, the full loop will play repeatedly. Notice that while you Option-drag a region, the help tag now reads Copy Regions.

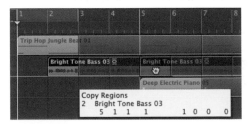

TIP ▸ In Logic, when you use modifier keys such as Shift, Control, Command, or Option while dragging, it is most important which key is depressed at the time you release the mouse button. In fact, you can switch modifier keys while dragging, and the help tag will reflect the change, displaying the appropriate operation. To successfully copy a region by Option-dragging it, make sure you release the mouse button before you release the Option key.

2   In bar 2, select the Bright Tone Bass region.

3   In the Inspector's Region Parameter box, click to deselect the Loop checkbox (or press L).

The region's Loop parameter is turned off, and the region does not loop anymore.

You are about to shorten the bass region, but first you will zoom in on it so that you can see individual bass notes in the waveform.

4   Press Z (the "Toggle Zoom to fit Selection or All Content" command).

The selected region fills the Arrange area, and you can clearly identify individual notes in the waveform.

5   Click the "Play from Selection" button in the Transport bar (or press Shift-Enter).

Listen to your bass pattern while looking at the waveform. You are going to shorten the bass region to remove the last three notes.

6   Press the Spacebar to stop playback.

7   Position your pointer over the lower-right corner of the region.

The pointer turns into a Resize tool.

You can use the Resize tool to adjust the start or end of a region.

8   While looking at the waveform, drag the corner of the region to the left, shortening the region to hide the last three notes.

Don't use the help tag for this operation. Look at the waveform and make sure you hide the last three notes. You will now zoom out. When no regions are selected, the "Toggle Zoom to fit Selection or All Content" key command zooms to fit all the regions in the Arrange area.

9   Click the background of the Arrange area to deselect all regions, and press Z.

You can see all your regions in the Arrange area.

You now have a nice short bass pattern in measure 2 that is perfect for the introduction.

10 Choose File > Save (or press Command-S).

The project is saved.

You need to repeat the same bass pattern twice in bars 3 and 4, before the full bass loop kicks in at bar 5.

11 Click the Bright Tone Bass region in bar 2 to select it.

12 In the Arrange area's local menu bar, choose Region > Repeat Regions (or press Command-R).

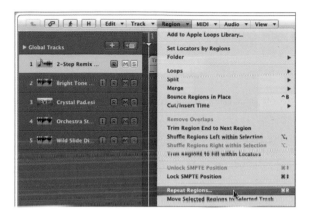

The Repeat Regions/Events dialog opens, allowing you to create copies of the region and snap them to the desired grid unit.

13 In the Number of Copies text field, enter *2*. From the Adjustment menu, choose Bar, and click OK.

The shortened bass region is copied twice on the downbeats of bars 3 and 4.

14 Press Command-S.

The song file is saved.

15 Go the beginning of the song and listen to your new introduction.

You now have a nice little introduction. The song starts with the drums groove; then a shortened version of the bass riff is introduced and played three times. On bar 5, the whole bass line starts just as the electric piano joins in.

Adjusting Loop Repetitions

Before you move on to arrange the strings and slide guitar parts, you will adjust the number of repetitions of the electric piano so that it stops on bar 9, leaving some space in the mix for the next section.

1 Position your pointer over the upper part of the piano loops (the dimmed parts to the right of the region).

The pointer switches to a loop tool. You can use the tool to precisely adjust the point where a region stops looping.

2 Hold down the Loop tool at bar 9.

The help tag reads *Loop 9 1 1 1 (2)*, meaning that the region is looped until the first downbeat of bar 9, and the loop plays twice.

> **TIP** ▶ Once you become more proficient with Logic, you can use the Loop tool by clicking where you want to cut off the loop without holding down the mouse button. For now, holding down the mouse button displays the help tag, which allows you to make sure the loop will stop exactly where you want. If the help tag doesn't read 9 1 1 1 (2), you can drag the mouse left or right until it does, then release the mouse button to perform the cut.

3   Press Command-S.

The song file is saved.

The song is starting to take shape! It has a nice sparse intro, then a fuller grooving section with the electric piano. Let's work on the strings and slide guitar section.

Arranging a Middle Section

One modern production trick is to re-create a music phrase composed of pieces of phrases from different instruments. It is the modern equivalent of the classic call-and-response dialogue that blues singers and guitarists perform when jamming: The singer sings a short phrase, and then the guitarist answers it with a short lick.

In this song, you are going to perform that trick using the strings for the call and the slide guitar for the response.

1   Select the Orchestra Strings region.

2   Press L.

That region's Loop parameter is turned off, and the region does not loop anymore.

3   Position the pointer on the lower-right corner of the strings region until the Resize tool appears. Drag to the left to halve the size of the region.

The help tag indicates that the resized region is one bar long.

4   Select the Wild Slide Distortion region.

5 Press L.

That region's Loop parameter is turned off, and the region does not loop anymore.

6 Drag the region's lower-right corner to bar 11.

The resized region is one bar long.

You have re-created a two-bar phrase composed of one bar of strings followed by one bar of slide guitar. The strings play a simple quarter-note motif. The slide guitar repeats and sustains the last note played by the strings, and then slides back into the first note of the strings motif. If you repeat that new phrase a few times, the slide guitar will take you right back into the strings motif.

You can use the same Repeat Regions command you used earlier to repeat a group of regions.

7 Click in the background and drag the pointer, making sure that the rectangular green highlight touches both the strings and the slide regions.

Both regions are selected.

TIP ▶ When selecting regions, make sure you always start dragging in the background. If the pointer is over a region when you start dragging, you will move the region.

8 In the Arrange area's local menu bar, choose Region > Repeat Regions (or press Command-R). Leave Number of Copies set to 2, set Adjustment to None, and click OK.

This time the whole selection, which contains two regions, is repeated twice.

9 Select the first Orchestra Strings region on bar 9.

10 Click the "Play from Selection" button (or press Shift-Enter).

Playback starts at the beginning of the selection, on bar 9, and you can listen to your new dialogue between the strings and the guitar.

11 Press the Spacebar to stop playback.

Ending the Song

Now would be a good time to wrap up the song. You will bring back the electric piano, let it groove for a while, and create an ending for the song on bar 21. First, you will need to zoom out of the Arrange area to make space for the ending.

1 At the lower right of the Arrange area, drag the horizontal zoom slider to the left (or press Option-Control–Left Arrow).

Vertical zoom slider
Horizontal zoom slider

The whole arrangement zooms out horizontally. Look at the Bar ruler, and try to display at least 23 bars in the Arrange area. Depending on your screen size, you might also want to zoom in vertically.

2 Drag the vertical zoom slider down (or press Option-Control–Down Arrow).

The whole arrangement zooms in vertically.

The zoom sliders are an easy means of zooming the whole arrangement. Once again, commit the Option-Control arrow key combinations to memory, and save your right arm a trip to the sliders every time you need to zoom. The commands are listed at the end of this lesson.

3   Option-drag the Deep Electric Piano region to bar 15, right after the end of the last Wild Slide Guitar region.

The region is copied along with its single loop. To create an ending for the song, you will stop all the still-looping regions at the same place. The last piano loop is still selected, so you will add the drum loop and bass loop to the selection by Shift-clicking them.

4   Shift-click the drum loop and the bass loop above the selected piano loop.

Shift-clicking allows you to select several regions at once when there is no easy way to drag a rectangle across them as you did earlier for the strings and guitar regions.

5   Position the pointer over the top part of one of the looping sections.

The pointer switches to the Loop tool.

6   Option-drag the Loop tool to bar 21.

All three regions stop looping on bar 21. When using the Loop tool on multiple regions, holding down Option makes all the looping sections stop at the same place.

7   In the lower half of the Bar ruler, double-click about a bar before the end.

The playback starts where you double-clicked. The song ending sounds a little abrupt: Usually musicians end a song by playing the last note on the downbeat of the last bar. Since the loops are cut off right on the downbeat, that last note is missing.

You can adjust the end of the bass and the piano loops so that they play one more note on the next downbeat.

8   Press the Spacebar to stop playback.

9   Click in the background of the Arrange area.

All the regions are deselected.

This time, you need to zoom in on the ending of the bass and the electric piano tracks to precisely adjust where both instruments will end.

10 Option-Control-drag around the last bar (bar 20) on both the bass and piano tracks.

The pointer switches to the Zoom tool, and the highlighted area is zoomed in.

11 On the bass track, drag the Loop tool to the right to uncover one more note, until the help tag reads 21 2 1 1 (16).

You can see the final note in the waveform.

12 On the piano track, drag the Loop tool to the right to uncover the beginning of the first note in bar 21.

On MIDI regions, notes are displayed as horizontal lines. Here, the low note is in the lower part of the looped region. As long as the attack of a note is visible, Logic will sustain the note for its whole length.

Now you can zoom out to see your entire arrangement.

13 Option-Control-click anywhere in the Arrange area.

The arrange area returns to the previous zoom level, showing you your complete arrangement.

14 Listen to your arrangement.

You should now have a basic understanding of how to manipulate regions to create an arrangement in Logic. Your basic editing techniques are as follows:

▶ Drag a region to move it.

▶ Option-drag a region to copy it.

▶ Place the pointer at one of the lower corners of a region to resize it.

▶ Place the pointer at the upper-right corner of a region to loop it.

You also learned basic zooming techniques:

▶ Option-Control-drag on an area to zoom in on that area, and Option-Control-click anywhere to return to the previous zoom level.

▶ Press Option-Control–Right Arrow to zoom in horizontally, Option-Control–Left Arrow to zoom out horizontally.

▶ Press Option-Control–Down Arrow to zoom in vertically, Option-Control–Up Arrow to zoom out vertically.

▶ Press Z to zoom in on the selection, and press Z again to return to the previous zoom level, or deselect all regions and press Z to see your entire arrangement.

Feel free to experiment on your own, and be creative! Try adding sections, or creating breaks in some parts. Use short breaks in the drums or bass tracks to trigger attention. They remove the foundation that listeners take for granted. You wake them up, then bring them back into the full groove.

As an additional exercise, try to stop the bass from looping just before the last section (on 14 2 1 1), and have it return for the end (on 15 1 1 1).

Mixing the Song

Once you have arranged the song, the next step is to mix the song before you can export it as a stereo file. Mixing is the art of blending the instruments, carefully balancing their volume and frequency spectrum, and giving them a place in the stereo sound field.

As you finish the project, you use the Mixer to adjust the level of each track and its stereo position, and add processing plug-ins to sculpt the sounds. In the following exercises, you will mix the middle section: the exchanges between the strings and guitar.

Preparing for Mixing

When mixing, you can use Cycle mode to repeat a section of the song, so you don't have to worry about navigating the song while you focus on making that section sound better as you work in the Mixer.

In this exercise, you will open the Mixer, rename the channel strips, and adjust the cycle area to match the middle section of the song.

1   At the bottom of the Arrange window, click the Mixer button (or press X).

The Mixer opens.

NOTE ▶ Depending on your screen size, you may need to resize the Mixer area so that you can still see your tracks in the Arrange area. You may also have to scroll the Mixer area vertically to see the entire channel strips.

The Mixer shows you the channel strips that correspond to the tracks in the Arrange area. All those channel strips are mixed onto the Stereo Out channel strip. The Arrange area stacks tracks vertically, while the Mixer stacks channel strips horizontally, so the channel strips are displayed left to right in the same order in which they are displayed top to bottom in the Arrange area.

The names of the channel strips are not really descriptive. You can rename a channel strip by double-clicking the name at the bottom of the channel strip, or in the corresponding track's header.

2   In track 1, double-click the drums track's name.

A text field appears.

3   Type *Drums*, and press Tab.

The first channel strip in the mixer displays the new name, *Drums*, and the text field moves to the next track.

Set the remaining track names:

▶ Track 2 to *Bass*

▶ Track 3 to *Piano*

▶ Track 4 to *Strings*

▶ Track 5 to *Guitar*

In the Mixer, all the channel strips display the new names.

Now let's adjust the cycle area to the middle section of the song.

4 Select all six Orchestra Strings and Wild Slide Distortion regions.

5 In the Toolbar, click Set Locators.

The Cycle mode is turned on, and the cycle area adjusts to fit the selection.

From now on, when you use the Spacebar to toggle between play and stop, playback will always start at the beginning of the first strings region at bar 9.

Adjusting Levels

Each channel strip has a level meter, a peak detector on top of the meter, a volume fader to adjust the level, and a Pan/Balance control to adjust the stereo position. Below the volume fader, a Mute button allows you to silence that channel strip, and a Solo button allows you to listen to that channel strip by itself.

TIP ▶ In Logic, selecting something in one area or window usually results in the same element being selected in other Logic areas or windows. For example, selecting a track in the Arrange area results in the selection of that track's channel strip in the Mixer, and vice versa.

1   Play the song.

The peak detector at the top of the Stereo Out channel strip is hitting the red. That's not good! Notice that it reads 3.0. That means Logic's output is overloading by 3 dB. You will turn down some of the instruments to avoid overloading the mix.

2   In the Drums channel strip, drag the level fader down –8.2 (dB).

3   On the Stereo Out channel strip, click the peak detector.

The peak detector is reset and starts tracking the new peak level. It no longer hits the red. Good.

4   On both the Drums and the Bass channel strips, click the Solo buttons.

The Solo buttons turn yellow, and you can hear only the Drums and the Bass tracks. This makes it easy to balance the level of the bass against the drums without the distraction of other instruments that are not yet mixed. Now that you've turned down the drums, you can hear that the bass needs a little taming.

5 In the Bass channel strip, lower the level fader to –2.7 (dB).

6 Option-click one of the yellow (engaged) Solo buttons.

Both Solo buttons turn off simultaneously.

In trip-hop, you want to keep the drums and bass "in your face." The only way to achieve that balance without overloading the mix is to turn down all the other instruments. If you feel your mix starts to sound weak, don't be fooled: Simply turn up the volume on your audio interface or monitoring system.

7 In the Strings channel strip, lower the level fader to –9.2 (dB).

8 In the Guitar channel strip, lower the level fader to –20.0 (dB).

9 Press the Spacebar to stop playback.

Using Processing Plug-Ins

At the top of each channel strip, a Setting button gives you access to thousands of factory channel strip settings for both software instrument and audio tracks. Again, a channel strip setting is a collection of all the plug-ins on a channel strip, along with their individual settings.

Below the Setting button are the EQ display and the Insert slots for processing plug-ins.

Another technique to keep the drums and bass sounding big is to make the other instruments sound thinner. First you will try a few channel strip settings to change the sound of the guitar.

1 At the top of the Guitar channel strip, click the Setting button to open the Channel Strip Settings menu, and choose 02 Electric Guitar > 01 Guitar Tone Sampler > Surf.

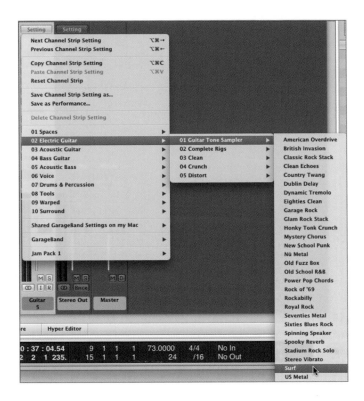

The channel strip setting loads, inserting an Amp Designer, Channel EQ and Compressor plug-in, and their settings to give that particular surf sound. The Setting button now displays this channel strip setting's name, *Surf*.

2   Press the Spacebar.

Playback starts at the beginning of the cycle area, and you can hear the effect of the chosen channel strip setting on the guitar.

3   Click the Setting button for a moment to open the Channel Strip Settings menu again, and choose Next Channel Strip Setting.

The next channel strip setting loads, and the Setting button displays its abbreviated name, *US Metal*. That setting doesn't seem to work as well for that song, but feel free to experiment with other settings until you find one you like. For this exercise, we'll go back to the Surf setting.

4 Click the Setting button again and choose Previous Channel Strip Setting.

The Surf setting is reloaded.

5 Press the Spacebar to stop playback.

Panning Instruments and Copying Plug-Ins

Remember that your initial goal is to get the strings and the guitar to have a conversation. You will realize this concept by panning them to either side of the stereo field while making them sound a little more alike, placing them in the same range of frequencies. In the Surf channel strip setting, the Amp Designer plug-in is mainly responsible for the resulting sound, so you will copy that plug-in and its settings on the Strings channel strip.

1 In the Strings channel strip, drag the Balance control down to –15.

Even though the Balance control is a rotary knob, you adjust it like any other setting in Logic: drag the Balance control vertically, starting dragging in the middle of the control knob.

The strings move to the left.

2 Drag the Guitar channel strip's Balance control up to +14.

The guitar moves to the right.

Now let's copy the Amp Designer plug-in from the Guitar channel strip to the Strings channel strip.

3 Command-Option-drag the Amp Designer plug-in to a Strings channel strip Insert slot on the left.

A copy of the plug-in, with identical settings, is inserted on the Strings channel strip. The Strings are now slightly too loud.

4 In the Strings channel strip, lower the fader to −19 (dB).

Now let's listen to a section with the electric piano to adjust its level.

5 In the Arrange area, select the Deep Electric Piano region at bar 5 and click the "Play from Selection" button (or press Shift-Enter).

Logic starts playing the song from the selection, even though you have Cycle mode turned on.

6 In the Piano channel strip, lower the fader to −5.3 (dB).

7 Click the Mixer button again to close the Mixer, click the Cycle area to turn off Cycle mode, and listen to your song.

The song is finished! You started from nothing and used the Loop Browser to select five loops; created an arrangement by moving, looping, and editing regions; and mixed the five instruments. You can now export the mix and share it with your friends and family.

Exporting the Mix

When you are finally happy with the way your song sounds, it's time to export it. In this exercise, you will export an MP3 file. The process of rendering the mix into a single stereo file that you can burn onto a CD or use in other applications is called *bouncing*.

First, you must adjust the project length to define the bounce range. At the top of the Arrange area, look at the Bar ruler. The last region in your song is the bass, and it stops a little after bar 21. If you listen to the song's end, you'll notice that the last piano note sustains for a while, so you will end the song on bar 24 to avoid cutting off the last note.

1   In the Transport bar, below the Tempo display, drag the Project End display down to set the project length to 24 bars.

Let's make sure the song plays until the end.

2   Double-click the lower half of the Bar ruler around bar 20 to play the end of the song.

The last electric piano note is not cut off.

The bounce range can also be defined by the cycle area, or by selecting regions. To bounce the entire song, make sure that Cycle mode is turned off and no regions are selected.

3   Click the background of the Arrange area.

All the regions are deselected.

4   Choose File > Bounce (or press Command-B).

You are going to bounce the project as an audio file, so the Bounce window looks like a Save As dialog with name, location, and bounce options at the bottom.

Make sure the Start and End positions correspond to your entire song. Start should read *1 1 1 1* and End should read *24 1 1 1*. If they don't, you can adjust them now by dragging the digits vertically.

Bounce destinations

Start and End positions

5   Name the bounce file *New Day*; and from the Where pop-up menu, choose Desktop (or press Command-D).

You can choose from four different destinations for your bounce file:

▶ PCM: uncompressed audio file (AIFF, WAVE, CAF, and Sound Designer II)

▶ MP3: compressed audio file

▶ M4A: compressed audio file format used by iTunes and iPod

▶ Burn: a file burned directly from Logic onto a CD or DVD-A

6 Deselect PCM, and select MP3.

7 Click Bounce.

A progress indicator appears, tracking Logic as it bounces the mix. A second progress bar tracks Logic as it converts the mix to an MP3 file.

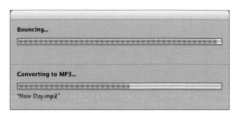

Once the Progress windows disappear, the file is ready.

8 On your desktop, double-click the file **New Day.mp3**.

TIP ▶ You can use Mac OS X key commands to help complete this last step. Press Command-Tab to switch to the Finder, and then press Command-Option-H to hide other applications so that you can see your desktop. Type the first few letters of your song or use arrow keys to select it, and press Command–Down Arrow to open it.

The file opens in iTunes (or in your default MP3 player), and you can listen to your very first Logic mix. Your MP3 file is ready to be shared in an e-mail or uploaded to a website!

Lesson Review

1. How many areas are in the Arrange window, and what are their names?
2. When the same key command can be used in different areas, how do you know which area will respond to key commands?
3. What are the two ways to adjust a setting (such as the tempo) in Logic?
4. Which kinds of regions go on software instrument tracks and audio tracks?
5. What units displayed in the help tag indicate a length or a position in the project?
6. How do you move or copy a region in the Arrange area?
7. In what order are channel strips displayed in the Mixer?
8. What is a channel strip setting?
9. What are the steps to take to export your mix?

Answers

1. There are six areas in the Arrange window: Arrange area, editing area, Media or Lists area, Inspector, Toolbar, and Transport bar.
2. The area that has key focus, indicated by a white frame.
3. Drag a value up and down to increase or decrease it, or double-click to access a data field in which you can directly enter a new value.
4. MIDI regions go on software instrument tracks; audio regions go on audio tracks.
5. Bars, beats, divisions, and ticks.
6. Drag a region to move it; Option-drag a region to copy it.
7. Channel strips are displayed left to right in the same order in which they are displayed top to bottom in the Arrange area.

8. The collection of all the plug-ins on a channel strip, including each plug-in's settings.

9. Adjust the project length, deselect all regions and turn off Cycle mode, choose File > Bounce, choose a name and a destination, and click Bounce.

2

Lesson Files   Logic 9 Files > Lessons > 02 New Day

Logic 9 Files > Lessons > 02 We Shared Everything

Logic 9 Files > Lessons > 02 We Shared Everything_end

Time   This lesson takes approximately 60 minutes to complete.

Goals   Choose digital audio settings

Record single and multitrack audio

Record additional takes

Record in Cycle mode

Punch record both on the fly and automatically

Adjust count-in, metronome, and other settings

Recording Audio

To build a song, you need to come up with the raw material you will later arrange and mix. You might start with an idea you have in your head, a part you rehearsed on an instrument, or a prerecorded sample or loop, or you can start experimenting until inspiration strikes. To sustain and develop that initial inspiration, you need to master the various techniques that Logic offers to record, create, or edit the audio and MIDI regions that constitute the building blocks for your project.

In addition to providing resources such as software instruments and Apple Loops, Logic Pro is a powerful digital audio workstation, offering you a complete set of tools to assist you in the most demanding recording sessions.

In this lesson, you will set up Logic for audio recording and study some situations that you will typically encounter when recording live musicians: recording a single instrument, recording additional takes of the same instrument, cycle recording, multitrack recording, punching on the fly, and automatic punching.

Setting Up Digital Audio Recording

When recording audio, Logic saves the digital data stream from the audio interface to an audio file on your hard disk. Assuming you have the correct settings, Logic does not exert any influence over the quality of your recordings. By choosing the right recording environment and using high-quality components in your signal chain, you ensure that the quality of your audio recordings will be the same as the quality produced by a professional studio.

In the following exercises, you will set up Logic to prepare for a music recording intended for use on an audio CD.

▶ **Digital Recording, Sample Rate, and Bit Depth**

When audio is recorded in Logic Pro, sound pressure waves are turned into a digital audio file, as follows:

1. The microphone transforms sound pressure waves into an analog electrical signal.

2. The microphone preamp amplifies the analog electrical signal. A gain knob lets you set a proper recording level and avoid distortion.

3. The analog-to-digital (A/D) converter transforms the analog electrical signal into a digital data stream.

4. The audio interface sends the digital data stream from the converter to the computer.

5. Logic Pro saves the incoming data as an audio file displayed on the screen by a waveform representing the sound pressure waves.

To transform the analog signal to a digital data stream, the converters sample the analog signal at a very fast time interval, or *sample rate*. The sample rate identifies how many times per second the audio is digitally sampled. The *bit depth* identifies the number of data bits (0s and 1s) used to encode the value of each sample. The sample rate and bit depth settings both influence the quality of a digital audio recording.

NOTE ▶ Most audio interfaces include converters, and many include microphone preamps. Also, most modern Macintosh computers ship with a built-in audio interface. Many Mac notebooks and iMacs even have internal microphones. While they are not intended for professional-quality recording, internal microphones will allow you to perform the exercises in this lesson in the absence of an external microphone.

Setting the Sample Rate

The sample rate of a project should be set before starting your first recording. All the audio files used in a project should be recorded and played at the same sample rate. Playing an audio file at the wrong sample rate will result in the wrong pitch and tempo, much like playing back an audiotape or vinyl record at the wrong speed.

NOTE ▶ Make sure you read the section "Installing the Logic Lesson Files" in "Getting Started" before you continue.

1   Go to Logic 9 Files > Lessons, and open **02 New Day,** or continue working in the project file you created in Lesson 1.

NOTE ▶ Depending on your screen size, the regions in the Arrange area may appear too big or too small. To see the entire project, make sure all the regions are deselected and press Z.

2   In the Toolbar, click the Settings button and choose Audio.

The Project Settings window opens.

By default, the sample rate is set to 44.100 kHz.

Data for an audio CD is encoded at a sample rate of 44.1 kHz (44,100 samples per second), and audio data for a standard video DVD is encoded at 48 kHz. While you can choose to work at other sample rates, using 44.1 kHz for music projects and 48 kHz for video projects avoids the need to convert the sample rate.

Since you are working with a music file for a CD, you'll work at 44.100 kHz, the current setting.

3   Close the Project Settings window (or press Command-W).

NOTE ▶ In Logic, settings fall under two categories:

- Project settings, such as the sample rate, can be set individually for each project, so that each project can have unique project settings.
- Logic Preferences, such as the bit depth, which are the same in all projects.

Setting the Bit Depth

While it is problematic to mix audio sample rates, Logic handles audio files of various bit depths in the same project without causing problems at playback.

Let's set the bit depth and choose an audio interface.

1   In the Toolbar, click the Preferences button and choose Audio.

The Audio Preferences window opens.

2 From the Output Device and Input Device menus, choose the desired audio
interfaces.

The Output Device is the device connected to your monitors or headphones. The
Input Device is the device into which you plug your microphones or instruments.
You will often use the same device for both audio output and input.

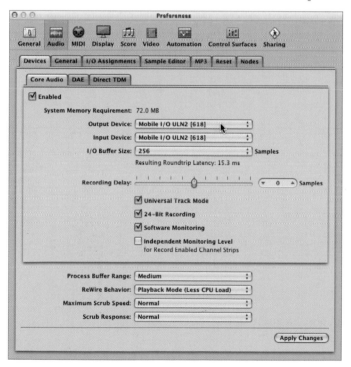

If you do not have an audio interface connected to your Mac, choose from the Built-in Output and Input devices.

When 24 Bit Recording is not selected, Logic records at 16-bit resolution. A 24-bit recording has a significantly greater dynamic range than a 16-bit recording. The extended dynamic range lets you record at lower levels without having to worry about digital noise, thereby decreasing the chances of clipping your recording.

3   Make sure 24-Bit Recording is selected.

4   Close the Preferences window (or press Command-W).

If you choose a new output or input device, Logic automatically reinitializes the Core Audio engine when you close the window.

MORE INFO ▶ Some additional options are available that seldom need to be changed from the default settings. For more information on these, see "Changing Recording and Metronome Settings," later in this lesson.

Recording a Single Track

In this example, you will record a single instrument. While the exercise describes recording an acoustic guitar, feel free to record any instrument you have, or your own voice if you do not have an instrument.

Preparing a Track for Recording

To record audio, you first have to create a new audio track, select the correct input (the input connected to your microphone), and enable that new track for recording.

TIP▶ To avoid feedback, turn off your speakers and monitor your recording using headphones. If you are working with a notebook computer's microphone, plug in the headphones or turn off the speakers before you enable a track for recording.

When adding tracks, the new tracks are inserted below the selected track. To create a new track at the bottom of the Arrange area, you first need to select the bottom track.

1 At the bottom of the Arrange area, make sure the Guitar track is selected.

2 At the top of the track list, click the New Tracks button (+) at the top of the track list (or press Command-Option-N).

The New Tracks dialog appears.

3 Make sure Number is set to 1, Type is set to Audio, and Format is set to Mono.

4 From the Input menu, choose the desired input of your audio interface. If you are using your Macintosh's built-in audio interface or your notebook's microphone, leave the option at Input 1.

5 Select Record Enable.

6 Select Open Library.

This selection will open the Library tab in the Media area so that you can select a channel strip setting for your new audio track.

7 Click Create (or press Return).

A new record-enabled mono audio track is created, and in the Media area, the Library opens showing all available audio channel strip settings. Logic automatically assigns the new track to the next available channel. Since three audio tracks were created when you dragged blue Apple Loops in Lesson 1 (remember that the green Apple Loops are on software instrument tracks), the new track is assigned to the Audio 4 channel and is automatically named Audio 4. Let's rename it.

You will record in an existing Logic project, and the audio files will automatically be placed in the audio folder inside that project folder.

NOTE ▶ If the Logic project was not already saved, a Save As dialog appears when you record-enable an audio track or create a new record-enabled audio track. Always save the project before you record audio, and make sure that Include Assets is selected at the bottom of the Save As dialog. This ensures that all audio files used in that project will be placed in the audio folder inside the Logic project folder.

8   In the Audio 4 track header, double-click the name.

A text field appears with the current name selected.

9   Enter *Acoustic*, and press Return or click outside the text field.

TIP ► Since Logic automatically assigns the name of a track to the audio files recorded on that track, it is a good idea to always name a track before recording on it. You will avoid populating your hard disk with files with nondescript names such as *Audio 04#06*, and more descriptive names will help you identify files later.

Before you start recording, you will expand the new track vertically to better see the waveform.

10 Position the Pointer tool near the lower-left corner of the track header.

The Pointer tool turns into the Finger tool.

11 Using the Finger tool, drag down to resize the new track.

TIP ► When the Pointer tool turns into a hand, it indicates that you can drag an element to move it. When it turns into an index finger, it indicates that you can drag an element to resize it.

Because your new audio track is record-enabled (the R button on the track header is red), the next recording will create an audio region on that track. You can monitor the audio routed to record-enabled tracks while Logic is stopped, playing, or recording.

NOTE ► If you are already using a hardware mixer or your audio interface's software to monitor the audio being routed to record-enabled tracks, turn off Software Monitoring in Logic's Audio Preferences. Otherwise, you will be monitoring the signal twice, resulting in a flangy or robotic sound.

Adjusting the Recording Level

Before recording, make sure you can monitor the sound through Logic, and adjust the source audio level to avoid overloading the converters. On the channel strip, look at the clip detector, and make sure it never hits 0 dBFS (decibels full scale), which would indicate that you are *clipping* the input of your converter. Keep in mind that you need to adjust the audio level *before the converter input*, so use your microphone preamp gain knob. Allow for some headroom, especially if you know that the artist might play or sing louder during the actual recording. It's better to work with a low-level recording than clipping the input.

 — Clip detector

MORE INFO ▶ If you are using the Macintosh built-in line input or microphone, you can adjust the input level in the Sound pane's Input tab in System Preferences.

Let's adjust the recording and monitoring levels, tune the guitar, and find a cool acoustic guitar sound.

1   Ask the musician to play the loudest part of the performance you are about to record, and adjust the level on the microphone preamp as you watch the clip detector on the channel strip. If the clip detector turns red, lower the gain on the preamp and click the clip detector to reset it. Make sure the maximum peak sits comfortably below 0 dBFS: The wider the dynamic range of the source, the more headroom it needs to limit the risk of clipping.

NOTE ▶ You may hear a small delay between when you play a note and when you hear it. This delay is called *latency*. You will learn how to reduce latency at the end of this lesson, in the section "Setting the I/O Buffer Size."

2   Press the Spacebar to start playback, and play along with the song. If the acoustic guitar is now too loud or too soft in comparison to the other tracks, adjust the monitoring level using the channel strip's fader.

During recording, the channel strip's volume fader adjusts the monitoring level, but it does not alter the recording level. After the recording, the fader stays at the same position to play back the track at the same level.

3   In the Library tab, choose 03 Acoustic Guitar > Bright Acoustic.

The Bright Acoustic channel strip setting opens. The channel strip displays the name of the setting, and Channel EQ and Compressor plug-ins are inserted. The guitar sounds a little brighter, fitting better into the mix. The settings even include a Tuner plug-in, so you can verify that your instrument is in tune before you start recording.

4   Press the Spacebar to stop playback.

5   Double-click the Tuner plug-in in the first insert slot.

The Tuner plug-in opens. The Bypass button is orange, indicating that the plug-in is bypassed.

6   Click the Bypass button to turn off the bypass function.

The Bypass button turns black, indicating that the Tuner is now on.

7   Play the guitar's individual strings one after another, making sure that the Tuner displays the correct note and the meter stays as close as possible to the center position (blue bar).

8   Bypass the Tuner.

9   Close the Tuner window.

You have set the desired sample rate and bit depth, adjusted the recording and monitoring levels, found a good-sounding channel strip setting, and tuned the instrument. You are now ready to start recording.

Recording Audio

Let's record a guitar part from bar 5 to bar 9.

1   In the Transport bar, click the Forward or Rewind button as needed—or press > (right angle bracket) or < (left angle bracket)—to position the playhead on bar 5.

2   Click the Record button (or press R).

TIP ▶ If no track is record-enabled, Logic automatically record-enables the selected track.

The playhead jumps one bar earlier and gives you a four-beat count-in with an audible metronome click before the recording starts. The Bar ruler turns red to indicate that Logic is recording. A progress window appears that shows the remaining recording time and the elapsed time. A new region with a red halo is created behind the playhead on the record-enabled track, and you can see the recording's waveform drawn in as you play or sing.

MORE INFO ▶ By default, the metronome automatically turns on when recording, and you get a four-beat count-in. You will learn how to adjust both the metronome and the count-in settings later in this lesson.

3   After you've recorded a few bars, in the Transport bar, click the Stop button (or press the Spacebar).

Your new recording appears as an audio region on the Acoustic track. Note that this new region is selected, making it easy to play, or to delete if you're not happy with it.

4   In the Transport bar, click the Play from Selection button (or press Shift-Enter).

The playhead jumps to the beginning of the recording and starts playing.

5   Stop playback.

6   Make sure the Arrange area has key focus, and press Delete on the main keyboard.

A Delete dialog appears. You can still click Cancel if you change your mind; but if you select Delete and click OK, the audio file will be permanently deleted from your hard disk. If you select Keep and click OK, the region is removed from the Arrange area, but the file remains on your hard disk.

7   Click Cancel (or press Esc).

The new recording remains on the track.

Using the Audio Bin

When recording or importing audio files into a project, Logic uses the Audio Bin, located in the Media area, to track all the audio files and audio regions imported or recorded in the project. You can open the Audio Bin to make sure that files are recorded at the correct sample rates and bit depth settings and are properly named.

1   At the top of the Media area, click the Bin tab.

The Audio Bin opens, showing you the new **Acoustic#01.aif** file, as well as the three blue Apple Loops that you dragged into the Arrange area in Lesson 1.

For each audio file, the Info column displays the following:

▶   Sample rate

▶   Bit depth

▶   Status icon

▶   File size

You can click the disclosure triangle to the left of an audio file to display the regions associated with that audio file.

2   Click the disclosure triangle next to Bright Tone Bass 03.aif.

The regions associated with that audio file are displayed, including the one you shortened in Lesson 1 for the intro of the song. The blue segment indicates which portion of the audio file the region contains.

Notice that the new **Acoustic#01** audio region you just recorded is selected, in both the Audio bin and the Arrange area. The path of the selected region's parent audio file is displayed at the top of the Audio Bin (or the beginning of the path if the path is too long to fit).

This is a quick way to ensure that the audio file was recorded in the correct location: in the audio folder inside the project folder.

In this case, the path is too long to be displayed in its entirety.

3   In the Bin, Control-click the **Acoustic#01.aif** audio file and choose Show File(s) in Finder.

A Finder window opens, showing the selected audio file.

MORE INFO ▶ In Logic, you can also choose Window > Audio Bin to open the Audio Bin window, which displays the full path for each audio file.

4   Click the Arrange window (or press Command-Tab) to go back to Logic.

5   Click the first Bright Tone Bass 03 region in the Audio Bin.

Bright Tone Bass 03 is selected in both the Audio Bin and the Arrange area. In the Arrange area you can see that it's the first shortened region used in the intro. Experiment by clicking regions in the Audio Bin or the Arrange area, and observe the same region being selected in the other location.

6   Click the disclosure triangle for the Bright Tone Bass audio file.

The regions associated with Bright Tone Bass are hidden.

Keep the Audio Bin open for the rest of this lesson to look at the new audio files created when recording.

Recording Additional Takes

When recording a live performance, musicians can make mistakes. Rather than deleting the previous recording and repeatedly recording until you get a flawless performance, you can record several *takes* (performances of the same musical part) and later choose the best take, or even the best parts of each take, to create a *comp track* (composite track).

To record new takes in Logic, you can record the new performance over the previous one. All of the takes (including the original recording) will be placed into a *take folder*.

1 Make sure the track used to record your first performance (the Acoustic track) is still selected and record-enabled, and the Arrange area has key focus.

2 Position the playhead on bar 5.

3 In the Transport bar, click the Record button (or press R).

Record a second take of about the same length as the first take.

The new recording seems to be recorded over the previous audio region.

4 Stop the recording.

Disclosure triangle

Take Folder menu arrow

Take folder

Both the original take and the new take have been packed into a take folder. You can tell that the region is a take folder by the presence of a disclosure triangle in front of the region name, and by the Take Folder menu arrow at the upper right of the region. Clicking the disclosure triangle displays all takes on individual sub-tracks. Clicking the Take Folder menu arrow allows you to access take-editing features.

5 Record a third take.

6 In the Acoustic track header, click the Record Enable (R) button.

The Record Enable button is disabled: The track is disarmed, and you can no longer hear the incoming sound.

If you listen to the song now, only the last recorded take will play back. The previous takes are muted. If the last take is shorter than another take you recorded previously, then playback automatically switches to that previous take at the end of the last take.

7 Click the disclosure triangle next to the take folder's name.

The take folder opens, showing you all the takes on lanes.

When the take folder is open, you can select the take you want to listen to.

MORE INFO ▶ The take turns blue and the others are dimmed (muted). Take folders and comping (creating a comp track) will be discussed in Lesson 3.

8 Click the disclosure triangle on the take folder.

The take folder closes.

TIP ▶ You can also double-click a take folder to open and close it.

Recording Takes in Cycle Mode

If you are both the engineer and the musician, it's not always practical to switch from playing your instrument to operating Logic between each take (and it can really destroy the vibe). Recording in Cycle mode allows you to repeatedly record a single section, creating a new take for each pass of the cycle. When you stop the recording, all the takes are packed inside a take folder.

1 Click the Go to Beginning button (or press Return).

2 Drag the horizontal zoom slider to the right (or press Option-Control–Right Arrow a few times) to zoom in on the intro, so that you can see at least the first five bars.

3   Drag a cycle from left to right between bars 3 and 5.

4   Start recording.

The playhead jumps a bar ahead of the cycle for a one-bar count-in and starts recording the first take. When it reaches bar 5, the end of the cycle area, it jumps back to
bar 3 and starts recording a new take.

TIP ▶ You don't have to position the playhead when recording in Cycle mode:
Recording automatically starts at the beginning of the cycle, after the count-in.

Logic keeps looping the cycle area, recording new takes until you stop recording.
Record five or six takes.

5   Click Stop (or press the Spacebar).

All the takes recorded in Cycle mode are placed in a take folder.

6 Look at the new audio file in the Audio Bin.

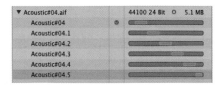

All the takes recorded in Cycle mode are displayed as successive regions of a single audio file.

Let's turn off the Cycle mode and return the Acoustic track to its original size.

7 Click the cycle area in the Bar ruler (or press C).

Cycle mode is turned off.

8 Position your Pointer tool over the lower-left corner of the Acoustic track header.

The Pointer tool turns into the Finger tool, ready to resize.

9 With the Finger tool, Shift-click the track header.

The track zooms out and returns to the same height as the other tracks.

TIP ▶ When tracks have different heights, Shift-clicking the lower-left corner of any track header using the Finger tool resets all the tracks to the same height.

Recording Multiple Tracks

You can use the same single-track techniques to record multiple tracks simultaneously. This allows you to record several instruments at once, placing each instrument on a separate track.

You first create as many tracks as needed, making sure each track is set to a different input and is record-enabled. (You can't record-enable channel strips that are set to the same input on your audio interface because they would all record the same input.)

In the following exercise, you will record two mono tracks at the same time, which you can do using the built-in Macintosh audio interface. To record more than two tracks simultaneously, you need an audio interface with more than two inputs.

1 At the bottom of the Arrange area, click the last track header.

This ensures that the tracks you create now will be added below the last track.

2 At the top of the track list in the Arrange area, click the New Tracks button (+) (or press Command-Option-N).

The New Tracks dialog appears.

3 Use the following settings:

▶ Number: 2

▶ Type: Audio

▶ Format: Mono

▶ Input: Input 1

4 To the right of the Input pop-up menu, select Ascending.

When creating multiple tracks, selecting the Ascending checkbox automatically sets the inputs (or outputs) to ascending settings. In this case, it will create two tracks and assign the first to Input 1 and the second to Input 2.

5   Make sure Record Enable is selected.

6   Deselect Open Library.

The Library won't open. The Audio Bin will stay open, and you can see the audio files created as you record.

7   Click Create (or press Return).

Two audio tracks are created, automatically assigned to the next available audio channels (Audio 5 and Audio 6). Their inputs are set to Input 1 and Input 2, and both are record-enabled.

TIP ▶ If you need to reassign a track's input, hold down the Input slot in the I/O section on the track's channel strip. A menu opens, allowing you to choose any input on your audio interface.

8   Rename the tracks *Piano* and *Voice*, or whatever you wish.

9   In the Transport bar, click the Go to Beginning button, or press Return.

10 Start recording.

The multitrack recording starts, and after a one-bar count-in, you see the playhead appear on the left of the Arrange area, creating two regions, one on each record-enabled track.

11 After a few bars, stop the recording.

You have a new audio region on each track.

You can use the same procedure to simultaneously record as many tracks as needed. If the tracks already exist in the Arrange area, make sure you assign them the correct inputs, record-enable them, and start recording.

Recording Additional Takes on Multiple Tracks

You can record additional takes on multiple tracks as you would record a single track: by recording over the existing multitrack recording.

1   Return the playhead to the beginning of the song.

2   Make sure both the Piano and Voice tracks are still record-enabled.

3   Start recording.

A new take is recorded on each record-enabled track.

4   Stop recording.

You have a new take folder for each track.

You can also use cycle recording to record multiple takes on multiple tracks.

First, let's clean up the project by deleting all the Piano and Voice recordings.

5   Make sure both the Piano and Voice take folders are selected.

6   Choose Edit > Delete (or press Delete).

A Delete dialog appears.

If you select Keep and click OK, the operation is nondestructive. The selected regions or take folders disappear from the Arrange area but remain in the Audio Bin, and the audio files remain on the hard disk.

If you choose Delete and click OK, the operation is destructive. The audio files are deleted from the hard disk. In that case, you cannot undo the operation and the audio files are removed permanently.

TIP ▶ Be very careful when deleting audio files. When in doubt, click Cancel to abort. Then you can open the Audio Bin to preview all of the selected audio files before deciding what to do with them.

If you do not wish to keep the piano and voice recordings, delete them.

7 Make sure Delete is selected.

8 Select "For all."

When "For all" is selected, the choice of deleting or keeping the first audio file will be applied to all selected audio files.

9 Click OK (or press Return).

The take folders disappear, and the corresponding audio files are removed from the Audio Bin and permanently deleted from the hard disk.

10 In the upper half of the Bar ruler, click the gray cycle area to turn on Cycle mode.

11 Make sure both the Piano and Voice tracks are still record-enabled.

12 Start recording.

Logic counts in four beats, and then records one take on each track for every pass through the cycle area.

13 Stop recording.

You have two take folders containing each track's multiple takes.

14 Choose File > Close Project. Save the project only if you want to keep your work in this lesson.

Punching In and Out

When you want to correct a specific section of a recording—usually to fix a performance mistake—you can start playback before the mistake, punch in to engage recording just before the section you wish to fix, and punch out to stop recording immediately after the section. A take folder is created, automatically edited to play only the new recording between the places where you punched in and out. Punching is nondestructive. At any time, you can open the take folder and select the original recording.

There are two punching methods: on the fly and automatic. Punching on the fly allows you to use a key command to punch in and out while Logic plays, whereas automatic punching requires you to set the Autopunch area in the Bar ruler before recording. Punching on the fly is fast but usually requires an engineer to perform the punch in and punch out while the musician is performing. Automatic punching is ideal for the musician-producer who is working alone.

Punching on the Fly

In the next exercise, you will get familiar with the song, turn on the "Punch on the Fly" mode, and then use the Record Toggle key command (Shift-R) to punch on the last acoustic guitar track, Acoustic Right.

1   Go to Logic 9 Files > Lessons, and open **02 We Shared Everything**.

2   Play the song.

   The last track, Acoustic Right, is missing an entire section. The guitar player made a mistake and stopped playing between bars 14 and 18. To make it easier to focus on that track, you can mute all the tracks except for the drum tracks.

3   Starting on the High Cello tracks, hold down the Mute button and drag down to the Acoustic Left track.

Tracks 7 through 14 (High Cello to Acoustic Left) are muted. Holding down a button in a track header and dragging down or up emulates the way engineers quickly mute or solo a whole section of the arrangement by sliding a finger across the buttons on a real mixing board.

4   Choose Options > Audio > Punch on the Fly; or in the Transport bar, hold down the Record button and choose Punch on the Fly from the pop-up menu.

If you look at the menu again, a checkmark appears next to Punch on the Fly, indicating that the mode is active.

5   Click the lower half of the Bar ruler at bar 12 to position the playhead.

6   At the bottom of the Arrange area, record-enable track 15 Acoustic Right.

7   Check your recording and monitoring levels.

Now that the project is ready to record, save it. You will revert to this record-ready state in the next exercise.

8   Choose File > Save (or press Command-S).

9   Start playback.

10 When the playhead reaches bar 14, press Shift-R (the Record Toggle key command), and play your instrument.

You just punched in. Logic starts recording over the current Acoustic Right audio region.

11　When the playhead reaches bar 18, click the Play button, or press Shift-R again.

This time you punched out. Logic stops recording and reverts to playing back the current Acoustic Right audio region on the track.

12　Stop playback.

The Acoustic Right track now displays a take folder.

13　Open the take folder.

You can see that the comp take contains the original recording and the new recording between bars 14 and 18 where you punched in and out.

Using Automatic Punching

To prepare for automatic punching, you turn on the Autopunch mode and adjust the Autopunch area. You will also temporarily hide all tracks except for the one you record on, to clearly see what occurs.

1　Choose File > Revert to Saved.

An alert message appears, indicating that you are about to discard the changes you've made since the last time the song was saved.

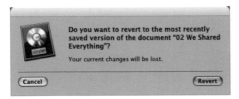

2   Click Revert.

The current project is closed without being saved, and the last saved version of **02 We Shared Everything** opens. It should be ready for recording, as you saved it before punching on the fly in the previous exercise.

Let's hide all the tracks but the one you're going to record on.

3   At the top of the Arrange area, click the Hide View button (or press H).

The Hide View button turns green, and a Hide button (with the letter H) appears in each track header.

4   Hold down the first track's Hide button, and drag down to the Acoustic Left track to engage the Hide Track function for those tracks.

5   Click the Hide View button again (or press H).

The Hide View button turns orange, and all the tracks with Hide buttons engaged are now hidden.

6   Press Option-Control–Down Arrow a few times to zoom in vertically.

7   In the Transport bar, click the Autopunch button.

In the Bar ruler, a red autopunch strip appears from bar 2 to bar 4. The Autopunch area defines the section to be rerecorded.

TIP▶ You can also toggle the Autopunch mode by Option-clicking the upper half of the Bar ruler.

8   Adjust the Autopunch area so that it extends from bar 14 to bar 18.

You can drag the edges of the Autopunch area to resize it or drag the entire area to move it. The red vertical guidelines will help you to align the punch in and out points with the waveform.

9 Position the playhead before the Autopunch area.

10 Record-enable the Acoustic Right track.

11 Click the Record button (or press R).

Playback starts. When the playhead reaches the beginning of the Autopunch area, Logic starts recording over the current Acoustic Right audio region. When the playhead reaches the end of the Autopunch area, Logic stops recording and reverts to playing the current Acoustic Right audio region.

12 Click Stop (or press Return).

The Acoustic Right track now displays a take folder.

13 Open the take folder.

You can see that the comp take contains the original recording and the new recording between bars 14 and 18 (corresponding to the Autopunch area).

You can hear the results of a successful punch recording in **02 We Shared Everything_end**, where the guitar player used Autopunch mode to replace bars 14 through 18 with a new take.

14 Close, but don't save, the current project and open **02 We Shared Everything_end**.

The Acoustic R track is soloed and its take folder is expanded. The second take, Acoustic Right#2, is colored light red, so you can clearly see it in the comp at the top, under the Autopunch area.

TIP ▶ To change the color of a region or take, click the Colors button in the Toolbar (or press Option-C) to open the Color palette. Then select the region(s) and click the desired color in the palette.

15 Position the playhead just before the Autopunch area and start playback.

Listen to the transitions between the takes. Not bad!

16 In the Acoustic R track header, click the Solo button to unsolo the track.

17 Click the Hide View button at the top of the Arrange area (or press H).

All tracks are now visible.

18 Listen to the Autopunch area again.

Notice the nice chorus effect produced by the two acoustic guitars panned left and right.

TIP ▶ You can speed up the Autopunch recording process by using the Marquee tool described in Lesson 3. When a marquee selection is present, starting a recording automatically turns on the Autopunch mode, and the Autopunch area matches the marquee selection.

19 In the Bar ruler, Option-click the Autopunch area to turn Autopunch mode off.

Changing Recording and Metronome Settings

Some settings do not affect the quality of the audio recording but can change the behavior of your project when recording or the audio file format used for recordings. Although you can record audio using the default settings, sometimes you'll want to change them. The next few exercises will show you how those settings affect the audio recording process, and how to adjust them.

Setting the I/O Buffer Size

When communicating with the audio interface, Logic does not receive or transmit just one sample at a time. It places a number of samples in a buffer. When the buffer is full, Logic processes or transmits the entire buffer. The larger the buffer, the less work is required from the CPU. The advantage of using a larger buffer is that the CPU has more time to calculate other processes and you can use more plug-ins. The drawback to a larger buffer is that you have to wait a bit longer for the buffer to fill before you can monitor your signal. That means a longer delay between the original sound and the one you hear through Logic. That delay is called *latency*.

Usually, you want to have the smallest possible latency when recording and the most CPU processing power possible when mixing, so that you can use more plug-ins. You can adjust the I/O buffer size depending on the situation.

1 In the Toolbar, click the Preferences button and choose Audio.

2 Click the I/O Buffer Size pop-up menu.

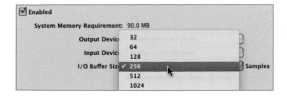

The menu allows you to set the buffer size anywhere between 32 and 1024 samples.

3   Choose 32, and click Apply Changes.

Wait for the Core Audio engine to reinitialize. Note the very small resulting latency displayed below the I/O Buffer Size menu.

4   Play the song.

Look at the CPU meter in the Transport Bar. Depending on your computer's CPU, you might see pretty big spikes. You might even hear pops and cracks while the song plays back, or get a Core Audio overload alert.

5   Set the I/O Buffer Size to 1024, and click Apply Changes. Note the difference in the resulting latency displayed below the menu.

6   Play the song.

The CPU meter should hit much lower. It doesn't have to work as hard with the larger buffer size. However, if you try to record audio with that setting, you will hear a delay between the notes you play and the notes you hear. That's latency. If you intend to do more audio recordings, find the lowest I/O buffer size setting that allows a clean monitoring.

TIP ▶ To monitor CPU and HD usage with more precision, double-click the CPU or HD meter in the Transport bar. A floating high resolution CPU/HD monitor window opens.

Setting the Recording File Type

Logic can record in three digital audio file formats: AIFF (the most commonly used audio file format on Macintosh computers), Broadcast Wave File (BWF, or WAVE), and Core Audio Format (CAF). The Audio Engineering Society recommends using BWF for most applications. CAF is practically unlimited in file size and can contain more than two channels, so it can be used for large audio files and multichannel surround audio files.

1 At the top of the Audio Preferences window, click the General tab.

2 Set the Recording File Type to WAVE (BWF).

3 Close the Preferences window.

From now on, any new audio recorded in Logic will create BWF files.

Setting the Count-In

The count-in is the time you have to prepare yourself and get in the groove before the actual recording begins.

1 In the Toolbar, click the Settings button and choose Recording; or in the Transport bar, hold down the Record button and choose Recording Settings.

The Recording Project Settings window opens.

2   From the "When Beginning" options, select Count-in, and set it to 2 Bars.

3   Record-enable any track.

4   Go back to the beginning of the song.

5   Start recording.

This time you can hear eight beats (two bars in 4/4) before the playhead appears and starts recording on the first downbeat of bar 1.

6   Stop the recording.

7   Choose Edit > Undo Recording (or press Command-Z).

Setting the Metronome

You can adjust the sound of the metronome in the Metronome project settings.

1   At the top of the Project Settings window, click the Metronome button.

TIP ▶ You can also access the Metronome project settings by holding down the Metronome button in the Transport bar and choosing Metronome Settings.

The Metronome Project Settings window opens. The Software Click Instrument settings are on the right of the window.

MORE INFO ▶ Preferences (such as the I/O buffer size and the Recording File Type set in previous exercises) are global settings that affect Logic's behavior in any project you work on. Project settings (such as count-in or metronome settings) are local settings that affect only the current project and are saved with the project.

2   Start playing the song.

3   Click the Metronome button in the Transport bar.

4   In the Metronome Project Settings window, drag the Volume slider to the right.

The metronome click increases in volume.

5   Drag the Tonality slider to the right.

The metronome sound changes and you can distinctly hear a pitch. Adjusting the tonality of the metronome is important: A pitched sound (slider to the right) will cut better through a busy mix but will also bleed through the musician's headphones into the microphone. A more muted sound (slider to the left) is more suitable for quiet mixes when you can't tolerate any metronome bleed.

Adjust the metronome so that it is loud and clear.

When a project already contains a drum track, you may need the metronome only during the count-in to get into the groove before the song starts.

6   Under Options, select "Only during count-in," and deselect "Click while playing."

7   Position the playhead on bar 2, the beginning of the song.

8   Start recording.

You hear the metronome for two bars; then it stops playing as the song starts on bar 2.

9   Stop and undo the recording.

NOTE ▶ If you want your metronome to play a specific sound on an external hardware MIDI synthesizer or sampler, use the MIDI Metronome. From the MIDI Port menu, choose a port, and connect a MIDI cable from that MIDI Out port on the MIDI Interface to the MIDI In port on your hardware sampler/synthesizer.

Lesson Review

1. Which settings affect the quality of a digital audio recording?

2. Where can you adjust those settings?

3. How do you record on one or several tracks?

4. How do you record additional audio takes?

5. What happens when you record in Cycle mode?

6. How do you punch on the fly?

7. How do you use the Autopunch function?

8. Where do you adjust the I/O buffer size?

9. How do you choose the best I/O buffer size?

10. Where do you set the recording file type?

11. Where do you adjust the count-in?

12. Where do you adjust the metronome settings?

13. How can you quickly access recording and metronome settings?

14. How can you hide tracks?

Answers

1.   Sample rate and bit depth.

2.   You adjust the sample rate in File > Project Settings > Audio. Adjust the bit depth in the Devices tab of the Audio Preferences.

3.   Record-enable the desired track(s) and click the Record button in the Transport bar.

4.   Record over an existing audio region.

5.   A new take is recorded for each pass of the cycle, and all the takes are packed into a take folder.

6.   Make sure Punch On the Fly is enabled (choose Options > Audio > Punch On the Fly to toggle it on and off), start playback, and press the Record Toggle key command (Shift-*) to punch in and out.

7.   In the Transport bar, click the Autopunch Mode button. Adjust the Autopunch range in the Bar ruler, and click the Record button.

8.   In the Devices tab of Audio Preferences.

9.   Choose a lower I/O buffer size when recording (for less latency), and a higher I/O buffer size when mixing (for more CPU processing power).

10. In the General tab of Audio Preferences.

11. In the Toolbar, click the Settings button, and choose Recording.

12. In the Toolbar, click the Settings button, and choose Metronome.

13. Hold down (or Control-click) the Record or Metronome buttons in the Transport bar.

14. At the top left of the Arrange area, click the Hide button. Click individual Hide buttons on track headers, and click the main Hide button again.

3

Lesson Files	Logic 9 Files > Lessons > 03 New Day
Media	Logic 9 Files > Media > Additional Media
Time	This lesson takes approximately 60 minutes to complete.
Goals	Create a composite take from multiple takes
	Assign Left-click and Command-click tools
	Edit regions in the Arrange area
	Apply fades and crossfades
	Import audio files
	Quantize audio regions
	Move individual notes inside an audio region using the Flex tool
	Edit audio destructively in the Sample Editor
	Position audio regions in the Arrange area

Lesson 3
Editing Audio

Audio engineers have always looked for ways to edit recordings. In the days of magnetic tape, they used razor blades to cut pieces of a recording, and then connected the pieces with special tape. They could create a smooth transition (or crossfade) between two pieces of magnetic tape by cutting them at an angle.

Digital audio workstations revolutionized audio editing the same way that word processors revolutionized text editing. A waveform displayed on the screen gives you a visual representation of the digital audio recordings stored on the hard disk. The ability to read that waveform and manipulate it using Logic's editing tools is the key to precise and flexible audio editing.

In this lesson, you will develop waveform-reading skills to identify musical notes in the waveform. With the multiple takes you recorded into a take folder in the previous lesson, you will use Quick Swipe Comping to create a single composite take. You'll also edit audio regions nondestructively in the Arrange area, and import an audio drum loop, quantize it, and use the Flex tool to change its groove. Finally, you'll apply destructive audio editing in the Sample Editor to reverse a hi-hat sound.

As your ability to read waveforms and use Logic's editing tools develops, never forget to use your ears and trust them as the final judge of your work.

Comping Takes

In the previous lesson, you recorded several takes of acoustic guitar and packed them into a take folder. Now you will learn how to preview the individual takes and assemble a composite take by choosing sections from different takes, a process called *comping*.

Comping techniques are useful when you have recorded several takes of the same musical phrase, each with its own good and bad qualities. Maybe in the first take the musician messed up the beginning but got the ending perfectly, and in the following take he nailed the beginning and made a mistake at the end. You can create a comp using the beginning of the second take and the ending of the first take.

You can use the same comping techniques to create a single musical passage out of multiple musical ideas. As they improvise, musicians will often record a few takes and later comp the best ideas of each performance into a new virtual performance.

Previewing the Takes

In this exercise, you'll comp three different performances of the same acoustic guitar riff, keeping only the best parts of each take. Before you start comping, you need to get familiar with the takes you are going to comp.

1   Go to Logic 9 Files > Lessons and open **03 New Day**.

A take folder is present on the Acoustic track (track 6).

2   Double-click the take folder to open it.

3   Press Z.

The selected take folder and its takes fill the Arrange area. The take folder is still displayed on the Acoustic track (track 6), with a disclosure triangle before its name and a take folder menu at the top right. The individual takes are displayed on lanes below the Acoustic track, with a take symbol before their name.

You can see that the Bright Acoustic #1 take at the top is selected (it is highlighted and has a black title bar). That's the one currently playing (the other takes are dimmed to indicate that they are muted).

Notice the name of the take folder: Acoustic: Bright Acoustic #1. It's the name of the track and the name of the selected take.

4   In the Bar ruler, drag a cycle area from bar 5 to bar 9.

5 Press the Spacebar.

Playback starts on bar 5, and you can hear the first take, Bright Acoustic #1. The beginning of that take is a bit messy, but bars 7 and 8 sound very good.

6 Stop playback.

7 Click the Bright Acoustic #2 take.

The Bright Acoustic #2 take is selected, and the name of the take folder is now Acoustic: Bright Acoustic #2. Notice that this take has a different color, and the color of the selected take is reflected in the take folder.

8 Press the Spacebar.

You are now listening to the second take, Bright Acoustic #2. This time, the guitarist really nailed the first bar but missed most of the notes in the rest of the take.

9 Stop playback.

MORE INFO ▶ Logic can continue playing in Cycle mode as you select different takes. In that case, a brief delay will occur as Logic switches playback between takes.

Repeat these steps to listen to the three takes, while watching the waveforms and determining the usable sections of each take. You will use the following sections of each take:

Bright Acoustic #1: bars 7 and 8

Bright Acoustic #2: bar 5

Bright Acoustic #3: bar 6

Comping the Takes

Now you'll select the best sections of each take to create a single, flawless composite take using a feature called *Quick Swipe Comping*. You will swipe your mouse across the parts of the takes you want to hear in your comp.

1 Click the Bright Acoustic #2 take.

The entire take is selected, and its color and name are displayed in the take folder.

2 Click Bright Acoustic #3 on the downbeat of bar 6, and drag to the right to select one measure.

Don't worry about being very precise in your selection. You will fine-tune the edits later in this lesson, but right now, let's get it in the ballpark.

A comp is created, and the name of the take folder is now Acoustic: Comp 1. By examining the colors, you can see that the take folder will play the selected parts of each take: Bright Acoustic #2 from the beginning to bar 6, Bright Acoustic #3 for the duration of bar 6, and Bright Acoustic #2 from bar 7 to the end.

For the end section, you'll use the Bright Acoustic #1 take. Once a section has been highlighted in a take, you can click the same section in another take to highlight it instead.

3   Click the Bright Acoustic #1 take in the bar 7 and 8 section.

That section of the Bright Acoustic #1 take is now highlighted and will play in the comp. This technique makes it easy to compare the same section in several takes after you've determined the locations of your edit points.

TIP ▶ If you're not happy with your comp and want to start over, Option-click a take to select the entire take.

4   Listen to your comp.

You now have a flawless performance for the entire four-bar section. Let's listen to it closely.

5   In the Acoustic track header, click the Solo button, and continue listening.

You may find that some of the edits (the points where you're switching from one take to another) don't sound very clean.

6   Option-Control-drag around the first edit to zoom in on it.

7   Place your pointer over the beginning of the selection in the Bright Acoustic #3 take, and drag so that the edit is positioned just before the attack of the first note you want to hear in that selection (the note just before bar 6).

8   Option-Control-click the waveform to zoom out.

9 Option-Control-drag around the second edit to zoom on it.

10 Place your pointer over the beginning of the selection in the Bright Acoustic #1 take, and drag so that the edit is positioned before the attack of the first note you want to hear in that section (the note just before bar 7).

11 Option-Control-click the waveform to zoom out.

12 Listen to your comp and make sure that it sounds right.

MORE INFO ▶ When using Quick Swipe Comping inside a take folder, classic audio editing features (such as cutting, moving, and resizing) are disabled. To edit the takes inside a take folder, you can turn off Quick Swipe Comping by clicking the Take Folder Editing Mode button.

Take Folder Editing Mode button

Once you're happy with your comp, you can commit to it. You will flatten the take folder, replacing it with the audio regions that compose the current comp, Comp 1.

13 At the top right of the take folder, click the arrow to open the take folder menu.

14 From the take folder menu, choose Flatten.

The take folder is replaced by the current comp, and the selected sections of the takes in the take folder are now replaced by audio regions. Crossfades are displayed at the edit points, and a fade-out is displayed at the end of the last region.

15 Click the Acoustic track's solo button to unsolo the track, and listen to the result.

Using the take folder's Quick Swipe Comping feature, you have created a flawless virtual performance by dragging over the good parts of three different imperfect performances.

Assigning Mouse Tools

Until now, you have worked exclusively with the default tools. You have also used keyboard modifiers such as Option-Control to choose the Zoom tool, and you have used features that change the pointer to tools such as the Resize tool or Loop tool, depending on its position.

When editing audio in the Arrange area, you will need to access more tools.

Two Tool menus are located at the upper right of the Arrange area. The left menu assigns the Left-click tool, and the right menu assigns the Command-click tool, which you access by holding down the Command key while clicking.

1 Position the pointer over the Arrange area, and hold down Command.

The pointer changes to the Command-click tool—the Marquee tool, in this case. Let's assign the Text tool to the Command-click tool.

2 From the Command-click Tool menu, choose Text Tool.

The Command-click Tool menu now displays the Text tool. The Comp 1 regions are still selected, and you need to deselect them to rename them individually.

3   Click the background of the Arrange area with the Pointer tool.

All Comp 1 regions are deselected.

4   On the Acoustic track, Command-click the first Comp 1 audio region.

A text field appears, in which you can rename the region.

5   Type *Beginning* and press Return to rename this region.

6   Rename the second region *Middle* and the third region *End*.

Instead of moving the pointer back and forth from the tracks to the Tool menus at the top right of the Arrange area, you can press the Esc (Escape) key to open a Tool menu at the current pointer position.

7   Make sure that the pointer is positioned over the Arrange area, and press Esc.

A Tool menu appears at the pointer position. This key command will save you a lot of trips to the Tool menus.

TIP ▸ Each area of the Arrange window has its own set of tools. You can change an area's tools in the Tool menus in its title bar, or by positioning the pointer over that area before pressing Esc.

8 Choose the Solo tool.

The Left-click tool switches to the Solo tool.

TIP ▸ Instead of choosing a tool from the menu using the mouse, you can use the keyboard shortcuts listed in the menu. For example, when the Tool menu is open, pressing 7 chooses the Solo tool as the Left-click tool.

9 Hold down the Solo tool over the Beginning region, just before bar 5.

The region is outlined in yellow, and Solo mode is temporarily turned on. Playback starts where you clicked, and you can hear the Beginning region play by itself until you release the mouse button.

TIP ▸ When using the Solo tool, to start playback at the beginning of the region, hold down Option and hold down the mouse button over the region.

Let's return the Left-click tool to the Pointer tool.

10 Press Esc twice.

The Left-click tool switches to the Pointer tool. Now let's assign the Solo tool to the Command-click tool.

11 Press Esc.

The Tool menu appears. You can Command-click a tool to assign it to the Command-click tool.

12 Press Command as you choose the Solo tool.

The Solo tool is the Command-click tool. Now you can perform edits with the Pointer tool, and you can Command-click any region to hear it in Solo mode.

TIP ▸ If you have a two-button mouse, you can assign a third tool to the right mouse button by choosing Logic Pro > Preferences > General and clicking the Editing tab. Choose "Is Assignable to a Tool" from the Right Mouse Button pop-up menu. The Right-click Tool menu will appear to the right of the two existing Tool menus.

Editing Audio Regions in the Arrange Area

Editing audio regions in the Arrange area is nondestructive. Regions are merely pointers that identify parts of an audio file. When you cut and resize regions, or add fades and crossfades in the Arrange area, only those pointers are altered. No processing is applied to the original audio files, which remain unaltered on your hard disk. You can always adjust your edits later. As a result, editing in the Arrange area provides a lot of flexibility and room for experimentation.

Adding Fades

When editing audio, you want to avoid abrupt transitions on edit points—the region boundaries and the junctions between regions. You can use nondestructive fades in the Arrange area to create smooth transitions. For this exercise, you'll temporarily raise the volume of the acoustic guitar to clearly hear your fades.

1   In the Inspector, Option-click the Acoustic channel strip's volume fader.

The volume fader jumps to 0.0 dB.

2   In the Bar ruler, click the Cycle area to turn off Cycle mode.

3   On the Acoustic track, select the End region.

4   Click "Play from Selection" (or press Shift-Enter).

Listen to the transition from the guitar part to the orchestra strings part in measure 9. The last acoustic guitar note is sustained too long and clashes with the melody of the strings.

5   Drag the lower right corner of the End region toward the left to shorten it so that it stops around bar 9, just when the strings come in.

As you drag to resize the region, notice that the pointer snaps to certain positions. When you need to edit with more precision, you can temporarily disable snapping by holding down Shift-Control after you start dragging.

6   Click "Play from Selection" (or press Shift-Enter).

The transition works better. Let's try it without the fade out at the conclusion of the End region.

7   Press Esc and choose the Crossfade tool (or press Esc-0).

The Left-click tool changes to the Crossfade tool. Using the Crossfade tool, you can Option-click a fade to delete it. You might need to zoom in to use the Crossfade tool.

8   At the end of the End region, Option-click the fade-out to delete it.

9   Listen to the transition.

Now the guitar dies abruptly on bar 9. Let's add a new fade out at the end of the End region.

10   Drag the Crossfade tool over the region's boundary.

Make sure that you drag over the region's boundary, or nothing will happen. You can create fades only over region boundaries. Here, the green shaded rectangle should cover the end of the region.

A fade-out is created. The length of the drag area determines the length of the fade.

 TIP ▶ You don't have to use the Crossfade tool to apply fades. To apply fades using the Pointer tool, Shift-Control-click inside the region and drag over the region's boundary.

11 Listen to the fade-out.

Depending on the sound you're going for, you may want to adjust the fade's length and shape. To adjust the length, you can drag the white vertical line to the left of the fade-out with the crossfade tool, or while holding Shift-Control.

12 With the Crossfade tool, drag the fade's white vertical line to the left.

The fade is now a bit longer. To adjust the fade's curve, you can bring the Crossfade tool to the middle of the fade and drag to the left or right.

 13 Position the Crossfade tool over the fade, and drag toward the right.

The fade now has a curved shape: The volume starts dropping slowly at the beginning of the fade and drops much faster at the end of the fade, creating a more natural result.

14 In the Inspector, drag the Acoustic volume fader down to –11.6 dB and listen to your result.

Feel free to continue adjusting the fade's curve and length until it sounds just right. There are no rules as to what the perfect shape of a fade should be, so experiment and trust your ears.

Cutting and Copying Regions

You will now use the Marquee tool to select a portion of a rhythm acoustic guitar region and make a copy to use later in the song, using the No Overlap Drag mode to make sure that the regions don't overlap.

1 On the Rhythm GT track (track 7), select the Rhythm Guitar region.

2 Click "Play from Selection" (or press Shift-Enter) to listen to that section.

The guitar plays the same two-bar chord pattern twice: once in bars 15 and 16, and once in bars 17 and 18. However, bars 19 and 20 don't have any rhythm guitar. You will now select the first two-bar chord pattern in bars 15 and 16, and copy it to bars 19 and 20.

3 At the upper right of the Arrange area, from the Drag menu, choose No Overlap.

When No Overlap is chosen, dragging one region over another automatically trims the region underneath to make space for the new one, which avoids region overlaps.

4 With your pointer over the Arrange area, press Esc to open the Tool menu, and then Command-click the Marquee tool.

5 With your pointer over the Arrange area, press Esc twice to reset the Left-click tool to the Pointer tool.

The Command-click tool is now the Marquee tool, and the Left-click tool is the Pointer tool. This is a very powerful tool combination when editing audio in the Arrange area. You can select a portion of an audio region with the Marquee tool, and move or copy that selection with the Pointer tool.

6 Zoom in on the Acoustic track for the whole last section (bars 15 to 21).

7 Command-drag in the Rhythm Guitar region from bar 15 to bar 17 to select that portion of the region.

8 Press the Spacebar.

The playhead jumps to bar 15 and plays the marquee selection. It corresponds exactly to a two-bar pattern of the guitar, what you need to add at the end to complete the rhythm guitar part.

TIP ▶ When a marquee selection is present, playback starts at the beginning and stops at the end of the marquee selection, even if Cycle mode is turned on.

9 Option-drag the marquee selection to bar 19.

Option-dragging a marquee selection automatically divides, copies, and pastes the selection to a new location regardless of region boundaries. When the mouse button is released, the original region is automatically restored.

Here the two-bar guitar pattern is copied and pasted at bar 19. The end of the original region is trimmed at bar 19 so that it does not overlap with the region you just pasted.

Now that the rhythm guitar part is complete, you can fine-tune the junction between the two regions and add a crossfade to avoid any clicks at that junction.

10 Zoom in on the junction between the two Rhythm Guitar regions.

It looks as though the edit point is in the middle of the note's attack. It would be better if placed a little earlier, in the silence before bar 19.

11 Position the pointer over the junction on the upper half of the waveform.

Junction pointer

The pointer switches to the Junction pointer. Dragging the Junction pointer horizontally changes the position of the junction between the regions while keeping both regions connected, without any gaps or overlaps.

12 Drag the Junction pointer to the left.

> **TIP** When you use the Junction pointer, the help tag can sometimes get in the way, hiding part of the waveforms in the audio regions. To fix this, position the pointer in the upper part of the junction to get the Junction pointer, and drag the Junction pointer down to the lower part of the regions; then drag horizontally to adjust the edit's position.

Now the junction of the two regions occurs in the silence.

It's usually a good idea to add a short crossfade to an edit point between two regions to avoid any clicky noise. Remember, you can apply a fade with the Pointer tool by holding down Shift-Control.

13 Shift-Control-drag a green-shaded rectangle over the junction.

A crossfade is created when the mouse button is released. Let's change its shape.

14 Position the pointer in the middle of the crossfade, and Shift-Control-drag toward the right to change the crossfade's shape.

Now that you know how to apply fades, take a minute to create a fade-in at the beginning of the first Rhythm Guitar region and a fade-out at the end of the last Rhythm Guitar region. If you decide to resize the beginning of the first region to eliminate the noise in the guitar recording during the first bar of count-in, remember to first deselect the second region, or you will be resizing both regions at the same time.

Deleting Unused Audio Files

When recording audio in Logic, storage space appears unlimited at first. When you are not totally happy with a recording, you usually keep it "just in case" and record another take. And another. ... You focus on recording the best performance, delaying the process of sorting out the good takes from the bad for the editing stage.

Once in the editing stage, you choose the best takes and comp them, or you edit the regions you need in the Arrange area. The leftover regions sit unused in the Audio Bin and can quickly pile up, crowding your hard disk space and bloating the project folder.

In the next exercise, you will delete unused audio files from your hard disk to reduce the size of the project folder.

1   In the Toolbar, click the Media button (or press B).

The Bin opens, listing all the audio files that were imported or recorded in the project, even if they are no longer used in the Arrange area. The Info column displays the audio files' information: sample rate, bit depth, status, and file size. The status icon indicates whether the file is mono or stereo (one or two symbols), and whether it's an Apple Loops file, a regular audio file, or a compressed audio file. In front of each region, the dark gray bar represents the audio file's length, and the colored section represents the region.

2   In the Audio Bin's local menu bar, choose Edit > Select Unused (or press Shift-U).

All the audio files that are not in use in the Arrange area are selected.

If you need to make sure that you won't need the unused files again, you can select them one by one and listen to them by clicking the Speaker button at the lower left of the Audio Bin. If you are sure that you want to delete them all, press Shift-U again to select all the unused audio files and regions.

You have two choices: You can delete the unused audio files from the Audio Bin but keep them on your hard disk (if you think you might need them later), or you can permanently delete them from the hard disk.

First, try deleting them from the Audio Bin, but keep them on your hard disk.

3   From the Audio Bin local menu bar, choose Edit > Delete (or press Delete).

The selected audio files and regions are deleted from the Audio Bin but not from your hard disk. This will not reduce the size of your project folder, but it will clean up your Audio Bin.

Since the operation is nondestructive, you can undo it and see the files again.

4   Press Command-Z.

All the audio files are once again displayed in the Audio Bin.

This time, you will delete the files from your hard disk. Be very careful whenever you permanently delete audio files: The operation is destructive, and you will not be able to recover those deleted files.

5   Choose Audio File > Delete File(s).

After a few seconds, an alert appears. Read it carefully! Make sure that you want to delete the audio files forever before you click Delete.

6   Click Delete.

The files are permanently deleted from the Audio Bin and from the hard disk.

MORE INFO ▶ In reality, the files are moved to the Trash in the Finder. If you just performed this operation by mistake, you still have a chance to undo it right now. But when you empty the Trash, the files are permanently deleted from the hard disk.

Quantizing an Audio Drum Recording

If you are not happy with the timing of an audio recording, you can quantize it to correct the positions of individual notes. In the following exercises, you will import an audio drum loop to your project, select a Flex mode to have Logic detect the attacks (or transients) or the individual drum hits in the audio file, and quantize the audio region to time-correct the positions of those transients.

> **NOTE** ▸ In Lesson 4, "Recording MIDI," you will quantize MIDI regions.

Previewing and Importing Audio Files

In the Media area, the File Browser allows you to search your hard disk for any kind of media files supported by Logic. In this exercise, you'll use the File Browser to locate, preview, and finally add a drum loop to your project.

1 In the Media area, click the Browser tab to open the File Browser.

The Browser is like a mini-Finder window inside Logic. At the top, you can see Back and Forward navigation buttons with which to step through your navigation history. The Path menu displays the current folder and allows you to move up in the Finder hierarchy. Three bookmark buttons provide quick access to the volumes on your computer, your home folder, or the project folder.

2 Click the Home button to display the contents of your home folder in the search results.

You can choose the way the search results are displayed by clicking the List and Column buttons. Column view displays columns, allowing you to see the folder hierarchy.

3   Click the Column button to display the search results in two columns.

List button
Column button

4   Click the Desktop folder to display the contents of your Desktop folder in the right column.

5   Navigate to Logic 9 Files > Media > Additional Media and select **TripHopLoop.aif.**

The file's information (file type, sample rate, bit depth, format, and length) is displayed at the top of the Browser.

TIP ▶ If you know the name of your file, use the search field at the top of the Browser. You can also click the plus (+) button to the right of the search field to set conditions that will limit your search by date, comments, length, and so on.

6   At the lower left of the Browser, click the Speaker button (or press the Spacebar).

The selected file starts playing. You can already tell that it has a very "lazy" groove and will need to be quantized to fit your New Day song.

7   Drag **TripHopLoop.aif** to the Arrange area at bar 15, below the last track.

A new audio track is created at the bottom of the Arrange area, and the TripHopLoop audio region is added to that track at bar 15.

8   In the Media area, click the Bin tab.

You can see the **TripHopLoop.aif** audio file in the Audio Bin.

9   Listen to the section of the song with the TripHopLoop region.

You can hear that this trip hop drum loop should work fine for that song, but right now it has a feel that is way too laid back and clashes with the drums on track 1.

Quantizing an Audio Region

You will now quantize the TripHopLoop audio region to make it better fit the groove of your song. To quantize an audio region, you first have to choose a Flex mode, which allows Logic to detect the transients in the audio file.

1   In the Arrange area, click the TripHopLoop track (track 8).

2   Press Z ("Toggle Zoom to fit Selection or All Content").

The selected TripHopLoop audio region fills the Arrange area.

3   In the Inspector, click the disclosure triangle in front of the track name to open the track parameter box (below the region parameter box).

Track parameter box

4   Click the Flex Mode parameter and choose Slicing.

A quick progress bar appears as Logic analyzes the audio file on the TripHopLoop track. The slicing Flex mode allows you to move slices of audio between transients without performing any kind of time stretching on the audio material.

You will now quantize the TripHopLoop region, so watch the result in the Arrange area as you perform this next step.

5   In the Region parameter box, set Quantize to 1/8 – Note.

In the Arrange area, the waveform in the TripHopLoop region changes shape as the individual drum hits are aligned to an eighth-note grid.

6   Click the "Play from Selection" button (or press Shift-Enter).

You can hear the TripHopLoop lose its laid-back feel. It is now perfectly in time and fits the groove of your song much better.

7   Stop playback.

Flex audio editing provides a powerful way to time-correct any audio file. Now that you have detected the transients of each note, you are not restricted to automatically lining them up with a grid. You can manually move individual notes where you want them. Enter the Flex tool, which you'll use in the next exercise.

Manipulating the Waveform with the Flex Tool

Until now, you've edited audio by manipulating audio regions in the Arrange area: You know how to move, resize, and copy a region, and even how to select a portion of it with the Marquee tool. However, when the inspiration strikes and you're ready to experiment with individual notes inside a region, you can use the Flex tool to manipulate the waveform without changing the region's integrity.

1   Place your pointer over the Arrange area, and press Esc to open the Tool menu.

2   At the bottom of the tool menu, click the Flex tool.

3   Zoom in on the first three or four notes in the TripHopLoop region.

4   Place the Flex tool over the attack of the second note in the waveform (at 15 1 3 1).

Depending on its position on the waveform, the Flex tool can have different actions, indicated by different tool icons, so make sure that the tool is precisely over the note's attack and looks like the icon in the preceding figure.

5   Drag the Flex tool to the right to move that hi-hat one sixteenth note later (at 15 1 4 1).

The waveform moves along with your pointer. You are changing the hi-hat note's position without modifying the rest of the audio region.

6   Click the "Play from Selection" button (or press Shift-Enter).

By moving the second hi-hat one sixteenth note later in the groove, you've created an interesting syncopation that changes the character of your drum loop. You can play with Command-Z to undo and Command-Shift-Z to redo your flex editing, and compare the groove before and after.

7   Press Esc twice to return to the Pointer tool.

8   Zoom out so that you can see the entire end section (from bar 15 to bar 20).

You can now fill in the rest of the section with your drum loop.

9   Drag the upper right corner of the TripHopLoop region to the right to loop it twice.

10 Stop playback.

Flex editing is a powerful new feature in Logic 9 that allows a fluid manipulation of individual notes directly on the waveform, without resorting to the cutting and dicing of regions. It lends itself very well to experimenting with note placement, changing the phrasing of a melody, or quickly correcting the timing of a note that was poorly performed. You will dive further into flex editing and its time-stretching modes in Lesson 7, "Manipulating Tempo and Time Stretching."

Editing Audio Destructively in the Sample Editor

The Sample Editor allows you to perform destructive audio editing. Although performing nondestructive editing on audio regions in the Arrange area keeps the parent audio file intact, processing an audio region in the Sample Editor actually modifies the audio file associated with that region. You will use the Sample Editor to reverse a single hi-hat note, creating a swelling sound that will be a perfect introduction for the last section of your song where you just added a drum loop.

Saving a Selection as a New Audio File

Instead of performing destructive audio editing on the original audio file, you can save the desired selection as a new audio file and work on that file while leaving the original unaltered. In this exercise, you'll save a single hi-hat note as a new audio file so that you can later edit the hi-hat file destructively without modifying the original trip hop drum loop.

1   In the Arrange area, double-click the TripHopLoop audio region.

Region marker

The region opens in the Sample Editor and appears in the editing area. You may need to resize your screen or scroll down to see the editing area. Notice that the Sample Editor displays the whole audio file. The region you double-clicked is selected (white waveform over a dark gray background) and displayed as a region marker in the region area below the waveforms. The region marker has the same color and name as the region in the Arrange area or the Audio Bin. Make sure you scroll all the way to the left so that you can see the hi-hat note (the second note on the waveform).

2 Drag over the waveform to select the second note.

TIP If you need to adjust your selection with more precision, you can Option-Control-drag over one of the edges of your selection and Shift-drag that edge precisely where you want it. Then Option-Control—click to zoom out, and repeat for the other edge.

3 From the Sample Editor's local menu bar, choose Audio File > Save Selection As.

The Save Selection As dialog appears.

4 Name the new audio file *Reversed Hat* and choose the desktop.

Leave the "File conversion settings" menu options unchanged, but make sure that "Add resulting files to Bin" is selected.

5   Click Save (or press Return).

A new Reversed Hat audio file is created and added to the Audio Bin.

6   At the bottom of the Sample Editor, click the Sample Editor button to close the Sample Editor.

At the bottom of the Bin, you should see your new Reversed Hat.aif audio file. In the Arrange area, you may need to zoom out a bit to clearly see where you're going to add the reversed hat.

7   From the Audio Bin, drag **Reversed Hat.aif** to the Arrange area, below the TripHopLoop track, at bar 15.

Reversing a Sample

Now for the fun part of using the editor! You will reverse the waveform on the time axis, meaning that your hi-hat will play backward, starting at the end of its tail and slowly building up into a swooshing sound until it reaches its attack.

1   In the Arrange area, double-click the Reversed Hat region.

The Reversed Hat region opens in the Sample Editor.

2   In the Sample Editor, click the Preview button (or press the Spacebar) to play the Reversed Hat file once.

3 From the Sample Editor's local menu, choose Functions > Reverse.

The waveform is reversed.

4 Click the Preview button (or press the Spacebar).

You can now hear your reversed hi-hat. It sounds like it's going to suck you in! That's the perfect kind of fun sound to add to a production to announce a new section.

5   In the Arrange area, listen to your song from around bar 14.

The reversed hi-hat starts on bar 15, which creates an interesting syncopation effect with the TripHopLoop.

To make the reversed sound really shine and pull the listener into the next section of the song, the reversed hat should start toward the end of the break, and its attack should be on the first downbeat of bar 15. Obviously, you could just drag the region in the Arrange area until it sounded right, but there's a more accurate way to position a region, which you'll discover in the next exercise.

Positioning an Audio Region in the Arrange Area

Audio regions have an anchor, which is used to position the region in the Arrange area. When you drag a region in the Arrange area, the anchor position is the position displayed in the help tag, and the anchor is used to snap the region to the grid.

By default, the anchor is located at the start point of an audio region. While this makes sense for most audio regions, sometimes the part of the audio region you want to align with the grid is not at the beginning of a region. To line up the attack of a reversed sound with the grid, you need to position the anchor right on the attack (the loudest part, or *amplitude peak*), near the end of the region.

In this exercise, you will move the anchor to the amplitude peak of the reversed hi-hat. In the Arrange area, the anchor of the Reversed Hat region is on the first downbeat of bar 15, so you will end up with a reversed hi-hat sound that has its amplitude peak on the first downbeat of bar 15.

1   In the Arrange area, zoom or scroll so that you can clearly see the Reversed Hat region.

Before you move the Reversed Hat region's anchor, you need to unlock the region's Arrange position. You want the region to move so that its new anchor position is still on the downbeat of bar 15.

2   From the Sample Editor's local menu, deselect Edit > "Lock Arrange Position when moving Anchor."

At the lower left of the Sample Editor, you can see the anchor, represented by an orange indicator below the waveform.

3   Drag the anchor to the maximum amplitude on the waveform, almost at the end of the Reversed Hat region.

In the ruler, the downbeat of bar 15 follows the anchor to end up where you drag it: to the amplitude peak. In the Arrange area, the Reversed Hat region moves so that its anchor stays on bar 15.

4 In the Arrange area, zoom in on the Reversed Hat region.

The anchor's position is represented by a white vertical line, and you can see it aligned with bar 15. You can try adjusting the anchor's position in the Sample Editor and see the region's position change in the Arrange area.

5 Zoom out and start playback around bar 14.

Listen to the effect of the reversed hi-hat. It sounds great! Now the reversed hi-hat really draws you into that final section of the song.

To go a little further with this song, try choosing interesting "lo-fi" channel strip settings for the TripHopLoop and Reversed Hat tracks: Some Electric Guitar settings will work great for those drum tracks, or you may want to experiment with settings in the "09 Warped" category.

You now know how to read a waveform, identifying notes and their attacks to perform precise and clean edits. You acquired skills with a number of editing tools—such as the Marquee tool, Crossfade tool, Junction pointer, Flex tool, and take folders—that you will continue using as you edit recordings and arrange projects. You can now increase your workflow by choosing the appropriate Left-click and Command-click tools for the job. As you produce more music in Logic, you will continue sharpening those skills, becoming a proficient audio engineer.

Lesson Review

1. How do you open a take folder?

2. How do you preview the takes?

3. How do you comp takes?

4. How can you see the result of your comp as regions?

5. How can you assign the Left-click tool?

6. How can you assign the Command-click tool?

7. How do you add a fade-in or fade-out to a region?

8. How do you crossfade between two regions?

9. How can you import an audio file into your project?

10. How can you select a portion of an audio region?

11. When you choose Edit > Select Unused in the Audio Bin, which files are selected?

12. What do you need to do before you can quantize an audio region?

13. Which tool allows you to move an individual note inside an audio region, without altering the region?

14. What kind of audio editing can you do in the Sample Editor?

15. What is the anchor?

Answers

1. Double-click a take folder to open it.

2. Click the takes you want to preview. The highlighted take is the take playing; the others are muted.

3. Open the take folder, and drag over each take to highlight the desired sections. The take folder assembles a comp comprising all the highlighted sections.

4. From the take folder menu, choose Flatten.

5. From the Left-click Tool menu, choose the desired tool, or press Esc and choose the desired tool.

6. In the Command-click Tool menu, choose the desired tool, or press Esc and Command-click the desired tool.

7. Drag the Crossfade tool over the boundaries of a region (or Shift-Control-drag the Pointer tool).

8. Drag the Crossfade tool over the junction of the regions (or Shift-Control-drag the Pointer tool).

9. You can locate and preview it in the File Browser, then drag it to the Arrange area.

10. Use the Marquee tool.

11. Choosing Edit > Select Unused selects all the audio files and regions that are not currently used in the Arrange area.

12. You need to first select a Flex mode in the Track Parameter box.

13. The Flex tool.

14. Destructive audio editing.

15. The anchor is a point in an audio region used to position the region to the grid in the Arrange area.

4

Lesson Files Logic 9 Files > Lessons > 04 Rock Song

Time This lesson takes approximately 60 minutes to complete.

Goals Record MIDI performances

Quantize MIDI recordings

Merge a MIDI recording with an existing MIDI region

Record MIDI in take folders

Punch record a MIDI recording

Capture a performance as a recording

Record MIDI using Step Input mode

Filter incoming MIDI events

Lesson 4
Recording MIDI

MIDI (the Musical Instrument Digital Interface) was created in 1983 to standardize the way electronic musical instruments communicate. Today, MIDI is extensively used in the music industry, from cell phone ringtones to major-label albums. Most TV and film orchestra composers use MIDI to sequence large software sound libraries, getting ever closer to productions that sound like a real orchestra.

MIDI sequences can be compared to piano rolls, the perforated paper rolls once used by mechanical player pianos. Like the punched holes in piano rolls, MIDI events do not contain audio. They contain note information such as pitch and velocity. To produce sound, MIDI events need to be routed to a software instrument or to an external MIDI instrument.

There are two basic types of MIDI events: MIDI note events that trigger musical notes, and MIDI continuous controller (MIDI CC) events that control parameters such as volume, pan, or pitch bend.

For example, when you hit C3 on a MIDI controller keyboard, the keyboard sends a Note On MIDI event. The Note On event contains the pitch of the note (C3) and the velocity of the note (which indicates how fast the key was struck, measuring how hard the musician played the note).

By connecting the MIDI controller keyboard to Logic, you can use Logic to route the MIDI events to a virtual software instrument or to an external MIDI instrument. The instrument reacts to the Note On event by producing a C3 note, and the velocity typically determines how loud the note sounds.

MORE INFO ▶ To learn more about the MIDI standard specification, visit the MIDI Manufacturers Association website at http://www.midi.org/.

Recording MIDI

In Logic, the techniques used to record MIDI are very similar to the techniques you used to record audio in Lesson 2. When a MIDI controller keyboard is connected to your computer, and its driver is properly installed (some devices are class-compliant and don't require a driver installation), you can use that keyboard to record MIDI in Logic. Logic automatically routes all incoming MIDI events to the record-enabled software instrument or external MIDI track.

TIP ▶ If you don't have a MIDI controller keyboard, press the Caps Lock key on your computer keyboard to turn your Mac keyboard into a polyphonic MIDI controller keyboard. A representation of your computer keyboard is displayed, showing the letter keys assigned to musical notes. The number keys allow you to choose the octave range, and the lower row of keys lets you choose the note velocities. Keep in mind that you may need to disable the Caps Lock keyboard to access some of Logic's key commands. Press the Caps Lock key again to disable the Caps Lock keyboard.

To record a MIDI performance triggering a software instrument, you need to create a software instrument track, insert an instrument plug-in or choose a channel strip setting from the Library, and click Record.

1   Go to Logic 9 Files > Lessons and open the **04 Rock Song** project.

That project has a single audio track with a drum loop, which will provide a timing reference to record your new instrument.

2   At the top of the track list, click the New Tracks button (+) (or press Command-Option-N).

The New Tracks dialog appears.

3   Make sure that Number is set to 1, Type is set to Software Instrument, and Open Library is selected. Then, click Create.

A software instrument track is created, and it is automatically record-enabled. The Library opens, displaying software instrument channel strip settings.

By default, audio tracks have a blue icon and audio regions are blue. Software instruments have a green icon and MIDI regions are green.

4   Choose a channel strip setting from the Library.

For this exercise, choose 05 Keyboards > 01 Electric Piano > Suitcase V2.

LOGIC EXPRESS ▶ For this exercise, choose 05 Keyboards > 01 Electric Pianos > Tines Electric Piano, and in the following exercises, substitute Tines Electric Piano when you see Suitcase V2.

In the Inspector, the software instrument channel strip loads the necessary plug-ins. In the Arrange area, the name *Suitcase V2* is displayed on the Inst 1 track header.

Processing plug-ins

Software instrument plug-in

While audio channel strip settings contain only processing plug-ins, software instrument channel strip settings also contain the software instrument plug-in. On the channel strip, the software instrument plug-in is loaded in the Instrument slot of the I/O section.

5   Play some notes on your MIDI controller keyboard.

You should hear the electric piano. In the Transport bar's MIDI In display, the incoming MIDI note events are displayed as notes are played. If you play a chord, the display shows the chord name.

You are now ready to record, but first open the Piano Roll Editor so that you can see the MIDI notes appear as you record them.

6   At the bottom of the Arrange area, click the Piano Roll button (or press P).

The Piano Roll Editor opens in the editing area.

7   Go to the beginning of the project.

8   In the Transport bar, click the Record button (or press R).

The playhead jumps back one bar, giving you a four-beat count-in with an audible metronome click before recording starts. The Bar ruler turns red to indicate that Logic is recording.

9   When you can see the playhead, play some notes.

Play a simple bass line in an eighth-note pattern. You will record more notes in that region later in this lesson.

When you play the first MIDI note, a new MIDI region with a red halo is created on the record-enabled Suitcase V2 track. The region's length constantly updates to include the most recent MIDI event played.

The MIDI notes appear in the Piano Roll Editor as you record them.

10 Stop recording.

MIDI notes

In the MIDI region, the notes are displayed as small beams.

11 Go back to the beginning and listen to your MIDI recording.

If you are not happy with your performance, you can undo it (Command-Z) and try again.

> **TIP** ▶ If you record-enable several software instrument tracks, incoming MIDI events will be routed to all record-enabled tracks, allowing you to layer the sounds of several instruments.

Quantizing MIDI Recordings

If you are not happy with the timing of your MIDI performance, you can correct the timing of the notes. The time-correction process is called *quantization*. To quantize a MIDI region, you choose a grid resolution from the Quantize menu in the Region Parameter box. Each note inside the region will snap to the nearest position on the chosen grid.

Quantizing MIDI Regions

In the following exercise, you will quantize the recording you made in the previous exercise to correct its timing, so that the piano notes are in sync with the drums.

1   Make sure the new #default MIDI region is selected.

First, you'll rename the region so that you can easily identify it later.

2   In the Inspector's Region Parameter box, double-click the name of the region and enter *Piano*.

The region is renamed *Piano*.

Now choose the Quantize value, which determines the resolution of the grid used to quantize the notes.

3   Set the Quantize parameter to 1/8-Note while looking at the notes in the Piano Roll Editor.

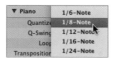

All the MIDI notes snap to the nearest eighth note.

4   Go to the beginning and start playback.

You can hear your performance, perfectly in time with the drums. Unless of course the performance timing was really poor, in which case some of the notes may not snap to the desired 1/8 note.

In Logic, quantizing is a nondestructive operation. You can always go back to the way the performance was originally recorded.

5   With the Piano region selected, open the Quantize parameter menu and choose "off (3840). "

The MIDI notes return to their original recording positions.

MORE INFO ▶ The (3840) indicator identifies the shortest resolution of Logic's MIDI sequencer, the tick. When the time signature is 4/4, there are 3840 ticks in a bar (or 240 ticks in a sixteenth note). When Quantize is set to "off (3840)," the notes snap to the closest tick.

6   From the Quantize parameter menu, choose 1/8-Note again.

The notes snap back to the grid.

MORE INFO ▶ The Quantize menu also offers Swing settings. The Swing settings delay the position of every other note in the grid to obtain a swing, or shuffle groove, common in many music genres such as blues, jazz, hip-hop, and house music. The amount of delay goes from no delay (A = no swing) to a lot of delay (F = hard swing). For example, 8B Swing will subtly delay the second eighth note of each beat.

Setting a Default Quantization Grid

You can set a default quantization value so that any new recording will automatically be quantized to that grid resolution. This is very useful if you are not confident of your timing chops. Since the Quantize setting is nondestructive, you can always adjust it or turn it off for that region after the recording is done.

1   Click in the background of the Arrange area.

All regions are deselected, and the Region Parameter box now displays the MIDI Thru settings. The MIDI Thru parameter settings are automatically applied to any new MIDI region that you record.

2   Set the Quantize parameter to 1/16-Note.

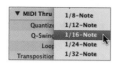

3   Select the Piano region.

The Region Parameter box displays the region's name and settings. You can see the Quantize setting you applied to that region in the previous exercise: 1/8-Note.

4   Press Delete.

The region is deleted.

5   Go to the beginning of the track and click the Record button (or press R).

Record a new simple bass line as you did previously.

6   Stop recording.

In the Piano Roll Editor, the notes immediately snap to the nearest 1/16 note. The new MIDI region is selected, and the Region Parameter box now displays its parameters: Quantize is automatically set to 1/16-Note, the MIDI Thru Quantize setting you set in step 2.

7   Set the Quantize parameter to "off (3840)."

The notes return to their original recorded positions.

8   Set the Quantize parameter back to 1/16-Note.

Merging Recordings into a MIDI Region

Sometimes you may want to record a MIDI performance in several passes. For example, when recording piano, you can record only the left hand and then record the right hand in a second pass. Or, when recording drums, you can record the kick drum in the first pass, the snare in a second pass, and the hi-hat in a third pass.

In Logic, when recording MIDI events on top of an existing MIDI region, you can choose to merge the new events with the existing ones.

Recording into a Selected MIDI Region

In the previous exercise, you recorded a simple bass line onto a piano track. Now you will play chords as you listen to the bass line and record the new chords inside the same MIDI region. First, you will choose the correct recording setting to merge your new recording with the selected region.

1 In the Toolbar, click the Settings button and choose Recording.

2 Under MIDI, set Overlapping Recordings to "Merge with selected regions."

Now you only have to select the existing MIDI region before recording, and the new notes will be recorded inside the selected region.

3 Make sure the Piano region is still selected.

4 Go to the beginning and start recording.

Try to play some chords that complement the bass line you recorded previously.

NOTE ▶ While you are recording, you are temporarily recording a new region on top of the existing one. The new region will be merged with the existing one as soon as you stop recording. The Piano Roll Editor displays the contents of the new region you are recording, and although the contents of the existing region are not displayed while you are recording, you can still hear the existing notes played back.

5   Stop recording.

The new recording is merged with the existing region and you can see all the notes in the Piano Roll Editor. (You might have to scroll or resize the Piano Roll Editor window to see all the notes.) Note that the notes you just recorded snap to the nearest 1/16 note, the default quantize resolution you chose in the previous exercise.

TIP ▸ You can also use this technique to add MIDI Controller events such as pitch bend or modulation to a region after you have recorded the MIDI notes.

Merging Recordings in Cycle Mode

Recording in Cycle mode allows you to continuously repeat the same section and only record new events when you are ready. This can be very useful when recording a drum pattern, for example. When repeating a one-bar or two-bar section, you can add new elements to the pattern during each pass of the cycle, while listening to everything that you have recorded.

When you are recording in Cycle mode, notes recorded in all consecutive passes of the cycle are merged into a single MIDI region. In this exercise, you will use Cycle mode to record drums—first recording the kick, then the snare, then the hi-hat.

1   In the Arrange area, mute both existing tracks.

Remember that you can click the Mute button on the first track header and drag down the mouse to mute both tracks.

2   At the top of the track list, click the New Tracks button (+) (or press Command-Option-N).

The New Tracks dialog appears.

3   Make sure that Number is set to 1, Type is set to Software Instrument, and Open Library is selected. Then, click Create.

This time, you will insert the software instrument in the Inspector, on the Arrange channel strip.

4   In the I/O section of the channel strip, click the Instrument slot.

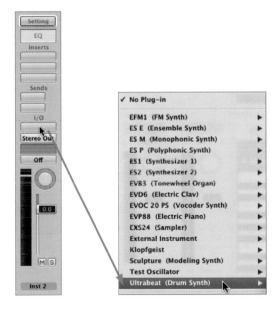

A menu appears, allowing you to choose one of Logic's software instruments.

5   Choose Ultrabeat (Drum Synth).

NOTE ▶ When you place your pointer over Ultrabeat (Drum Synth), a menu opens on the right that allows you to choose between Stereo and Multi-Outputs. For now, do not use the lower-level menu, and simply choose Ultrabeat (Drum Synth). By default, a stereo Ultrabeat will be inserted.

The Ultrabeat plug-in is inserted in the Instrument slot of the channel strip, and the Ultrabeat plug-in window opens.

6 Close the Ultrabeat window.

MORE INFO ▶ For now, you will use Ultrabeat to produce drum sounds as you record MIDI in Cycle mode. In Lesson 6, "Programming Drums," you will use the Ultrabeat interface to program a drum pattern.

Notice the white frame around the Ultrabeat plug-in on the channel strip. A white frame indicates the selected section of the channel strip, whose settings are automatically displayed in the Library. The Library now displays Ultrabeat settings.

7 In the Library, choose 01 Drum Kits > Funk Boogie Kit.

Wait a few seconds while Ultrabeat loads the kit. When the kit is fully loaded, the drum kit name is displayed on the track 3 track header in the Arrange area.

Selecting a software instrument track automatically record-enables it, but the instrument is not always in live mode. (An instrument in live mode requires more CPU resources) When an instrument is not in live mode, the first note you play will take about 100 ms (milliseconds) to trigger the instrument, which is then placed in live mode.

You can put an instrument in live mode by sending any MIDI event to it (playing a dummy note, moving the modulation wheel, and so on) or by clicking the Record Enable button in its track header.

Record-enabled instrument not in live mode

Record-enabled instrument in live mode

First, locate the notes on your controller keyboard that trigger the kick, the snare, and the hi hat. In Ultrabeat, you will use the following:

▶ C1: kick

▶ E1: snare

▶ F♯1: hi-hat

8 Play the lowest C note on your MIDI controller while watching the MIDI Activity display in the Transport bar.

If the MIDI In display doesn't show a C1, press your MIDI controller keyboard Octave Up and Down buttons until the lowest C plays a C1.

NOTE ▶ If your MIDI keyboard has a C lower than C1, locate the C1 on a higher octave.

MORE INFO ▶ If you are using the Caps Lock keyboard, press 4 to set the right octave, and press A to trigger a C1 MIDI note.

When you can trigger a kick with C1, locate E1 (two white notes to the right) to play the snare and F♯1 (the next black note to the right) to play the hi-hat.

9 In the Bar ruler, click the cycle area.

Cycle mode turns on, and the cycle area is shown as green.

10 Resize the cycle area so that it spans one bar starting at the beginning of the song.

You will now record the drums, one at a time.

11 Click in the background of the Arrange area.

The Region Parameter box displays the MIDI Thru parameters.

12 Set the Quantize parameter to 1/8-Note.

13 Start recording.

You hear a four-beat count-in before the playhead reaches the beginning of the cycle area. Play two C1 notes: one on the first beat, one on the third beat. In the Piano Roll Editor's Bar ruler, the first beat is on 1, the third beat on 1.3 (bar 1, beat 3).

When a new cycle begins, you can hear the kick drum notes you just recorded. Notice that the notes snap to the nearest 1/8 note because you chose that grid resolution for your default MIDI Thru parameters.

You have all the time in the world before you continue to record. As long as you don't play anything, there are no MIDI events, and Logic keeps cycling over the existing region, playing back your kick drums. If you feel the need to practice the snare before recording, you can return to play mode while cycling continues.

14 Click the Play button (or press Shift-Return).

Logic is no longer in record mode (and the metronome stops clicking), but playback continues as Logic repeats the cycle area without interruption. Notice that the two C1 notes are now quantized to the grid.

On your MIDI keyboard, locate the snare (E1) and practice a snare pattern. Try to hit the snare on beats 2 and 4.

15 Click the Record button.

Playback continues without interruption, but Logic reenters record mode.

16 Click your drum region on track 3 to select it. When you feel ready, record the snare.

When the playhead jumps to the beginning of the cycle, you can see the two kick notes and the two snare notes in the Piano Roll Editor.

Use the same techniques to record your hi-hat (F#1) on every eighth note in the same MIDI region.

17 Stop recording.

The merge MIDI-recording techniques you used in the two previous exercises provide a lot of flexibility and allow you to take your time, recording a single part of a performance. These techniques will work in many situations. For example, consider recording a violin or cello on a software instrument track; then, on a second pass, record the movements of the pitch bend wheel to add vibrato to some of the notes.

Recording MIDI Takes

When you want to nail a performance or experiment with various musical ideas, you can record different takes and later choose the best one. The techniques to record MIDI takes are similar to the techniques you used to record audio takes in Lesson 2. You can record over an existing MIDI region, or you can use cycle recording to record one take for each pass of the cycle.

Cycle mode should still be turned on from the previous exercise. Let's record takes in Cycle mode and experiment using different melodies for a bass line.

1   In the Transport bar, hold down the Record button and choose Recording Settings from the pop-up menu.

   The Recording Project Settings window opens.

2   In the MIDI area, from the Overlapping Recordings pop-up menu, choose "Create take folders."

3   Close the Project Settings window.

4   In the Arrange area, unmute track 1 (Drums/Audio 1) and mute track 3 (Funk Boogie Kit/Inst 2).

5   Create a new software instrument track and open the Library.

6   In the Library, choose 03 Bass > 02 Electric Bass > Aggressive Fretless.

   LOGIC EXPRESS ▶ Choose 03 Bass > 02 Electric Bass > Rock Fretless, and in the following steps, use Rock Fretless instead of Attitude Bass.

7   Start recording and play a different melody for each pass of the cycle until you have three or four takes.

A MIDI take is recorded for each pass of the cycle where you play MIDI notes. If you don't play anything for a whole cycle, no take is recorded. The takes are packed into a take folder.

When a new cycle begins, the take you just recorded is automatically muted. You can listen to it by switching to play mode.

8   Click the Play button (or press Shift-Return).

You are now in play mode, and you can hear the last take you recorded.

9   Open the take folder menu and choose the take you want to hear.

You can also double-click the take folder to open it and click the take you want to hear. Double-click the take folder to close it.

MORE INFO ► Unlike audio take folders, you cannot comp the takes in a MIDI take folder.

10 Stop playback and turn off Cycle mode.

Using Punch Recording

You can use the punch-on-the-fly and autopunch techniques you learned for audio recording to punch on MIDI recordings. The only difference is that you'll have to turn on the Replace mode.

In the next exercise, you will record a piano performance, and then use both the Replace and Autopunch modes to rerecord a section of the performance.

1   Mute the Aggressive Fretless track.

2   Select and unmute the Suitcase V2 track.

The track is record-enabled, and the MIDI region on the track is selected. If you have several MIDI regions on that track, all the regions are selected.

NOTE ▶ Make sure that Cycle mode is turned off. If Cycle mode is turned on, selecting a track selects only those regions within the cycle area (and the regions that overlap the cycle area).

3   Press Delete.

All the selected MIDI regions are deleted.

4   Press Record, play your keyboard for four or five bars, and stop the recording.

You will now correct a bar of your performance.

5   Click both the Autopunch and Replace buttons.

In order to merge the new events you are going to record over the Autopunch area with the existing region on the track, you need to change your recording settings back to the default settings.

6   In the Transport bar, hold down the Record button and choose Recording Settings from the pop-up menu.

The Recording Project Settings window opens.

7   In the MIDI area, from the Overlapping Recordings pop-up menu, choose "Merge only in Cycle record."

8   In the Bar ruler, adjust the Autopunch area around a section of the Piano that you want to record over.

Make sure the Autopunch area is placed over a section of the piano performance you captured in the previous exercise.

9   Go to the beginning of the project and make sure the Suitcase V2 track is still record-enabled.

10   Click the Record button and start playing right away.

On the Piano track, the section below the Autopunch area is deleted.

Notes are deleted.

You can hear the notes you are playing over the previous recording, but only the notes played within the Autopunch area are recorded inside the MIDI region.

11 Turn off the Autopunch and Replace modes.

Using Step Input Recording

Instead of recording a real-time performance, you can record notes one at a time. In Step Input mode, you position the playhead and play a note or chord on your MIDI keyboard. The note(s) are recorded, and the playhead moves one step ahead, waiting for the next note(s).

This mode is very useful for recording complex musical phrases that you can't perform in real time, such as complicated chord patterns or really fast arpeggios (a great technique for dance music).

1 Select the Suitcase V2 track and press Delete.

All the regions on the track are deleted.

 TIP If you don't want to select the regions on a track when selecting the track, hold down Option as you select the track.

You start by creating an empty MIDI region using the Pencil tool (as the Command-click tool). You will step-record notes inside that new region.

2 Press Esc and Command-click the Pencil tool.

3 Command-click the Suitcase V2 track between bars 1 and 2.

The Pencil tool creates an empty one-bar MIDI region.

4 Resize the region so that it is four bars long.

5 At the upper left of the Piano Roll Editor, click the MIDI In button.

The button turns red and MIDI Step Input Recording is turned on.

MORE INFO ▶ You can also enable Step Input Recording in the Score Editor or the Event List.

6 Go to the beginning of the project.

7 Play a single note on your MIDI keyboard.

A 1/16 note is recorded at the playhead position, and the playhead moves forward one 1/16 note. The recorded note has the pitch and velocity of the note you played.

The length of a step is identified by the division setting in the Transport bar, below the time signature.

8   In the Transport bar, click the division setting and drag down until it reads /8.

In the Piano Roll Editor, the grid resolution is the same as the division setting. The vertical grid lines are now placed at eighth-note intervals.

9   Play a chord.

An eighth-note chord is recorded at the playhead position, and the playhead moves forward one eighth note.

You can also use the Step Input Keyboard to exercise more control over your step input recordings.

10   From the main menu bar, choose Options > Step Input Keyboard.

Note-length buttons

The floating Step Input Keyboard appears. The selected note-length button overrides the division setting in the Transport bar.

11 On the Step Input Keyboard, click the quarter-note button.

12 Play a note.

A quarter note is recorded at the playhead position, and the playhead moves forward one quarter note.

If you were recording a quarter-note pattern and wanted to record a single half note, you could click the half-note button, record your half note, and click the quarter-note button again to record the next quarter note.

An easier way is to use the Sustain Insert Note button.

13 Play a note and hold down the key on your MIDI keyboard.

A quarter note is recorded. You need to hold down the MIDI key for the next step, so that the note you are recording remains selected in the Piano Roll Editor.

TIP You can also release the key on your MIDI keyboard and click the inserted note to select it.

14 On the Step Input Keyboard, click the Sustain Inserted Notes button.

The selected note is lengthened by a quarter note, so it is now a half note. You can click the Sustain Inserted Notes button several times to lengthen the selected notes by the current step length. You can now release the key on your MIDI keyboard.

Now let's record quarter notes starting on bar 2.

15 With the pointer positioned over the lower half of the Piano Roll Bar ruler on bar 2, hold down the mouse button.

The playhead snaps to bar 2.

16 Play three notes, one at a time.

Now you want to insert a quarter-note rest.

17 On the Step Input Keyboard, click the Sustain Inserted Notes button.

The playhead jumps forward one quarter note. When no notes are selected, the Sustain Inserted Notes button makes the playhead move one step ahead, and you can resume step input recording.

Try using step input recording techniques to record fast 1/16-note arpeggios or even crazy chord patterns. With a little experimentation, you will quickly end up with cool musical phrases that couldn't possibly be performed live.

18 Click the MIDI In button to turn off Step Input recording, and close the Step Input keyboard window.

Filtering Incoming MIDI Events

Sometimes your MIDI controller keyboard sends MIDI events that you may not want to record in Logic. Maybe you are using a faulty MIDI keyboard that generates random pitch bend events, or your keyboard is sending aftertouch MIDI events when you apply pressure to the keys, but the instrument you are recording does not react to aftertouch.

Logic allows you to filter out undesired incoming MIDI events so that they are not recorded. Since input filter settings are project settings, you can adjust them to filter various types of events in different projects.

1 In the Toolbar, click the Settings button and choose MIDI from the pop-up menu.

2   Click the Input Filter tab.

In this tab, you can select the MIDI events you want to filter.

3   In the Arrange area, click the Suitcase V2 track header.

The track is selected and record-enabled.

4   Play some notes on your MIDI controller keyboard and move the pitch bend wheel.

You can hear the note pitches change as you move the pitch bend wheel.

5   In the MIDI Project Settings window's Input Filter tab, select Pitch Bend.

6   Play some notes on your MIDI controller keyboard and move the pitch bend wheel.

This time the pitch bend MIDI events are filtered at their input into Logic, and your pitch bend wheel movements have no effect on the pitch of the notes you play.

Separating the MIDI data from the audio signal produced by the instrument allows for very flexible recording. Throughout this lesson you quantized your notes to a grid and chose to merge new recordings into an existing MIDI region or to record separate takes in a MIDI take folder. You also used step input recording to enter notes one step at a time, without the pressure of recording a real-time performance.

After a MIDI performance is recorded, you can still change the sound of the instrument independently of the MIDI events, or edit the MIDI events independently of the instrument's sound. Those vast sound- and performance-editing possibilities take you to a new realm of experimentation. Enjoy it!

MORE INFO ▶ To learn how to use external MIDI instruments with Logic, read the Appendix, "Using External MIDI Devices."

Lesson Review

1. How does Logic route incoming MIDI events?
2. How can you time-correct a MIDI region?
3. How do you choose the default quantize settings for new MIDI recordings?
4. How do you record MIDI takes?
5. What do you need to do before you can punch in on a MIDI track to replace a portion of a MIDI region?
6. How do you turn on Step Input mode?
7. When recording in Step Input mode, identify two ways you can adjust the step length.

Answers

1. All incoming MIDI events are routed to the record-enabled track(s).
2. In the Inspector's Region Parameter box, choose a grid resolution value from the Quantize menu. The MIDI notes in the region will snap to the nearest position on the chosen grid.
3. Deselect all regions to choose the MIDI Thru parameters in the Region Parameter box.
4. Open the Recording project settings and choose Overlapping Recordings > Create take folders, and then record on top of an existing record, or record in Cycle mode.
5. You need to turn on the Replace mode.
6. Click the MIDI In button in the Piano Roll Editor, Score Editor, or Event List.
7. In the Transport bar, adjust the division setting; or open the Step Input Keyboard and use the note-length buttons.

5

Lesson Files	Logic 9 Files > Lessons > 05 Funky Groove
Media	Logic 9 Files > Media > Additional Media
Time	This lesson takes approximately 60 minutes to complete.
Goals	Import MIDI files into a project
	Insert and edit MIDI notes in the Piano Roll and Score editors
	Quantize and mute individual notes
	Edit note velocity and pitch using a MIDI keyboard
	Draw and edit MIDI continuous controller automation using Hyper Draw and the Hyper Editor
	Clean up MIDI regions in the Event List

Lesson 5

Programming and Editing MIDI

When you work with MIDI sequences, the flexibility of separating the performance data from the instrument playing it gives you total control over the performance data, even after it is recorded. You can open the MIDI region in a MIDI editor to precisely fine-tune each note's position, pitch, velocity, and length. You can edit or add MIDI controller events to automate the instrument's volume, panning, pitch, and many other parameters. You can also write music from scratch, creating notes in MIDI editors using only your mouse, similar to the way a composer writes music on staff paper.

Writing music in MIDI editors is also called *programming MIDI sequences*. Logic includes several MIDI editors for this purpose, and though they all display the same MIDI events, each does it in its own way. For example, the Score Editor shows you musical notes on a staff, while the Piano Roll Editor shows you notes as beams on a grid.

In this lesson, you will use Logic's MIDI editors to program and edit MIDI events. You will write a bass line and a simple horn riff, edit a real-time recording of a MIDI performance, and program MIDI control automation to breathe life into your MIDI sequences.

Programming in the Piano Roll Editor

The Piano Roll Editor is the most straightforward MIDI editor. It borrows its name from the perforated paper roll used by mechanical player pianos, in which the position and length of a punched hole determined the pitch and length of the note it triggered. In Logic, the Piano Roll Editor represents MIDI notes as beams on a grid, positioned below a Bar ruler, much as the Arrange area displays regions on a grid below a Bar ruler. In fact, most of the techniques for editing regions in the Arrange area also apply to notes in the Piano Roll Editor.

Creating Notes with the Pencil Tool

In the Piano Roll Editor, you create notes by clicking in the grid with the Pencil tool. As you write your musical part using the Pencil tool, you can also use it to resize, move, copy, or delete notes.

You will use the Pencil tool to program a simple bass line in the key of A minor (using only the white keys on the musical keyboard).

1 Go to Logic 9 Files > Lessons > and open **05 Funky Groove**.

Cycle mode is turned on, and the cycle area spans the first two bars. You are going to write a two-bar bass line, so leave Cycle mode on and listen to the drums.

2 In the Arrange area, make sure that the Attitude Bass track is selected.

You will use the Pencil tool (currently the Command-click tool) to create an empty MIDI region on that track.

3 Command-click the Attitude Bass track in bar 1.

An empty one-bar MIDI region is created.

4   Resize the region so that it is two bars long.

In the editing area, the Piano Roll Editor displays the contents of the selected Attitude Bass region, which is currently empty. You can use the piano keyboard on the left to audibly preview the notes before you create them.

5   In the Piano Roll Editor, click the keys on the piano keyboard.

The keys trigger the bass software instrument and you can hear the bass notes. Scroll down to find A1, two white keys below C2.

6   In the Piano Roll Editor, make the Pencil tool the Left-click tool and the Velocity tool the Command-click tool.

The Pencil tool and the Velocity tool are the two most important tools when you're creating notes in the Piano Roll Editor, and this tool combination will make you proficient at programming MIDI.

As you position the pointer over the grid, look at the info display at the top of the Piano Roll Editor. It displays the pitch and position of the note you are about to create.

Info display

In the Piano Roll Editor's grid, light gray lanes correspond to the white keys on the piano keyboard, and dark gray lanes correspond to the black keys. This song is in the key of A minor, and you will use the natural A minor scale, which contains only white keys. Therefore, you will insert notes only on the light gray lanes.

7   Using the Pencil tool, click the light gray lane at 1 1 1 1 in front of the A1 key.

Light gray lane (white key)

Dark gray lane (black key)

TIP ▶ You can customize the colors of the Piano Roll Editor lanes in View > Piano Roll Colors.

8   Position the Pencil tool over the lower-right corner of the A1 note.

The pointer changes to a Resize pointer.

9   Drag the corner of the note toward the right to lengthen the note to make it a quarter note.

Note length

The help tag shows the note length as . 1 0 0 (period one zero zero), which indicates the length as 0 bars, 1 beat, 0 divisions, and 0 ticks. In other words, a single quarter note.

10 Insert a C2 on 1 2 1 1 (the second beat).

Remember to watch the info display as you position the Pencil tool. When the info display shows the desired note pitch and position, you can click to insert the note.

C2 1 2 1 1

A quarter note C2 is inserted. The Pencil tool inserts notes of the same length and velocity as the last note selected with the Pencil tool.

11 Shorten the C2 so that it is an eighth note.

While you resize to an eighth note, you may need to hold down Control-Shift to disable snapping. The help tag shows the note length as . . 2 0 (two divisions, or two sixteenth notes, make an eighth note).

Instead of creating the note and then resizing it, you can hold down the Pencil tool to insert the note, and then drag the tool left or right to resize the note. This allows you to insert and resize a note in one action.

12 Hold down the Pencil tool to create an A1 on 1 2 3 1 (right after the last note), and drag toward the left to shorten the note to a sixteenth note.

To make the note a sixteenth note, drag until the help tag displays the note length as . . 1 0. Depending on your zoom level, you may have to hold down Control-Shift as you drag the Pencil tool to disable snapping.

13 Hold down the Pencil tool to insert an E1 note right on 1 2 4 1 (right after the last note), and drag to lengthen it to a quarter note.

You have just written a one-bar bass riff.

14 Press the Spacebar.

Listen to your bass riff. It works well with the drums. You will fill in the second bar in the next exercise.

Copying and Deleting Notes Using the Pencil Tool

Writing music is often about repeating musical phrases while introducing subtle differences. When programming MIDI, it is easy to select all the notes that form a musical phrase, copy them, and edit the copy to slightly change the repeated phrase.

In the following exercise, you will use the Pencil tool to copy the one-bar bass riff to bar 2 and delete a note to change the second riff.

1 Make sure that the Piano Roll Editor has key focus, and then choose Edit > Select All (or press Command-A).

All the notes are selected in the Piano Roll Editor.

Now you will copy the whole bass riff to bar 2. When you position the Pencil tool over the middle of a note, it turns into a Pointer tool. You can then use the Pointer tool to move the notes or Option-drag to copy the notes.

2   Position the pointer over the middle of the first note.

The Pencil tool becomes a Pointer tool.

After you start dragging notes in the Piano Roll Editor, you can hold down Shift to limit the dragging to a single direction, either horizontal or vertical. Holding down Shift while you Option-drag the selection will ensure that you don't accidentally copy the notes to another pitch.

> **TIP** Limiting dragging to a single direction is a very useful feature. If you prefer it, you can make it the default behavior. Choose Logic Pro > Preferences > General, click the Editing tab, and select Limit Dragging to One Direction In (Piano Roll and Score) and (Arrange). When those options are selected, you can hold down Shift when you do *not* want to limit the dragging to one direction.

3   Option-drag the whole selection to 2 1 1 1, but press Shift immediately after you start dragging, to limit dragging to horizontal.

To align the copy of the riff on 2 1 1 1, watch the help tag and also the vertical and horizontal white dashed guidelines that appear when you drag a note.

The riff now plays twice. To make the second riff slightly different, you can delete its first A1 note by double-clicking the note with the Pencil tool. But first you need to deselect all the notes.

4   Choose Edit > Deselect All (or press Command-Shift-A).

> **TIP** Holding down Shift with a key command often gives you the result opposite to the command. In this case, Command-A selects all, Command-Shift-A deselects all.

5   Double-click the first A1 note of the second bass riff.

The note is deleted.

6   Start playback and listen to your bass line.

Editing Note Velocity

When you play a MIDI keyboard, you need to control how loud each note is played. To judge how hard you press the keys, MIDI keyboards measure the speed at which each key is depressed. That speed is called *velocity*. When you press a key, the MIDI keyboard sends a *note-on* MIDI event that contains the pitch and velocity values of the note.

Higher velocities usually result in louder notes. Depending on the patch or program you're using, higher velocities can also trigger different sounds or different samples, as they do in the sampler instrument you're using on the Attitude Bass track. The result will sound more real, as the higher-velocity notes trigger samples of a bass string that was actually plucked harder.

You assigned the Velocity tool to the Command-click tool in the first exercise. You will now use the Velocity tool to edit the velocities of the bass notes to extend the dynamic range of your bass line and make it sound more natural. Using the Velocity tool, you can drag a note up to increase its velocity or drag down to decrease it.

1   Command-drag the first bass note up and down.

Note velocity   Line indicating velocity

In the help tag, you can see the value of the note velocity (to the right of the note pitch), ranging from 1 to 127.

The velocity value is indicated by the color of the note, ranging from violet (the lowest velocity) through blue, turquoise, green, yellow, orange, and red (the highest velocity). It is also represented by the length of the line in the middle of the note beam.

While you drag the Velocity tool up and down, the MIDI note is triggered repeatedly so that you can hear the sound of the note at different velocities. Notice how high-velocity (red) notes trigger bass sounds that are plucked very hard, and very low-velocity (violet) notes trigger ghost bass sounds in which the string is barely touched.

2   Adjust the velocities of the other notes to make the bass line more dynamic.

You can experiment with placing accents on individual bass notes by raising their velocities to change the groove of the riff. Subtle random differences in velocities also help make the bass line sound more realistic.

3   Choose Edit > Select All (or press Command-A).

4   Using the Velocity tool, drag up and down on one of the notes.

When the Velocity tool is used on multiple notes, all of the note velocities are offset by the same amount, and the differences in velocity between the notes are retained.

5   Choose Edit > Deselect All (or press Command-Shift-A).

6   Start playback.

7   Adjust the velocity of some notes while the project is playing.

As you drag the Velocity tool, MIDI notes are triggered over the playback, making it difficult to hear the result of your velocity changes on the bass line.

At the upper left of the Piano Roll Editor, you will see a MIDI Out button. By default, that button is turned on (green), and any note you create, select, or edit is automatically played. While you play the project in Cycle mode, it's a good idea to turn off MIDI Out.

8 Click the MIDI Out button.

The MIDI Out button is dimmed, and MIDI notes are no longer triggered when you're editing them. You can keep the project playing and adjust velocities while listening to the result.

9 Keep the project playing, and adjust the velocities of some notes while listening to the result, then stop playback.

Editing a MIDI Recording

When you're recording a MIDI performance, MIDI events are created in real time at the playhead position and placed in a MIDI region on the record-enabled track. You can then use the MIDI editors to fine-tune the performance.

In the following exercises, you will import a MIDI file containing a piano recording. You will use editing tools to mute undesired notes, shorten notes to get a better musical feel, and quantize individual notes to correct their timing.

Importing a MIDI File

To import any MIDI file into an existing project, just drag the MIDI file to a track.

1 In the toolbar, click the Media button. Then, in the Media area, click the Browser tab (or press F).

2 In the File Browser, click the Home button, navigate to Desktop > Logic 9 Files > Media > Additional Media, and locate **Piano.mid**.

3 Drag **Piano.mid** to the Suitcase V2 track, at 1 1 1 1.

A Piano MIDI region is created.

4 Click the background of the Arrange area, then click the Piano MIDI region to display its contents in the Piano Roll Editor.

You may have to scroll or zoom to see all the notes in the Piano MIDI region.

5 Listen to the piano performance you just imported.

Editing a Recorded MIDI Sequence

When opening a MIDI performance in the Piano Roll Editor, you can see all of the imperfections. Some notes shouldn't have been played, and some are sustained for too long. This is a good time to polish the performance.

In the current project, the Piano region includes several elements that could be improved. First, the two blue A notes on the fourth downbeat of measure 1 play at the same time as the snare. This is a funky groove, and one of the "rules" of groove is to leave space for the snare! You could delete the two notes, but you might change your mind later. For now, you can just mute the notes.

1 Make sure that the pointer is positioned over the Piano Roll, and press Esc (Escape) twice to revert the Left-click tool to the Pointer tool.

2 Drag to select the two blue notes at the end of measure 1.

3 Press Esc.

The Tool menu appears.

4 Choose the Mute tool.

5 Click one of the two selected notes.

The notes are dimmed, indicating that they are muted. Although the notes are still present in the region, they will not trigger any MIDI events. This is a great way to experiment with removing notes nondestructively. You can always unmute the notes later by clicking them again with the Mute tool.

To mute notes, you don't have to select them before clicking them with the Mute tool; but if you select multiple notes, one click of the Mute tool will mute them all.

TIP You can also mute and unmute selected notes by pressing M.

6   Press the Spacebar to start playback.

When the playhead reaches the fourth beat, the muted notes don't play, making room for the snare. That snare really snaps now! Much better.

7   Press Esc and choose the Quantize tool.

8   Drag to select the two first notes.

9   Hold down one of the selected notes with the Quantize tool.

The Quantize menu appears.

10 Choose 1/4-Note.

The selected notes snap to the nearest quarter-note grid line, on the first downbeat.

11 Listen to your edited piano.

Using the Score Editor

The Score Editor displays MIDI notes as standard musical notation. If you have classical training, this could become your editor of choice. In these exercises, you will use the Link modes to change the relationship between the Score Editor and the Arrange area displays, and use the Score Editor to create a simple horn part.

Using the Link Modes

You can use Link modes to control what an editor displays when you work in another area. By default, MIDI editors open in Content Link mode (indicated by a yellow link button) and display the contents of the selected MIDI region in the key focus area.

1 At the bottom of the editing area, click the Score button.

Link button

The Score Editor opens in Content Link mode and displays the contents of the Piano region. The notes you are seeing are the same notes you just edited in the Piano Roll Editor, but they're displayed as musical notation.

NOTE ▶ If the Score Editor doesn't show you the contents of the Piano region in the Arrange area, click the background to deselect all the regions, and then click the Piano region to select it. Click the background of the Score Editor to give it key focus.

Notice that the Inspector updates to display the score parameters and a Part box full of score symbols. You will use these in the next exercise to create notes on a staff.

2 In the Arrange area, click the Attitude Bass region to select it.

The Score Editor displays the contents of the Attitude Bass region, and you can see your bass line as musical notation.

When you unlink an editor, it will keep displaying the same contents independently of your actions in other areas. This is useful when you need to manipulate regions in the Arrange area without changing what a MIDI editor displays.

3   In the Score Editor title bar, click the Link button.

The button is dimmed, and the Score Editor is now in No Link mode.

4   In the Arrange area, select different regions.

The Score Editor does not update and still shows the contents of the Attitude Bass region.

In the Same Level Link mode, a MIDI editor displays all the contents of the key focus area. When the Arrange area has key focus, the Same Level Link mode allows a MIDI editor to display all the MIDI regions in the Arrange area.

5   In the Score Editor title bar, click the Link button.

TIP   You can also hold down the Link Button and choose a link mode from the pop-up menu, which allows you to switch from the Content Link mode to the Same Level Link mode without clicking the Link button twice.

The button is purple, indicating that the Score Editor is in the Same Level Link mode. The Score Editor now displays the contents of all the MIDI regions in the Arrange area.

On the top staff, the high notes are hidden under the title bar. You can drag the first clef vertically to move the staves down.

6 Drag the first G clef down.

All the staves move down, and you can now see the highest notes.

In the next exercise, you must see the contents of a new MIDI region to create a horn line, so you will need to reset the Content Link mode.

7 Double-click the Link button.

The Link button turns yellow, and the Score Editor is in Content Link mode. It displays the contents of the selected region in the Arrange area.

Creating a Horn Line in the Score Editor

You will now use the Score Editor to program a simple horn riff. First you need to create a new software instrument track and load a horn channel strip setting.

1 Create a new software instrument track, making sure that Open Library is selected.

2 In the Library, choose 08 Pop Horns > Studio Horns.

You may have to scroll to the left to see all the instrument categories.

You can play a few notes on your MIDI keyboard to hear the sound of the studio horns.

3 Command-click in bar 1 of the Studio Horns track.

An empty one-bar region is created and displayed in the Score Editor.

4 Resize the region so that it is two bars long.

5 Zoom in the Score Editor by dragging its vertical zoom slider at the bottom right.

The Score Editor has key focus again, and the Inspector displays the Part box.

In the Score Editor, you can insert notes and symbols by dragging them to the staff from the Part box.

6 In the Part box, drag a quarter note to the upper staff as an A3 at 1 1 1 1.

When creating notes in the Score Editor, look at the help tag to make sure that you drop the note at the desired pitch and position. Notice the note length in the help tag. The inserted note is a few ticks shorter than a quarter note. This is done to avoid creating overlapping notes in the Score Editor.

The note is green to indicate that it is selected. If you click the background, the note is deselected and turns black again.

You could continue to drag notes from the Part box, but in the Score Editor it is usually easier to copy existing notes.

7 Option-drag the A3 note to A2 (one octave below) at 2 1 1 1.

A new quarter note is inserted on the lower staff as an A2. Listen to your horns. Does it sound like the simplest horn line you have ever heard? Well, in funk music, sometimes simple works the best. Still, let's add a little lead-in note just before that last note, to make it groove.

8 From the Part box, drag a sixteenth note to G2 at 1 4 4 1.

As you drag the note to 1 4 4 1, it looks as though it's going to be dropped inside the second bar, but don't trust the display; always trust the help tag, and make sure that it reads 1 4 4 1 before you release the mouse button. When you do, the Score Editor will display the correct position and automatically fill in the blanks with the necessary rest symbols.

9   Click the Piano Roll button (or press P).

Your new horn notes are displayed as note beams in the Piano Roll Editor.

The Inspector now displays the Studio Horns channel strip.

10   Adjust the Studio Horns volume to suit yourself, and listen to your groove.

Editing Notes with a MIDI Keyboard

You can adjust the pitch and velocity of selected notes using your MIDI controller keyboard. The notes will retain their position and length, and they will update their pitch and velocity according to the note you played on the MIDI keyboard.

In this exercise, you will use your MIDI keyboard to experiment with the pitch and velocity of the horn notes you just entered in the Score Editor.

1   In the Arrange area, make sure that the Studio Horns track is record-enabled.

2   At the bottom of the editing area, click the Score button.

The Score Editor opens, showing you the three horn notes you inserted in the previous exercise.

3   Click the first note.

The note turns green to indicate that it is selected.

4   At the top of the Score Editor, double-click the MIDI In button.

The MIDI In button is the button you clicked to activate step input recording in the previous lesson. When you double-click the MIDI In button, the MIDI connector icon inside the button turns black, and you can now edit the selected note's pitch and velocity using your MIDI keyboard.

5   Play a note on your MIDI keyboard.

The selected note is changed to the pitch and velocity of the MIDI note that you played.

You will actually keep the A3 pitch but experiment with different velocities using the keyboard. Try to find the original A3 pitch on your keyboard (you can use the MIDI In display in the Transport bar).

6   Start playback.

With that first note still selected in the Score Editor, on your MIDI keyboard, press the A3 really hard or really softly. You can hear the note you play, and you can watch the selected A3's velocity update depending upon how hard you pressed the key. Each time the playhead jumps back to the beginning, you will hear the A3 played with the new velocity.

Continue experimenting in the same way with the other two horn notes. Try placing the accent on the second note or the third note, and listen to how it affects the groove.

Let's use the same technique in the Piano Roll Editor to alter the velocities of the notes in the bass riff.

7   At the top of the Score Editor, click the MIDI In button to turn it off.

8 In the Arrange area, click the Attitude Bass track header.

The Attitude Bass track is selected and record-enabled.

9 Double-click the Attitude Bass region.

In the editing area, the Piano Roll Editor opens and displays the contents of the Attitude Bass region.

10 At the top of the Piano Roll Editor, double-click the MIDI In button.

11 Select the first bass note, and play a note on your MIDI keyboard.

If the note you play has a very high pitch, the selected note will disappear from the visible area in the Piano Roll Editor. Play a few lower-pitched notes until the selected note reappears.

Find the original pitch (A1) on your MIDI keyboard, and experiment with hitting the note at various velocities while playing the project.

12 Click the MIDI In button to turn it off.

Editing Note Velocity Using Hyper Draw

While the Hyper Draw area is typically used to edit MIDI CC events, as you'll see in later exercises, you can also use it to adjust note velocities. Hyper Draw is especially useful for creating velocity ramps, crescendos, and decrescendos.

Let's apply a decrescendo to the bass line.

1   In the Arrange area, make sure that the Attitude Bass region is selected.

The bass line is displayed in the Piano Roll Editor. If necessary, zoom to make sure that all the bass notes are visible, and switch your Left-click tool back to the Pointer tool.

2   Solo the Attitude Bass track.

3   At the bottom left of the Piano Roll Editor, click the Hyper Draw button.

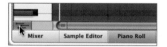

The gray Hyper Draw area appears at the bottom of the Piano Roll Editor.

Hyper Draw area

Since no MIDI CC events are present in the region, the Hyper Draw area displays the velocity of each MIDI note as a node along with a line representing the length of the note. The height of each line represents the velocity of the note above it on the grid, according to the scale on the left. You can adjust the velocity of a note by dragging the node (not the line) vertically.

4 Drag a node up or down.

A help tag shows you the note's velocity as you adjust it. When you release the mouse button, the note's beam changes color to reflect the new velocity.

Let's use the Line tool to create a decrescendo.

5 Hold down the mouse button in the background of the Hyper Draw area.

A Start Line help tag appears, helping you to precisely adjust the position and value of the beginning of the decrescendo. Keep holding down the mouse button as you position the pointer where you want to start the decrescendo.

6 Drag to the upper left of the Hyper Draw area until the help tag reads 1 1 1 1, Velocity = 127.

7 Release the mouse button and locate the End Line position, where you want the decrescendo to stop.

The help tag moves to the top of the Piano Roll Editor so that you can see the entire Hyper Draw area, and it now says *End Line*.

8   Position the pointer all the way down and to the right.

A green line appears between the Start Line position and the pointer position.

9   Click at the pointer position.

All the note velocities are aligned to the green line you just drew.

10   Listen to your bass line.

The Line tool can be very useful for creating velocity crescendos and decrescendos, but in this case, having a decrescendo on a bass line doesn't really work for a funky groove, and the last few notes are now too quiet to be heard.

11 Press Command-Z.

The original velocities reappear. The original accents you programmed by adjusting the note velocities with the Velocity tool work better for the bass line, so you will keep the note velocities as they are now.

Editing MIDI Continuous Controller Events

When playing a MIDI keyboard, you can add expression to your performance using knobs, sliders, or wheels, such as the pitch bend wheel or a volume pedal. Manipulating those controllers sends a stream of MIDI continuous controller (CC) events that represent the movement of the controller and trigger the intended action on the instrument.

When programming MIDI, you can draw the stream of MIDI CC events to automate an instrument's volume, pitch, and other parameters. In the following exercises, you will use Logic's MIDI editors to create pitch bend, volume, and pan automation in the bass and piano MIDI regions.

> **MORE INFO ▶** Automated MIDI CC events are often referred to as *region-based* automation, as opposed to *track-based* automation, which you'll explore in Lesson 10, "Automating the Mix and Using Control Surfaces."

Automating Pitch Bend Using Hyper Draw

Pitch bend events are MIDI CC events. Adding subtle pitch glides at the beginning or end of notes can help make a MIDI sequence more musical. By creating pitch bend automation on the first bass note, you will emulate the sound of the bass player sliding into the note.

1 At the upper left of the Hyper Draw area, click the arrow button.

A menu appears, allowing you to choose which MIDI controller automation you want to display in the Hyper Draw area.

2 Choose Pitch Bend.

The Hyper Draw area shows a blank slate where you can start creating and editing pitch bend events.

The black center line indicates the normal pitch of the note. You will create automation that starts at the minimum pitch bend value and goes back up to the normal pitch.

Although a single click is enough to create a node, dragging the pointer allows you to create the node and use the help tag to position it.

3 In the Hyper Draw area, position the pointer at 1 1 1 1. Hold down the mouse button and drag until the help tag displays the lowest possible pitch bend value (–64). Release the mouse button.

A node is created at the position where you released the mouse button.

Now you need to create a second node to return the pitch to the normal note pitch.

4 Click slightly to the right of the first node, as close to the black center line as possible.

A second node is created. Notice that the pitch bend value is displayed next to each node.

5 Drag the new node. While watching the help tag, position the node to a value of 0 (original note pitch) near the center of the first bass note.

6   Press the Spacebar to hear the results.

You can hear the pitch glide. It's getting there, but it still doesn't sound quite right. You can curve the pitch glide to make it sound more natural.

7   Control-Shift-drag the line between the two nodes.

Drag up or down to create a convex or concave curve, respectively. Drag left or right to create a horizontal or vertical S curve, respectively. Note that you can create a curve only between nodes of different values. You can't curve a horizontal line.

> **TIP** ▶ To revert to a straight line, hold down Control-Shift and click the line.

8   Try Control-Shift-dragging to the right to create a vertical S curve.

9   Press the Spacebar to hear the result.

The result sounds much more natural, very close to what a real bass player sliding into a note would sound like. Still, the slide is a little slow.

10 Drag the second node to the left.

The S curve is shortened. Keep listening and adjusting the position of the second node and the shape of the curve until you find the perfect-sounding slide.

11 In the Arrange area, click the Solo button on the Attitude Bass track header to turn it off.

Automating Volume Using Hyper Draw

You can add expression to a MIDI sequence by creating volume automation.

Because using MIDI CC automation intrinsically ties the automation to the MIDI region you are editing, it is called *region-based* automation. It is useful when you want to add expression to a musical phrase (for example, a volume swell on the first two notes), and want the same volume changes to occur every time you repeat the musical phrase. Copying or repeating the MIDI region in the Arrange area will copy or repeat all the notes and MIDI CC automation contained in the region.

In Lesson 10, you will use track-based volume automation, which is useful when you want to create dynamic changes that spread over several regions, such as a slow decrescendo over several copies of the same region.

You will now add dynamic expression to the piano performance by creating MIDI CC volume automation.

1 In the Arrange area, click the Suitcase V2 track header.

The Suitcase V2 track is selected, and its channel strip appears in the Inspector.

The Piano region is also selected, and its contents are displayed in the Piano Roll Editor. You may have to zoom and scroll to see the piano notes.

2   At the left of the Hyper Draw area, click the arrow to open the Hyper Draw menu, and choose Volume.

There are currently no MIDI volume events in this region, and a black horizontal line representing the current volume is displayed in the Hyper Draw area. It corresponds to the position of the volume fader on the channel strip in the Inspector.

To create the volume automation, you do not have to be precise when positioning the nodes. Click to create the nodes, and don't worry about the help tag. The goal is to accent the second beat.

3   Click the black line on the second beat.

Two nodes are created: one at the beginning of the line, and one where you clicked, both at the current volume.

4   Drag up the second node so that it is a bit higher than the current volume.

5   Create a node on the third beat to return to the original volume.

You may want to start dragging to insert the node and position it to the same value as the first node. If you can't get the same value, zoom in vertically, or hold down Control as you drag the node.

6   Shift-Control-drag the second line to curve it.

Don't hesitate to listen to the results and experiment as you're drawing automation. Also, close your eyes and focus on hearing the actual result, uninfluenced by the visual representation of the Hyper Draw automation.

If you make a mistake and create a node you don't want, click the node to delete it.

TIP ▶ You can also draw freehand automation by dragging the Pencil tool in the Hyper Draw area.

When you are happy with the accent in bar 1, you can copy the same accent to measure 2. To select several automation nodes, hold down Shift as you drag to select them.

7   Shift-drag to select all three nodes.

The whole automation is highlighted, indicating that it is selected.

8   Option-drag the selection to bar 2, using the help tag to position the copy as close as possible to 2 1 1 1.

Depending on your zoom level, the automation may snap to different values. If you want more precision when positioning automation nodes, you need to zoom in horizontally. In this exercise, it doesn't matter if the volume automation is a few ticks off.

The selected automation is copied to bar 2. Now copy the automation in measures 1 and 2 to measures 3 and 4.

9 Shift-drag around all the nodes in bars 1 and 2.

This time you will use a new technique to copy automation: You will copy the selection to the Clipboard, position the playhead where you want the copy, and paste the Clipboard contents.

10 Choose Edit > Copy (or press Command-C).

The selected automation is copied to the Clipboard.

11 Click and hold the lower half of the Bar ruler on the downbeat of bar 3.

The playhead is positioned on 3 1 1 1.

12 Choose Edit > Paste (or press Command-V).

The automation in the Clipboard is pasted at the new playhead position. Zoom out to see the whole region.

13 Turn off the Cycle mode, return to the beginning, and listen to the whole Piano region.

In the Inspector, the volume fader will move, following the volume automation you just created.

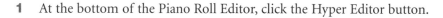 You can also display and edit MIDI CC automation in the Score Editor by clicking the Hyper Draw button, and in the Arrange area by choosing View > Hyper Draw and selecting the desired MIDI controller.

You have created volume MIDI CC automation in the Piano region. You could now arrange a song by copying, moving, or looping the Piano region. The volume automation you created would be present for each instance of the Piano region.

Automating Pan in the Hyper Editor

Although they share a similar name, Hyper Draw and the Hyper Editor are quite different. Hyper Draw is the name of the technique you previously used to draw MIDI CC automation by creating nodes and adding curves.

The Hyper Editor is a highly customizable MIDI editor, capable of displaying any type of MIDI event on its own lane. You can use the Pencil tool to draw events on a music grid, and each lane can have its own grid resolution. This makes it the editor of choice to draw drum rolls, as you will do in Lesson 6, "Programming Drums."

In the Hyper Editor, you can also display and edit multiple types of MIDI CC on their own individual lanes. Let's use the Hyper Editor to draw some pan automation in the Piano region.

1 At the bottom of the Piano Roll Editor, click the Hyper Editor button.

In the Hyper Editor, each lane allows you to display and edit one type of MIDI event, determined by its *event definition*. An event definition can be a MIDI note or a MIDI CC such as volume or pan. On each lane, events are represented by vertical beams on a grid. The height of a beam represents the value of the MIDI CC event, or the velocity of the MIDI note that the beam represents. A collection of event definitions is called a *hyper set*.

— Hyper Set menu

— Event Definition Parameter box

The Inspector now displays Hyper Editor parameters. The Hyper Set menu lets you choose which Hyper Set you want to display in the Hyper Editor. The Event Definition Parameter box allows you to adjust parameters for the selected event definition.

The default hyper set is called MIDI Controls. It includes the basic MIDI controller events: volume, pan, modulation, pitch bend, and a few others. If you are still looking at the Piano region, you can see the volume automation you created in the previous exercise.

2 Click the Pan event definition.

The Pan parameters are displayed in the Event Definition Parameter box.

3   Press Option-Control–Down Arrow a few times.

The Hyper Editor zooms in vertically so that you can better see the Pan event definition lane.

4   In the Inspector, set Grid to 1/32-Note.

The Pan lane's grid now has a finer resolution. Notice that the grids on the other lanes did not change.

Now you will enter some pan automation. You will use the Pencil tool (Command-click tool) to draw the automation in the lane.

5   In the first two bars, Command-drag in the Pan lane to create pan events.

You can now use the Line tool to shape the events you just created.

6   Press Esc and choose the Line tool.

The Line tool in the Hyper Editor works the same way as the Line tool you previously used in Hyper Draw to edit bass note velocities: Hold down the mouse button to find the Start Line position, release the mouse button, find the End Line position, and click to end the line. You will now use the Line tool to create a smooth movement of the Piano from one speaker to the other over the first two bars.

7   Hold down the Line tool in the Pan lane and find your starting position, at the top of the lane on 1 1 1 1.

8   Release the mouse button and find your ending position, over the last pan event just before bar 3.

A green line appears.

9   Click the end of the line.

All pan events are aligned to the green line, producing a smooth panning of the piano from right to left.

You can also use the Line tool to create events.

10 Using the same technique to start and end the line, use the Line tool in bars 3 and 4, which have no events at present.

Pan events are created on each grid mark, along the green line.

11 In the Arrange area, click the Suitcase V2 track header.

The Inspector shows the Suitcase V2 channel strip.

12 Go to the beginning and listen to the project.

You can hear the pan automation you just created, and see the Pan knob move in the Inspector.

With each lane placed in its own grid, and having the ability to draw events while snapping them to the grid of your choice, you can create interesting step automation. You could use swing grid resolution on a lane that controls the filter cutoff of a synth to generate some trippy filter sweeps! The Hyper Editor is also a great tool to program drum beats, as you will learn in Lesson 6.

Editing in the Event List

The Event List displays all the MIDI events contained in a region as text and numerical values. It offers powerful ways to filter events and to select and edit the desired events with the most accuracy, displaying the exact numerical value of each event's parameter.

Cleaning Up a MIDI Region

Sometimes a MIDI recording can contain undesired MIDI events that were not filtered during input. When you don't know which MIDI events a region contains, you might not know where to look for them in the other editors. The Event List can show all the MIDI events in a region, so you can use it to get a comprehensive view of the MIDI data that a region contains.

In this exercise, you will examine the contents of the Piano region that you imported at the beginning of this lesson and delete the unwanted events.

1   In the Toolbar, click the Lists button (or press E).

Hierarchy button

Event type

The Event List opens. It displays the contents of the Arrange area, listing all its regions and their positions and lengths.

NOTE ▶ If the Event List displays the contents of a region, click the Hierarchy button at the upper left of the Event List to see a list of all the regions in the Arrange area.

You can display the contents of a region by double-clicking the region in the Event List or by selecting the region in the Arrange area. When you are looking at the contents of a region, you can once again display all the regions in the Arrange area by clicking the Hierarchy button.

MORE INFO ▶ The Event List is the only MIDI editor that can display a list of regions and their positions. It is the only editor in which you can quantize the positions of regions in the Arrange area, which is very useful for quantizing the positions of audio regions (for example, to quantize drums).

2   In the Event List, double-click the Piano region.

A list of all the MIDI events contained in the Piano region is displayed.

If you look at the Status column, you'll see that some events are note events, some are controller events, and some are channel pressure (C-Press) events. In the Length/Info column, some of the controller events are volume; others are pan. Those are the MIDI controller events created by the automation you drew in the previous exercises.

Some MIDI controller keyboards send channel pressure events (also known as *aftertouch*) when pressure is applied to the keys. Channel pressure events can be configured to control instrument parameters such as vibrato or filter cutoff. But sometimes they are unused or may affect a modulation that you don't want.

Let's clean up the Piano region by deleting all channel pressure events.

3   At the top of the Event List Editor, make sure that the Filter button is turned on.

You can now click event type buttons to filter out the display of that event type.

4   Click the Notes button.

The Notes button is shaded, and all note events are hidden.

5   Click the Controller button.

The Controller button is shaded, and all controller events (volume and pan) are hidden.

Now only the channel pressure events are displayed. In the Event List, only the currently displayed events will be affected by editing commands.

6   Choose Edit > Select All (or press Command-A).

All the displayed events (the channel pressure events, in this case) are selected. Notice that the channel pressure events are also highlighted in the Hyper Editor. (You might have to scroll down to see the Channel Pressure lane.)

7   Press Delete.

All channel pressure events are deleted. You can also see the channel pressure events deleted from the Hyper Editor.

8   Click both the Notes and Controller filter buttons.

The Notes and Controller events are displayed again.

Quantizing Note Lengths

When playing a real drum kit, you do not usually control the length of the drum sounds. For example, when you hit a snare, the snare rings until the sound dies.

Similarly, when playing a MIDI drum kit, you don't usually control the length of the drum sounds. By default, drum synthesizers and samplers trigger mostly *one-shot* sounds. A one-shot sound always sustains only for its duration, independent of the length of the MIDI note that triggers it.

Since the length of the MIDI note generally does not influence the playback of your drum sounds, you may want to clean up a recording of MIDI drums so that all drum notes have exactly the same length, which makes them visually easier to edit in the Piano Roll Editor.

1   In track 1 of the Arrange area, click the Downtempo Funk Beat 05 region.

The contents of the selected region are displayed in the Event List.

2   At the bottom of the editing area, click the Piano Roll button.

The Piano Roll Editor also displays the contents of the drum region. You can see the notes as they were recorded. They all have different lengths, which can look confusing when you're editing drums.

3   In the Event List, choose Edit > Select All (or press Command A).

Holding down Shift-Option as you adjust a single value assigns the same value to all the selected events.

4   Shift-Option-drag down the length of one of the selected notes.

Position				Status	Ch	Num	Val	Length/Info			
1	1	1	1	Note	1	G-1	108	.	.	1	207
1	1	1	1	Note	1	A-1	108	.	.	1	207
1	1	1	1	Note	1	C0	73	.	.	1	207
1	1	1	1	Note	1	F5	90	.	.	1	207
1	1	1	1	Note	1	D#6	89	.	.	1	207
1	1	1	1	Note	1	D#7	112	.	.	1	207
1	1	1	11	Note	1	F#1	92	.	.	1	207
1	1	3	5	Note	1	F#1	57	.	.	1	207

All the note lengths are set to the same value. In the Piano Roll Editor, you can see that all the notes have the same length. A single tick can be a little short for viewing and manipulating notes in the Piano Roll Editor, so you should lengthen them.

5   Double-click the length of one of the selected notes.

A text field appears.

6   Type *200* and press Enter.

Position				Status	Ch	Num	Val	Length/Info
1	1	1	1	Note	1	G-1	108	200
1	1	1	1	Note	1	A-1	108	. . 1 207
1	1	1	1	Note	1	C0	73	. . 1 207

All note lengths are set to 200 ticks, which is a little shorter than a sixteenth note (a sixteenth note equals 240 ticks). Since the drum pattern is a sixteenth-note pattern, this ensures that you won't have overlapping notes.

The result sounds the same as before, but is visually clearer in the Piano Roll Editor.

7   Go to the beginning and listen to the project.

2	2	4	1	Note	1	D#6	82	. . . 200
2	2	4	1	Note	1	D#7	105	. . . 200
2	2	4	239	Note	1	F#1	84	. . . 200
2	3	2	1	Note	1	E1	59	. . . 200
2	3	2	235	Note	1	F#1	79	. . . 200
2	3	3	1	Note	1	G-1	38	. . . 200

Playhead position

In the Event List, the events scroll as they are played, and a white horizontal line indicates the playhead position.

In this lesson, you have used all the MIDI editors included in Logic, performing different tasks in each one. You have used the basic functions of each editor to create or edit simple sequences, but don't be fooled! The MIDI editors in Logic are powerful tools that include numerous options and features. When trying to perform a specific task, don't hesitate to look through an editor's local menu, or to Control-click an event or the editor's background area to access shortcut menus. Chances are, you will find the feature you are looking for and discover even more useful features you wouldn't have imagined.

Lesson Review

1. In the Piano Roll Editor, what can you do with the Pencil tool?
2. What does the MIDI Out button do?
3. Can you quantize individual notes? How?
4. How can you edit notes with a MIDI keyboard?
5. How can you edit MIDI continuous controller events in the Piano Roll Editor or Score Editor?
6. How do you insert nodes in Hyper Draw?
7. How do you curve a line in Hyper Draw?
8. How do you use the Line tool in Hyper Draw (when editing note velocities) or in the Hyper Editor?
9. How do you select automation in Hyper Draw?
10. How do you change the grid resolution of an event definition?
11. How do you draw automation in the Hyper Editor?
12. How do you hide a type of event in the Event List?

Answers

1. You can insert, resize, delete, move, and copy notes.
2. When the MIDI Out button is on, MIDI notes are triggered as you edit them.
3. Yes, you click the notes with the Quantize tool and choose a quantize setting from the pop-up menu.

4. Double-click the MIDI In button at the top of the MIDI editor, select the note you want to edit, and play a note on your MIDI keyboard.

5. Click the Hyper Draw button at the lower left of the editor.

6. Click in the Hyper Draw area to insert a node. You can also hold down the mouse button so that a help tag appears, and then drag the node to the desired position while looking at the help tag.

7. Shift-Control-drag the line.

8. Drag to find your Start Line position, release the mouse button, find your End Line position, and click to end the line.

9. Shift-drag around the desired nodes.

10. In the Inspector, in the Event Definition Parameter box, adjust the Grid parameter.

11. With the Pencil or Line tool.

12. When the Filter button is on, click an event type button to filter the corresponding events.

6

Media

Time

Goals

Logic 9 Files > Media > Additional Media

This lesson takes approximately 60 minutes to complete.

Program a drum pattern in Ultrabeat

Add rhythmic accents

Create drum rolls

Convert an audio drum loop to a sampler instrument

Lesson 6
Programming Drums

In most popular modern music genres, drums are the backbone of the instrumentation. They provide the foundation for the tempo and the groove of the piece. In recording sessions, when not all of the instruments are tracked at the same time, drums are usually recorded or programmed first, so that the other musicians can record to their rhythmic reference.

With today's high production standards, producing drum tracks usually involves using several techniques such as live recording, programming, sampling, audio quantizing, and sound replacement. For that reason, you will gain an edge by developing drum programming skills, and by knowing how to quickly convert MIDI patterns into audio loops, and audio loops into sampler instruments.

In this lesson, you will program a pattern in Ultrabeat, Logic's dedicated drum production plug-in. You will then import the pattern to the Arrange area and add a snare roll using Logic's MIDI editors. Finally, you'll turn your programmed MIDI groove into an audio loop and convert an audio loop into a sampler instrument.

Programming a Drum Pattern in Ultrabeat

Ultrabeat is a plug-in designed specifically to create drum sounds and to program drum patterns. It integrates all the classic drum synthesis techniques (phase oscillators, frequency modulation, ring modulation, noise generation, and physical modeling) with sample playback and a step sequencer.

In the next exercises, you will choose an existing drum kit and program a drum pattern using Ultrabeat's interface.

Choosing a Drum Kit and Previewing Drum Sounds

Before you start programming a pattern, you need to choose the drum sounds you will be using. In Ultrabeat, you can load a drum kit made up of 24 drum sounds, plus one bass sound that you can play chromatically.

Let's insert Ultrabeat on a software instrument's channel strip, choose a drum kit, get to know the layout of Ultrabeat's interface, and preview the individual drum sounds.

1   Choose File > New (or press Command-N).

2   In the Templates dialog, click the Empty Project template.

3   Create a software instrument track, and select Open Library.

A software instrument track is created, and its channel strip appears in the Inspector. The Library opens, displaying collections of software instrument channel strip settings.

You will insert the Ultrabeat plug-in directly into the software instrument channel strip.

4   Click the channel strip's Instrument slot, and choose Ultrabeat (Drum Synth) from the pop-up menu.

Ultrabeat is inserted, a default drum kit is loaded, and the Ultrabeat interface opens. The Library updates to display Ultrabeat settings.

All plug-in windows have a black header that contains buttons and menus to access plug-in settings and to navigate between plug-ins. For now, you can close that section to reduce screen clutter. You will use the Library to access the plug-in settings.

5   At the right of the plug-in window title bar, click the button.

The plug-in header is hidden.

TIP Drag out the lower-right corner of a plug-in window to make the window larger.

Ultrabeat's interface comprises three parts:

▶ The Assignment section, where you can assign drum sounds to MIDI notes and adjust each sound's volume, pan, mute, and solo settings. The currently selected sound is highlighted in white.

▶ The Synthesizer section, occupying most of the window, where you can tweak the parameters of the selected sound.

▶ The step sequencer, where you can program a sequence for the selected sound.

To the left of the Assignment section, a thin keyboard extends vertically. In front of each key appears the name of the sound assigned to it, and the sound's number. Sounds are numbered 01 through 25, from bottom to top. Each sound area also has a blue volume slider, a red Mute button, a yellow Solo button, and a Pan knob.

Let's listen to those drum sounds. You can click the keys of the vertical keyboard to preview individual sounds.

6   Click a key on the vertical keyboard.

The key is depressed and highlighted in blue, and the corresponding sound is played.

Using a MIDI keyboard is the best way to preview a drum kit, as you can play a little groove to get the feel of the sounds. MIDI notes C1 through B2 trigger sounds 01 through 24, used for drum sounds, while MIDI notes C3 and above play sound 25 chromatically, usually used for a bass sound.

7   Play the lowest C on your MIDI keyboard while watching the MIDI Activity display in the Transport bar.

If the MIDI In display doesn't show a C1, press your external MIDI controller keyboard's Octave Up or Down buttons until the lowest C triggers a C1.

In Ultrabeat, you can see the lowest key light up (in blue) and you'll hear sound 01, a kick drum.

8   Play a C♯1, and keep going up chromatically on your keyboard.

You see the corresponding Ultrabeat key light up, and the sound assigned to that key is played. When you reach C3 and up, you can play the bass sound chromatically.

Are you feeling adventurous? Try alternating two fingers of your left hand on C1 and E1 to play the kick and snare while using your right hand to play the hi-hat on F♯1. Skilled keyboard players can even play a drum groove with the left hand while the right hand plays a bass line!

Notice that sound 01 is highlighted in white. That's the currently selected sound. Its Synthesizer parameters are displayed in the Synthesizer section, and its sequence in the step sequencer.

9   Click the name of sound 02, Rim Shot.

Sound 02 is highlighted. The Synthesizer section and the step sequencer update to display the rim shot's Synthesizer parameters and sequence.

Let's try using other drum kits.

10 In the Library, choose 01 Drum Kits.

A collection of drum kits opens in the right column of the Library.

11 Choose Big Beat Remix Kit.

After the kit opens, the parameters update in Ultrabeat's interface. The name of the kit appears in the plug-in window's title bar and on the track header.

12 Use the mouse and the vertical keyboard, or play your MIDI keyboard, to preview the kit.

13 Make sure the Library has key focus, and press the Down Arrow key.

The next drum kit is loaded, and you can preview it.

14 Press the Up Arrow key.

The previous drum kit is reloaded. For this exercise, you are going to use an acoustic kit that includes live drum samples.

15 In the Library, choose Studio Tight Kit.

Drum kits using a lot of samples can take a while to load.

When the name of the drum kit (Studio Tight Kit) appears in the plug-in window's title bar and on the track header, the kit is loaded and you can preview its drum sounds.

Using the Step Sequencer

You can use the step sequencer at the bottom of the Ultrabeat interface to program or edit patterns. In Ultrabeat, you can save up to 24 patterns with each drum kit. Most factory settings include some prerecorded patterns, so let's listen to one and see what it sounds like.

1 At the upper left of the step sequencer, click the power button.

The power button icon turns blue, and the step sequencer becomes active.

2   Click the Play button next to the power button.

The Play button turns into a green Stop button. The step sequencer starts, and you can hear the first pattern. The notes on the keyboard in the Assignment section are highlighted as the sounds are played.

Ultrabeat's step sequencer is synchronized to the project and its tempo. To toggle the step sequencer playback on and off, you can also press the Spacebar to toggle the project playback, and the step sequencer will follow. Don't hesitate to leave playback on for the rest of this exercise, or to toggle it on and off frequently to listen to your results. If you choose to play the project, the playback will eventually stop when the playhead reaches the end of the project. When this happens, go to the beginning (press Return) and start playback again.

3   In the Assignment section, click Closed Hat (Sound 07).

Closed Hat is selected, and the step sequencer updates to show you the closed hi-hat sequence. Seeing the sequence of a single drum sound at a time can be useful for precise editing, but it does not give you an overview of the whole pattern.

4   At the lower right of the step sequencer, click the Full View button.

Now you can see the sequences for each sound directly across from the Assignment section. You can click anywhere on the grid to insert a new note.

5   Click step 1 on the Crash Cymbal 1 lane (sound 14).

A blue square is highlighted where you clicked, indicating that a crash cymbal is added on the first downbeat of the pattern. In the full-view grid, notice that downbeats are indicated by white vertical grid lines (on steps 1, 5, 9, 13, and so on).

You can also click an existing note to delete it.

6 On the Snare Light lane (sound 03), click the blue square on step 8.

The snare note is deleted.

You can access the setting's patterns in the Pattern menu at the lower left of the step sequencer.

7 Click the Pattern menu, and scroll all the way down so that you can see the entire menu.

The menu lists 24 available patterns. The *sq* indicates that a sequence is programmed for that pattern. For the Studio Tight Kit, patterns 1 through 10 already have a programmed sequence, while 11 through 24 do not.

MORE INFO ▸ Ultrabeat also has a Pattern mode that allows you to switch patterns in real time using a MIDI keyboard. The MIDI note in parentheses indicates the note that triggers each pattern when pattern mode is on.

8 Choose pattern 2.

Ultrabeat continues playing but switches to pattern 2, which is now displayed in the full-view step sequencer. You can choose from the Pattern menu to preview other patterns while the step sequencer is playing.

9   Choose pattern 4.

The step sequencer instantly updates to display pattern 4, and you can hear the pattern.

10   Stop playback.

Programming a Pattern

You are now ready to program your own pattern. You need to choose an empty pattern from the Pattern menu so that you can build your own groove from scratch.

1   From the Pattern menu, choose pattern 11.

The grid is empty and ready for a new pattern. In the menus to the right of the pattern menu, you can set the number of steps in the pattern and the step resolution. For now, you should keep the default settings: 32 steps with a sixteenth-note resolution, to create a two-bar pattern.

2   On the Kick 1 lane (sound 01), click step 1.

A kick note is added to the full-view grid. Since the kick sound is highlighted in the Assignment section, the step sequencer displays the kick sequence, and a blue vertical bar also appears on step 1 in the velocity/gate row. A blue square is also highlighted in the trigger row.

TIP ▶ Drag the pointer in the trigger row to quickly add notes on every step or to delete several existing notes at a time.

3   Continue entering kick notes every other beat (on steps 9, 17, and 25).

The step sequencer displays the entire kick sequence. Remember to regularly press the Spacebar to listen to the pattern as you build it. You can even choose to play the pattern continuously as you build it.

4   On the Snare light lane (sound 03), click step 5.

The snare sound is selected in the Assignment section, and the step sequencer displays the snare sequence, with the snare you just entered in step 5.

5   Continue entering snare notes every other beat (on steps 13, 21, and 29).

6   Control-click anywhere in the Closed Hat lane (sound 07).

A shortcut menu opens.

TIP Logic includes a number of shortcut menus that can be accessed by Control-clicking in various parts of the interface. When you are looking for a function, try Control-clicking!

7   From the shortcut menu, choose Add Every Downbeat.

Closed hi-hat notes are inserted on every downbeat (indicated by the white vertical grid lines).

8   Control-click the same Closed Hat lane (sound 07), and choose Add Every Upbeat.

You now have closed hi-hat notes every 1/8 note.

Often drummers will open the last hi-hat of a pattern to lead back into the first downbeat of the next pattern. Let's do just that!

9   Click the Closed Hat (sound 07) on step 31.

The last closed hi-hat is deleted.

10 Click the Open Hat lane (sound 11) on step 31.

The last hi-hat note is now an open hi-hat.

Editing Velocities and Accents

At this point, you have a basic rock pattern going. It sounds OK but a little mechanical. You can make it more exciting. Editing note velocities allows you to add variations in dynamics and make the sequence sound more human. You can also accomplish this using several randomization options available in a shortcut menu.

In the following exercise, you will insert a couple of softer kick notes, add accents to the hi-hat, and subtly randomize their velocities.

1 In the Kick 1 lane (sound 01), click step 11 to add a new kick at that step.

In the velocity/gate row, the blue bar's height represents the velocity of a note. The blue bar's width represents the length (or *gate time*) of a note.

2 In the velocity/gate row, drag down the top left of the new kick's vertical bar until the help tag reads Velo: 60.

MORE INFO ▶ Dragging a note's vertical bar horizontally adjusts the note length (or *gate time*), which affects only gated sounds.

The new kick note on step 11 sounds a little softer than the others.

You can also create notes and adjust their velocity and gate time in one operation by dragging directly in the velocity/gate row.

3   In the velocity/gate row, hold down the mouse button on step 27 to create a kick note, and drag vertically to adjust the velocity to 60.

Now let's work with accents. Accents can emphasize specific steps by raising the volume of multiple sounds in the kit. Whereas changing the velocity of a note can change the sound sample that it triggers, adding an accent changes only the volume of the sound.

At the top of the step sequencer, just above the trigger row, is a row of LEDs where you can select steps to accent. The Accent slider to the left adjusts the volume increase of the accents in decibels (dB). Although the accent slider setting and the accent steps are the same for all the sounds in the drum kit, the accent switch (the blue LED to the right of the Accent slider) lets you toggle the accents on and off for each drum sound.

Accent slider   Accent switch   Accent row

4   In the accent row, click steps 1 and 17, and listen to your beat.

Both the kick and the open hi-hat are accented on the first downbeat of each bar. The effect sounds good on the hi-hat, but not so good on the kick. Since the Kick lane is still selected, the step sequencer currently displays the kick sound parameters.

5   In front of the accent row, click the accent switch.

The kick is no longer accented, but the hi-hat is. The accent on the hi-hat could be a bit more pronounced.

6   Drag the Accent slider to the right until the help tag reads 8.0dB.

The difference in volume between the accented notes and the normal notes is now a little more pronounced.

Now let's adjust the velocities of the hi-hat notes and add a little randomness to make the pattern come alive.

7   In the Assignment section, click the Closed Hat name (sound 07).

The Closed Hat sound is selected, and the step sequencer displays its sequence.

8   Control-click in the velocity/gate row, and from the shortcut menu, choose Alter Vel.

The velocities of all closed hi-hat notes are randomly offset by a small amount.

Listen to the effect, and if the randomization is too subtle for your taste, repeat the procedure. If you went too far and velocity variations sound too drastic, you can reset all note velocities to their default values.

Remember that you made the last hi-hat an open one? Drummers like to accent that last open hi-hat to pull the groove back into the first downbeat of the next bar. Raising the velocity of the last hi-hat will accentuate that effect.

9 In the Assignment section, click the Open Hat name (sound 11).

10 In the velocity/gate row, drag the Open Hat note on step 31 up to a velocity of 113.

While dragging a note, notice that the velocity changes in increments of 2 or 3. To access every degree of velocity, you have to Shift-drag the note.

11 Shift-drag the same note to a velocity of 112.

The last open hi-hat is louder, which helps lead back into the downbeat of the next pattern.

Great job! You have programmed your first drum groove in Ultrabeat. Now you will import that groove as a MIDI region in the Arrange area and use Logic's MIDI editors to fine-tune the groove and create a snare roll.

Changing the Groove in the MIDI Editors

Musicians put many subtle timing and velocity variations in their playing, adding a human feeling to their performance that drum machines lack. If you reproduce those subtle inconsistencies when programming drums, your results will sound closer to a real performance.

In the previous exercises, you altered note velocities in Ultrabeat, helping to make the pattern sound more natural. While Ultrabeat's step sequencer is a powerful tool to program drum patterns, it lacks some of the advanced capabilities of Logic's other MIDI editors.

In the following exercises, you will import the Ultrabeat pattern to the Arrange window, open it in the Piano Roll Editor, and move the snare notes to change the feel of the groove.

Dragging the Pattern to the Arrange Area

You can insert the Ultrabeat pattern as a MIDI region in the Arrange area by dragging the button to the left of the Pattern menu in Ultrabeat's step sequencer. You will then be able to edit the MIDI region in Logic's MIDI editors.

1 Go to the beginning of the project.

You may have to move the Ultrabeat window to the right to see the first few bars of the Arrange area.

2 In Ultrabeat's step sequencer, position the pointer on top of the Pattern button.

A help tag appears that reads, "Drag to Arrange Window."

3 Drag the pattern to bar 1 below the track in the Arrange area.

NOTE ▶ As you drag the pattern to the Arrange area's grid, a green plus (+) icon appears, indicating that you can drop the pattern. You can drag the pattern to a specific track or drag it below the last track. If you drag the pattern below the last track, it will automatically create the MIDI region on the last track.

A MIDI region is created, containing your two-bar drum groove. It is called Ultrabeat.

You can now turn off Ultrabeat's step sequencer so that it doesn't play along with the MIDI region on the Studio Tight Kit track.

4 In Ultrabeat's step sequencer, click the power button.

The step sequencer is turned off and will no longer play along when you play the project.

5 Close Ultrabeat's window (or press Command-W).

6   In the Toolbar, click the Set Locators button.

Cycle mode is turned on, and the cycle area matches the length of the MIDI region.

7   At the bottom of the Arrange window, click the Piano Roll button (or press P).

The Piano Roll Editor opens and displays the drum groove in the Ultrabeat MIDI region. (You may have to scroll down to see the notes between C1 and C2.)

Let's open the Event List to see a detail of all the events in the Ultrabeat MIDI region.

8   In the Toolbar, click the Lists button (or press E).

The Event List opens. If the Event List does not show the contents of the Ultrabeat MIDI region, double-click the Ultrabeat MIDI region. Notice the polyphonic pressure (P-Press) events in the Status column. They turn the volume up and down just before and after the first downbeat of each bar to reproduce the accents you programmed in Ultrabeat.

You can now edit the contents of the MIDI region in both the Piano Roll Editor and the Event List. When editing MIDI data, it is a good idea to keep the Event List open to monitor how individual MIDI events are updated as you edit them in another editor.

With Cycle mode turned on, you will press the Spacebar in all the upcoming exercises to toggle playback on and off. Playback will always start at the beginning of the pattern and will continuously loop until you stop it.

Applying a Laid-Back Feel to the Snare

An interesting characteristic of a human performance is that a drummer never hits all the drums precisely on the time grid.

You can approach the qualities of a human performance by slightly changing the position of certain drum notes, either by dragging them or by using Logic's humanization functions.

First, you will give the groove a more laid-back feel by delaying the snare notes.

1   In the Piano Roll Editor, click the D1 key (one white note above C1) on the vertical keyboard.

All D1 MIDI notes (all snare notes) are selected. Note the functional similarity to the Arrange area, in which clicking a track header selects all the regions on that track.

2   Slowly drag the selection to the right while watching the help tag.

The notes snap to another position. The help tag shows that they are dragged from
1 2 1 1 to 1 2 1 81 (or another value, depending on your zoom level). That's an
80-tick delay.

3   Press the Spacebar to start playback, and listen to the new groove.

The snare notes are much too late and create a flam with the hi-hat notes. This almost
sounds like a very bad human drummer. You need to delay the snare by a smaller
amount. By pressing Shift-Control as you drag, you will have access to a greater degree
of precision.

4   Choose Edit > Undo Drag (or press Command-Z).

The snares return to their original positions.

5   Hold down the first snare note, and then Shift-Control-drag the note to the right.

Snapping is disabled, and you can now drag with tick precision.

6   While watching the help tag, drag the selection to 1 2 1 10.

Listen to the groove; the difference is very subtle.

NOTE ▶ If you hear a flange sound on the snare, you probably forgot to turn off Ultrabeat's step sequencer in the previous exercise. Turn it off now.

Let's keep the first snare note where it is and delay the other three a little more.

7   Shift-click the first snare note.

The Shift-clicked note is deselected, and the others remain selected.

TIP ▶ When multiple notes are selected, you can Shift-click one of the selected notes to deselect it, while leaving the other notes selected. You can also Shift-click a deselected note to add it to the selection.

8   Hold down the mouse button on the first selected note, and Shift-Control-drag the selection to 1 4 1 16 to delay the three selected notes by 16 ticks.

The first snare note is now 10 ticks later, and the three remaining snare notes are 16 ticks later.

Your groove already has a more laid-back feel. The difference in feel between the quantized snare and the new, laid-back snare is subtle, so let's compare the two.

Comparing the Quantized and Laid-Back Patterns
To compare the feel of the original quantized and the laid-back patterns, you are going to toggle the Quantize parameter on and off in the Inspector's Region Parameter box. In the

current pattern, the fastest notes are the eighth notes in the hi-hats. So, eighth note is the quantization value you should choose for the region.

The Region Parameter box displays the parameters of the selected region, so make sure that the Ultrabeat region is selected. The name of the region, Ultrabeat, should appear at the top of the Region Parameter box.

1   In the Inspector's Region Parameter box, set the Ultrabeat's region Quantize parameter to 1/8-Note.

In the Piano Roll Editor, all four snare notes snap to the grid.

2   Press the Spacebar to start playback, if necessary.

You are listening to the rigid groove, with the snare sounding right on the grid.

3   Choose Edit > Undo Parameter Change (or press Command-Z).

The Quantize parameter turns off, and the snare notes jump off the grid. You now are listening to the laid-back groove you created.

4   Choose Edit > Redo Parameter Change (or press Command-Shift-Z).

The Quantize parameter returns to 1/8-Note.

Keep pressing the Undo and Redo key commands to switch the quantization off and on while listening to the playback. Remember, because the last thing you did with your mouse was to turn the quantization on (by choosing the 1/8-Note value), the keys behave like this:

▶   Undo (Command-Z): The Quantize parameter turns off quantization (and plays the laid-back groove).

▶   Redo (Command-Shift-Z): The Quantize parameter turns on 1/8-Note quantization (and plays the quantized groove).

The difference is subtle, so focus your attention on the timing of the snare. After a while, the laid-back groove almost sounds normal, and the rigid groove sounds rushed! When the groove is quantized, the snare overpowers the hi-hat notes that are played at the same time, and the hi-hat seems to disappear every time the snare hits. But when the snare is delayed a bit, it opens space for the hi-hat notes, which more effectively cut through the mix.

If you still can't hear the difference, you can try dragging the snare notes farther off the grid to make the effect more obvious. You can also turn on the metronome to listen to the snare against the metronome click.

5   In the Transport bar, click the Metronome button.

> **NOTE** ▸ On smaller displays, the Metronome button may not be visible. To access it, click the right angle brackets (>>) in the Transport bar and choose Click from the pop-up menu.

6   Set Quantize to 1/8-Note.

You are listening to the rigid groove, and the snare plays precisely on the grid, as do the metronome clicks. In fact, the snare sound overlaps the sound of the metronome, and it almost sounds as if the metronome is not playing when the snare is playing.

7   Set Quantize to Off.

You are listening to the laid-back groove, and the snare is a little off the grid. If you focus your attention on the metronome and the snare, you can hear them *flam*; that is, they hit almost, but not quite, at the same time.

While the difference is subtle, this is the kind of detail that can breathe life into drum programming, so experiment with different amounts of delay for the snare until you get the feel you want.

> **TIP** ▸ To further humanize a groove, you can randomize note positions by selecting the notes to humanize. Choose Functions > Transform > Humanize, and click Operate Only. Try it on hi-hat notes for a great human effect! The Transform window is covered in more details in *Apple Pro Training Series: Logic Pro 9 Advanced Music Production* by David Dvorin with Robert Brock

Now you really have a good rock drum groove going. With careful manipulation of accents, note velocities, note placements, and a little randomization, you have transformed machine-like drum programming into a human-sounding groove.

Creating a Snare Roll Using the Hyper Editor

In the previous lesson, you used the Hyper Editor to draw and edit MIDI CC pan events. You can also use the Hyper Editor to create and edit MIDI note events. Its ability to adjust grid resolution independently for each lane makes the Hyper Editor a great choice for drum programming.

The Hyper Editor allows you to quickly enter many MIDI events at once, drawing them on the grid using the Pencil tool. This makes it easy to quickly draw a snare roll.

Creating a Custom Hyper Set

When you're programming a basic drum pattern, creating your own hyper set with just the MIDI notes you need will make the Hyper Editor easier to navigate.

In this exercise, you will create a custom hyper set that includes an event definition for each drum sound used in the pattern. You will then draw a snare roll using the Pencil tool and adjust velocities using the Line tool.

1   At the bottom of the Piano Roll Editor, click the Hyper Editor button (or press Y).

The Hyper Editor opens, and the Inspector updates to show you the Hyper Set menu, a couple of checkboxes, and the Event Definition Parameter box, which displays the parameters of the selected event definition lane.

There are two factory hyper sets in the Hyper Set menu: MIDI Controls, which you used in the previous lesson to add pan automation, and GM Drum Kit, which is used for drum programming.

2   In the Inspector, click the Hyper Set menu button and choose GM Drum Kit.

The Hyper Editor now shows event definitions for all the MIDI drum notes defined by the GM (General MIDI) standard.

MORE INFO ▶ The General MIDI standard defines many MIDI events left undefined in the MIDI standard. For example, it defines which sounds a MIDI note should trigger when playing a drum instrument: C1 is a kick drum, D1 is a snare drum, and so on.

3   Place the pointer between the Hyper Editor and the Arrange area, and drag up.

The Hyper Editor is resized, and you can see more event definitions.

Scroll vertically to see the whole set of GM drum sounds. When you have numerous event definitions for a variety of drum and percussion sounds that you don't need, the Hyper Editor can be difficult to navigate. Let's create a custom hyper set.

4   Click the background to deselect all notes.

5   In the Inspector, click the Hyper Set menu and choose "Create Hyper Set for Current Events."

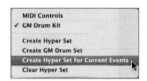

A new hyper set is displayed, called Ultrabeat, the name of the MIDI region. It contains event definitions only for the four drum sounds used in the region, plus an additional event definition, Pressure C-2, that corresponds to the accents used earlier in Ultrabeat (the polyphonic pressure events seen in the Event List).

To tidy up the display, you can delete the accent lane, then reorder and name the drum lanes.

6   Click the header of the Pressure C-2 lane.

The lane is selected.

7   Choose Hyper > Delete Event Definition.

The event definition is deleted from the hyper set. The accent events are not deleted from the MIDI region, and they remain visible in the Event List.

Now that you are working with a stripped-down hyper set, zoom in so that the four lanes fill the Hyper Editor display.

8 Click the first C1 note.

The kick note is played, and the C1 lane is selected. You can click the notes to trigger the sounds and determine which lane corresponds to which instrument, then rename the event definition. Even without clicking the notes, you should be able to visually identify the instruments by remembering their positions on the grid.

9 In the Inspector's Event Definition Parameter box, double-click C1.

A text field opens, and you can rename the event definition.

10 In the text field, type *Kick*.

11 Use the same technique to rename as follows:

> ▶ F♯1 to Closed Hat

> ▶ D1 to Snare

> ▶ A♯1 to Open Hat

You can drag lanes up and down by their header to reorder them so that the drums are in the same order as they are in Ultrabeat's step sequencer.

12 Drag the Kick event definition to the bottom of the window, below the Open Hat.

13 Drag the Open Hat event definition to the top of the window, above the Closed Hat.

This new custom hyper set is much cleaner looking. You have event definitions only for the four current drum sounds. With the event definitions renamed and reordered, you can tell at a glance which drum sound you are editing.

Drawing a Snare Roll

Now you're ready to draw that snare roll. First, you'll adjust the grid resolution of the snare lane and add a single snare note in the first bar. Then you will draw the snare roll at the end of the first bar.

In the Hyper Editor, the Pencil tool is assigned to the Command-click tool.

1 In the Snare lane, Command-click the grid line just before the second kick.

As in Ultrabeat's step sequencer, the height of the note represents its velocity. When using the Pencil tool, click higher to insert louder notes, or click lower to insert softer notes. You can also drag up and down with the Pencil tool to adjust the velocity of the note as you insert it, and drag with the Pencil or Pointer tool to adjust the velocity of an existing note.

Listen to the pattern. Let's make that snare softer than the other snares.

2   Drag down the new snare note to a lower velocity.

Listen to the pattern. Sounds good.

Drummers don't usually hit the hi-hat in the middle of a snare roll; so, before you add the snare roll at the end of the pattern, you will delete the last hi-hat note in the first bar.

3   On the Closed Hat lane, click the last Closed Hat note in the first bar to select it.

4   Press Delete.

The selected Closed Hat note is deleted.

You're ready to draw a snare roll at the end of the first bar. You first need to increase the resolution of the snare event definition grid so that you can draw the fast snare roll.

5   Select the Snare lane.

6   In the Event Definition Parameter box, set the Grid parameter to 1/48-Note.

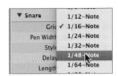

The higher-resolution grid is displayed on the Snare lane.

You should shorten the new snare note lengths so that the notes don't overlap when you look at them later in the Piano Roll Editor.

7   Double-click the Length parameter, and enter *20* to change the note length to 20 ticks.

Now you can draw the snare roll.

8   Zoom in on the area after the last snare in bar 1.

9   After the last snare, drag the Pencil tool to draw the snare roll, ending the roll just before the end of bar 1.

You can adjust the vertical position of the Pencil tool as you drag it to create notes of different velocities and to generate decrescendos and crescendos.

You can now use the Line tool to create a perfect crescendo.

10 Press Esc and choose the Line tool.

11 Hold down the Line tool and place it just before the first note in the snare roll, watching the help tag to ensure that the velocity is at 35.

12 Release the mouse button, and position the pointer just after the last note of the snare roll, so that the velocity reads 100 in the help tag.

13 Click to end the line.

The note heights are adjusted to the green line, forming a perfect crescendo.

Listen to the pattern. The snare roll is a little loud. Scroll to the end of bar 1 to examine the snare roll. All the notes from the roll are still selected. You will lower the velocities of the whole selection using the Pointer tool.

14 Press Esc twice.

15 Drag the last note down to a velocity of 76.

The velocities of all the selected notes are lowered. Listen to the drum pattern. If the snare roll starts a little too early, you can delete the first few notes of the snare roll.

16 Click in the background of the Hyper Editor to deselect all the notes.

17 Shift-drag the pointer over the first couple of notes you want to delete to select them.

18 Press Delete.

19 In the Arrange area, make sure the Ultrabeat region is still selected, and at the bottom of the editing area, click the Piano Roll button (or press P).

You can see the snare roll on the right. Imagine creating the snare roll in the Piano Roll Editor, one note at a time, and you will understand how powerful the Hyper Editor can be for that kind of job.

Converting a MIDI Sequence into an Audio Region

While programming MIDI sequences that trigger software instruments allows you to alter the sound of the instrument or the programmed sequence, there will be times when you're happy with your programming and instrument sounds and just want to convert your MIDI sequence to an audio file. Working with audio frees up the CPU to process the software instrument and processing plug-ins, and allows you to use audio editing techniques on your drum beat (to reverse one of the hits, for example). And audio drum loops are easy to share with anyone, regardless of the music production software they're using.

Bouncing a Region in Place

In the next exercise, you will bounce the Ultrabeat MIDI region in place. Logic will bounce your MIDI region to an audio region and place it on a new audio track at the same position as the MIDI region, then mute the MIDI region.

1 In the Arrange area, make sure that the Ultrabeat region is selected.

2 In the Toolbar, click Bounce Regions.

A dialog appears from the Arrange window's title bar.

3   In the Name field, type *Rock Drums,* and click OK.

The playhead quickly moves over your region, a new audio track is created, and the bounced audio region is placed on the new track. The MIDI Ultrabeat region is muted, freeing up the CPU that was used to process the Ultrabeat plug-in.

4   Listen to the bounced audio region.

The audio region is a drum loop that sounds exactly like the MIDI sequence you just programmed.

You have converted your MIDI sequence to an audio region. You can now modify the loop using the audio editing techniques learned in Lesson 3.

Converting an Audio Region into a Sampler Instrument Track

While the previous exercise showed you how to convert a MIDI region on a software instrument track into an audio region, this exercise will show you how to convert an audio region into a MIDI region on a software instrument sampler track. You might do this if you have a live drum recording or a drum sample from an old record that you want to play live, or you want to reprogram their grooves using the flexibility of MIDI.

The software instrument used is Logic's sampler, the EXS24. A sampler allows you to map bits of audio (samples) to MIDI notes. In this case, the audio region is sliced into samples that contain the individual drum hits of the drum loop. An EXS24 instrument made up of those samples is created and loaded onto a new track, and a MIDI region is created that contains the MIDI notes to trigger those samples. You can then freely alter the sound of the sampler instrument, play the samples live, or program a new MIDI sequence to create your own groove.

In this exercise, you will import an audio drum loop into the current project, then convert that audio region into a new sampler instrument track so that you can play the individual drum hits using your MIDI keyboard.

1   Mute the Rock Drums track (track 2).

2   In the Bar ruler, click the cycle area to turn it off.

3   In the Toolbar, click the Media button, and in the Media area, click the Browser tab (or press F).

    The File Browser opens.

4   Navigate to Logic 9 Files > Media > Additional Media, and drag **DrumLoop.aif** below track 2.

5   Listen to the drum loop to get familiar with the drum groove.

6   Make sure that the DrumLoop region is still selected, and from the Arrange area's local menu, choose Audio > "Convert Regions to New Sampler Track."

7   In the dialog that appears, select Transient Markers.

8   From the first Trigger Note Range menu, choose C1.

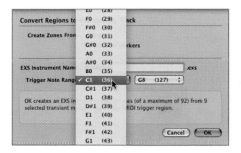

9   Click OK.

Be patient as Logic works in the background. Logic is detecting the transients in the audio region, and determining the start and end points of each sample. It then creates and loads the EXS24 instrument onto a new software instrument track, and places a new MIDI region on that track that triggers the samples sequentially. The original audio drum loop is then muted.

10   Play notes on your MIDI keyboard to trigger the individual drum hits. (Make sure that your MIDI keyboard is in the right octave, starting on C1).

You have turned an audio drum loop into a sampler instrument that you can play with your MIDI keyboard. Feel free to experiment by opening the MIDI region and moving the notes around, or programming a brand new pattern.

Programming drums is a skill that requires you to use your ears, not just to create the pattern, but also to add the little nuances that make the difference between a machinelike drum pattern and a drum groove that will fool the listeners into thinking a real drummer performed the part. Listen to live drummers, or recordings of live drummers, and focus on the dynamic variations, the use of accents to create the groove, and the timing of the snare and hi-hat. Then, use the tools and techniques you have learned in this lesson to incorporate those dynamic and timing subtleties into your drum programming. The ability to easily convert a live drum recording into a sampler instrument gives you the freedom of recycling virtually any drums you hear!

Lesson Review

1. Name the three main sections of the Ultrabeat interface.

2. In Ultrabeat, what sounds are triggered by which MIDI notes?

3. How do you insert a note on every downbeat?

4. How can you add accents to a pattern?

5. How can you add accents at different positions for different drum sounds?

6. In Ultrabeat, how can you randomize a sound's note velocities?

7. How can you view an Ultrabeat pattern as a MIDI region in the Arrange area?

8. In the Piano Roll Editor, how can you deselect a single note from a multiple note selection?

9. What editor is the best choice for creating a snare roll?

10. How do you create a custom hyper set containing event definitions only for the existing notes in the region?

11. How do you convert an audio region into a sampler instrument?

Answers

1. The Assignment section, the Synthesizer section, and the step sequencer.

2. Notes C1 through B2 play the 24 drum sounds; C3 and above play the bass sound chromatically.

3. Control-click the full view grid, and choose Add Every Downbeat from the shortcut menu.

4. By selecting steps in the accent row.

5. You can't. Accent positions are the same for all sounds. You can turn the accents on and off for individual sounds using the accent switch.

6. Control-click the step sequencer, and from the shortcut menu, choose Alter Vel.

7. Drag the Pattern button to the Arrange area.

8. Shift-click the note you want to deselect.

9. The Hyper Editor.

10. Make sure that all notes are deselected inside the region, and from the Hyper Set menu, choose "Create Hyper Set for Current Events."

11. Select the audio region and choose Audio > Convert Regions to New Sampler Track.

7

Lesson Files   Logic 9 Files > Lessons > 07 Sunday Morning

Media   Logic 9 Files > Media > Additional Media

Time   This lesson takes approximately 60 minutes to complete.

Goals   Match a project tempo to an audio file's tempo

     Use the Loop Browser

     Create Apple Loops

     Make an audio region follow the project tempo

     Insert tempo changes and tempo curves

     Time-stretch an audio region to match the project tempo

     Use Varispeed effects

     Apply Tape or Turntable speed-up and slowdown effects

     Use the Flex tool to stretch single notes on the waveform

Manipulating Tempo and Time Stretching

Modern music genres have seen the use of loops and samples increase exponentially over the last few years. New technologies encourage experimentation, and it is more and more common to find, say, a sample of a Middle Eastern instrument in a modern rock song, a sample of classical music in a pop song, or a sample of a pop song in a hip-hop track.

Mixing prerecorded material into a project can lead to exciting results, but the material must be carefully selected to ensure that it seamlessly blends into the project. The first challenge is to match the tempo of the prerecorded musical material with the tempo of a project.

But even when you record your own performances, the ability to stretch audio waveforms like a rubber band gives you new creative power as a producer. Furthermore, special effects such as Varispeed and tape speed-up or slowdown can trigger new inspiration.

In this lesson, you will import an audio file into a new project, changing the project tempo to match the audio file's tempo. You'll use existing Apple Loops and create your own Apple Loops. You will also create a tempo map for your project; use flex editing to make audio files follow the project tempo, or to stretch individual notes in an audio region; and apply the new Varispeed and Speed Fade features.

Matching the Project Tempo to an Audio Region's Tempo

Sometimes you start a new project with prerecorded material and want to use the tempo of that material for the new project. For example, you find a drum loop that you like because of the way it grooves at its original tempo. You need to adjust the project tempo to match that loop. When the project tempo matches the loop, you can use the grid to edit regions, program and quantize MIDI regions, or add Apple Loops while keeping everything synchronized with the prerecorded drum loop.

Detecting an Audio File's Tempo

In this exercise, you will import a drum groove recording into a new project, then have Logic detect the recording's tempo and set it as the new project tempo so that the drums are aligned to the project's grid.

1   Choose File > New (or press Command-N).

2   In the Templates dialog, click the Empty Project template.

3   Create a stereo audio track, and select Open Library.

4   In the Media area, click the Browser tab.

5   At the top of the Browser, click the Home button.

All the folders contained in your home folder are displayed in the Browser.

6   Click the Column button.

7 Navigate to Logic 9 Files > Media > Additional Media and locate the **Drums Recording.aif** file.

When you double-click an audio file in the Browser, an audio region is created on the selected track at the playhead position. Make sure that the playhead is placed at the beginning of the project.

8 Double-click **Drums Recording.aif**.

The audio file is imported into the project, and an audio region representing the entire audio file is inserted on the selected track, at the playhead position (bar 1).

9 In the Arrange area, zoom in vertically to clearly see the waveform.

You can use the metronome to check the project tempo (which in this case is the default 120 bpm for an empty project) and compare it with the audio file's tempo.

10 In the Transport bar, click the Metronome button to turn on the metronome.

11 Play the project.

The drums play more slowly than the metronome and rapidly drift out of sync.

12 Make sure that the Drums Recording region is selected, and choose Options > Tempo > "Adjust Tempo using Beat Detection."

Logic analyzes the file and then displays a dialog, which indicates a tempo of 90.6692 bpm, and allows you to create a tempo change. Because you want to use this loop throughout your song, you'll leave Globally selected.

13 Click OK.

In the Transport bar, the tempo is set to 90.6692 bpm, matching the tempo of the imported Drums Recording audio file.

14 Listen to your project. The metronome now plays in time with the drums.

15 Turn off the metronome.

You have matched the project's tempo to the audio file's tempo, and now you can start building the project using the grid. Before you go any further, you need to cut a loop out of the Drums Recording region to use as a drum loop throughout the song.

Cutting a Loop

You will now cut the best two bars out of the Drums Recording region and use the section as a drum loop, discarding the rest. To select the desired two bars, you will use the Marquee tool, your Command-click tool.

1   Command-drag in the Drums Recording region to select a section from bar 3 to bar 5.

You will now crop the marquee selection using the "Crop Regions outside Locators or Marquee Selection" key command (Control-C).

2   Press Control-C.

The marquee selection remains, and the unselected parts are discarded. You can now use your two-bar region as a drum loop.

3   Drag the region to bar 1.

4   In the Inspector, select the Loop checkbox (or press L).

The drums are now looped throughout the song.

Once you have set the project's tempo to match the drum loop you're using, you can use the Arrange area's grid to cut the region and loop it. You can then continue building your song using all the editing techniques you've learned in previous lessons. You can also add Apple Loops, which will automatically match the tempo of your drums.

Working with Apple Loops

Apple Loops are AIFF- or CAF-format audio files containing additional information that allows them to automatically match the tempo and key of a Logic project. They also contain descriptive information—such as instrument, genre, mood, and scale—that helps you search large libraries of Apple Loops using the Loop Browser.

> **MORE INFO ▶** Apple Loops are also supported by the GarageBand and Soundtrack Pro applications. When Apple Loops are imported into an application that does not support them, they behave like regular audio files.

Using the Loop Browser
You were introduced to the Loop Browser in Lesson 1, when you previewed and chose loops to create a project. Now you'll take a closer look at the Loop Browser.

1 In the Media area, click the Loops tab.

The Loop Browser opens. You are going to search for a major-scale acoustic guitar loop in the pop genre.

At the top of the Loop Browser, three menus—View, Signature, and Scale—allow you to filter searches of Apple Loops by collection (Jam Pack, GarageBand, or other), time signature, and type of scale (minor or major).

2 From the Scale menu, choose Major.

This will filter your next search to display only loops that work with a major scale. The Loop Browser needs a little more information and doesn't display any results yet.

At the upper right of the Loop Browser, you can choose one of three views: Column, Music, or Sound Effects. Each view enables a different way to filter the loops as they are organized in the Search Results list.

Column view
Music view
Sound Effects view

TIP ▶ You can customize the buttons displayed in the Music and Sound Effects views. Drag a button over another button to swap their positions, or Control-click a button to choose the category it should display. Those changes are saved as preferences and will be reflected in all your project files.

3   Click the Column button.

While the Music and Sound Effects views display only a selection of category buttons, the Column view lets you access all the existing descriptors: By Genres, By Instruments, and By Moods.

4   Choose By Instruments > Acoustic Guitar > Acousti...ar (365). Note that the last category name, *Acoustic Guitar (365)*, is abbreviated.

The number in parentheses (365) represents the number of results that match your search and may be different depending on the number of loops installed on your computer. The 365 major-scale acoustic guitar loops are displayed in the Search Results list at the bottom of the Loop Browser.

At the top of the Loop Browser, you can enter text in the search field and further filter the search results to display only the loops containing the search text in their names.

5   In the search field, type *pop*, and press Return.

The Search Results list now shows the 17 major-scale acoustic guitar loops that have *pop* in their name.

6   Click **Alt Pop Acoustic 01.**

	Name	▲	Tempo	Key	Beats	Match	Fav
	Alt Pop Acoustic 01		90	E	8	65%	☐
	Alt Pop Acoustic 02		90	E	8	65%	☐
	Alt Pop Acoustic 03		90	E	8	65%	☐
	Alt Pop Acoustic 04		90	E	8	65%	☐

The loop starts playing. It sounds like a detuned acoustic guitar, and you may hear some weird artifacts. In fact, in the Key column, you can see the loop's original key. This loop was performed in E major. When you preview a loop, it is transposed to match the key of the project (the default key signature for a project is C major—you will change the project's key signature in the next exercise). The further the playback key and tempo are from the loop's original key and tempo, the more artifacts are introduced.

At the bottom of the Loop Browser, the preview settings let you adjust the volume and key at which you preview the loops.

7   From the "Play in" pop-up menu, choose C#.

The loop plays in C#, one semitone higher than the project's default key.

8   From the "Play in" pop-up menu, choose Original Key.

The loop plays in its original key, E major. It now sounds like an acoustic guitar playing in a regular tuning, and the artifacts disappear.

9   Drag Alt Pop Acoustic 01 to bar 1, below the existing track in the Arrange area.

A new audio track is created, and the Alt Pop Acoustic 01 loop is inserted at bar 1.

10   In the Inspector, select the Loop checkbox (or press L) to loop the acoustic guitar.

11 Listen to the project.

The acoustic guitar plays in time with your drums! However, the loop plays in the project's key, C major. In the next exercise, you will change the project's key to make that loop sound better.

Setting a Project's Key Signature

In the previous exercise, you noticed that a loop sounds more natural when it is played in its original key. Its sound is closer to that of a regularly tuned instrument, and since there is no transposition to process, you hear fewer artifacts. It is usually preferable to choose Apple Loops with original keys and tempos that are closest to the project's key signature and tempo, in order to reduce the amount of processing necessary to match the loops to the project, thereby reducing audible artifacts.

Let's change the key of the project to E major, the original key of the acoustic guitar. To change the project's key signature, you need to access the global Signature track.

1 At the top left of the Arrange area, click the words Global Tracks (or press G).

The global Marker, Signature, and Tempo tracks are displayed. In the global Signature track you can see the time signature (4/4) and the key signature (C).

2 Double-click the key signature (C).

The Key Signature window opens.

3 From the Key pop-up menu, choose E. Keep Major selected.

4   Click OK.

On the global Signature track, the new key signature is *E*.

5   Listen to the project.

The loop plays in the new key signature, E major. It now sounds much more natural and matches the drums quite well.

You used the global Signature track to set your project's key, making sure that all Apple Loops in the project will now play at the new project key. If you want to go further and create an arrangement using Apple Loops, you can also insert key signature changes on the Signature track to build a chord progression, and all Apple Loops will change key according to the Signature track.

Inserting Tempo Changes and Curves

When you want to vary the tempo throughout a project, you can usAae the global Tempo track to insert tempo changes and tempo curves. All MIDI regions, Apple Loops, and audio regions that are set to follow tempo will automatically follow the project tempo, even when tempo variations occur in the middle of regions.

1   In the Global Tracks headers, click the global Tempo track disclosure triangle.

The Tempo track expands vertically. You can see the tempo value displayed (90.6692 bpm).

In the Tempo track header, you can choose between nine Alternative tempo maps. Let's leave Alternative 1 set to 90.6692 bpm, and choose Alternative 2. This will allow you to experiment with tempo changes in Alternative 2 but leave Alternative 1 available at the original tempo if you are not happy with the new results.

2   In the Tempo track header, click the Alternative menu and choose 2.

Tempo Alternative 2 is displayed, and the entire project is set to the default 120 bpm tempo.

3   Listen to the project.

The acoustic guitar Apple Loops automatically match the new tempo, and its region length is still exactly two bars. However, the drums audio region does not change its tempo and now plays too slowly. To make sure the drums follow the project tempo, you can use one of the flex modes.

4   In the Tempo track header, click the Alternative menu and choose 1.

The tempo goes back to 90.6692 bpm, and the drums are in time with the project again.

5   Select the Drums Recording track.

6   In the Inspector, click the Track parameters disclosure triangle.

7 Set Flex Mode to Slicing.

This Flex mode slices the audio where it detects a transient, and moves the slices without time-stretching them, which typically works great for drums.

8 In the Tempo track header, click the Alternative menu, and choose 2.

The tempo is set to 120 bpm again, but this time the Drums Recording region follows the new tempo and stays exactly two bars long.

9 Listen to the project.

Now both the guitar and the drums play in sync at the project tempo. From now on, you can insert tempo changes throughout the project, and both files will follow them.

The Tempo track displays tempo changes as nodes. At present, only one node is placed at the beginning of the project, and one horizontal line follows that node, indicating a constant tempo throughout the entire project. Let's first slow down the song.

10 In the Tempo track, position your pointer over the tempo line.

The pointer turns into the Hand tool to indicate that you can move the line.

11 Drag the line down to 100 bpm.

Although the line has to be dragged below the bottom of the Tempo track and seems to disappear, keep dragging down and watch the help tag to set the tempo to 100.

When you release the mouse button, the scale in the Tempo track header readjusts, and the line is visible again with the new value (100 bpm) visible next to the node.

Let's insert a tempo change at bar 5.

12   At bar 5, position the pointer far enough above the tempo line that it no longer looks like a hand, and double-click to insert a new tempo node.

The value of the new tempo is displayed next to the node. You can adjust the value of a tempo change up or down by dragging the node or the horizontal line that follows it.

13   To the right of bar 5, drag the new line up vertically to a value of 120.

You can move a tempo change left or right by dragging the node or the line that follows it.

14   To the right of the 120 bpm tempo node, drag the horizontal line to the left to move the tempo change to 3 1 1 1.

You will now create an accelerando during the first two bars. The goal is to gradually increase the tempo from 100 bpm to 120 bpm. To create a tempo curve, you need to position the pointer over the node placed above or below a tempo change. When the pointer changes into a pointing index finger icon, drag to the left.

15 At bar 3, drag the node below the 120 bpm tempo change, and drag it to the left and up.

You can precisely adjust the tempo curve by dragging the node farther to the left, up, or both.

16 Play back from the beginning of the song.

The whole project follows the new tempo map. Your results may vary, depending upon the Apple Loops you are using or the type of audio recordings that follow the tempo. Drastic tempo variations may create artifacts, so let your ear be the judge. Note that percussive material usually reacts better to tempo variations than melodic and harmonic material.

Let's revert to the first tempo alternative.

17 In the Tempo track header, click the Alternative menu and choose 1.

18 Close the global tracks (or press G).

You can now create complex tempo maps to add excitement to your arrangements. Sometimes, a chorus that's a bit faster than the rest of the song is all the song needs to really take off. Or you can use tempo curves to create the classic ritardando at the end of the song. All of your Apple Loops and MIDI regions will automatically follow the project tempo. To make audio files follow the tempo, you only have to choose a flex mode.

Creating Apple Loops

While flex modes make audio files follow tempo, Apple Loops follow both tempo and key signatures, and can be catalogued in the Loop Browser for easy access from any of your projects. When using audio regions to create Apple Loops, blue Apple Loops are produced.

Blue Apple Loops can be used only as audio regions on audio tracks. When you use MIDI regions, green Apple Loops are produced. Green Apple Loops can be used as audio regions on audio tracks or as MIDI regions on software instrument tracks, giving them the additional flexibility of being able to edit the sound of the instrument and the MIDI sequence.

1   Drag the Drums Recording region to the Loop Browser.

The "Add Region to Apple Loops Library" dialog appears. All the information you enter in this window will be used by the Loop Browser to index the loop. It is the same information you will use to search for that loop in the Loop Browser.

2   Enter or choose the following information:

▶   Name: Rock Groove

▶   Type: Loop

▶   Scale: Neither

▶   Genre: Rock/Blues

▶   Instrument Descriptors: All Drums > Beats

Click the tags Single, Clean, Acoustic, Relaxed, Cheerful, Dry, Grooving, and Part.

MORE INFO ▶ When dragging a region to the Loop browser, you can create blue Apple Loops only when the number of beats in a selected region is a whole integer. This function uses the project tempo to tag the transient positions and works best for audio files that match the project tempo. If the selected region's number of beats is not an integer, the Type parameter will be set to One-shot and dimmed.

To create blue Apple Loops with material that does not match the current project tempo, and to see a more refined transient analysis of your audio file, choose Audio > Open in Apple Loops Utility and use the Apple Loops Utility, as explained in *Apple Pro Training Series: Logic Pro 9 Advanced Music Production* by David Dvorin with Robert Brock. (Peachpit Press).

3 Click Create.

Logic temporarily solos the Drums Recording track, bounces the audio region as a new audio file, and then adds the loop to the Loop Browser. This process can take some time, depending upon the number of loops present on your system.

When the operation is completed, an Apple Loops file has been created and indexed, and is available in the Loop Browser. You can now access it from any project as you can any other Apple Loops file.

4   In the Loop Browser's search field, type *Rock Groove*, and press Return.

Your new drum loop is displayed in the search results. You can click it to preview it, and add it to any of your projects.

Now that you know how to create Apple Loops, try creating a green Apple loop. Create a new Software Instrument track, choose a channel strip setting in the Library, and use some of the techniques you've learned in the previous three chapters to create a MIDI region (recording, step input recording, programming, or even Pitch Bend automation in Hyper Draw, if you're feeling adventurous!). Then drag your MIDI region over the Loop Browser to create a green Apple Loop.

Remember the distinction between blue and green Apple Loops when you preview loops in the Loop Browser. When you like the sound of a green loop, you can add it to your project just to use the software instrument channel strip setting. Then, delete the MIDI region and record or program your own MIDI region. (Previewing green Apple Loops gives you a chance to audition their software instrument channel strip settings without loading the channel strip settings.) In contrast, if you like the melodic or rhythmic pattern played by a green loop, you can add it to the Arrange area and keep only the MIDI region, using another software instrument channel strip setting.

Change the Playback Pitch and Speed with Varispeed

In the days of analog tape recording, engineers performed all sorts of tricks by changing the tape speed. Many major albums were sped up ever so slightly during the mixing process to add excitement to tracks by raising their tempos. This simultaneously raised the pitch, giving the impression of the vocalist reaching higher notes in the most emotional passages of the song. On the other hand, engineers would sometimes slow the tape during recording, so that a musician could play a challenging passage at a more comfortable tempo. When played back at its regular speed during mixdown, the recording gave the illusion of the musician playing faster than he really was. DJs are probably the biggest users of Varispeed techniques, which gives them control over the tempo and pitch of a track, allowing for seamless transitions from one track to the next.

Logic takes this concept a step further, offering both the classic Varispeed—which, like a tape or record player, changes both the pitch and the speed simultaneously—and a mode called Speed Only, which allows you to change the speed without changing the pitch.

1 Close the current project, and don't save it.

2 Navigate to Logic 9 Files > Lessons, and open **07 Sunday Morning**.

3 Listen to the song to get familiar with it.

To use the Varispeed feature, you need to add the Varispeed display to the Transport bar.

4 Control-click the Transport bar, and choose Customize Transport Bar.

A dialog appears, in which you can select the buttons and displays you'd like to see in the Transport bar.

5 In the Customize Transport Bar dialog, select Varispeed and click OK.

A new Varispeed display appears in the Transport bar.

6   In the Varispeed display, drag the 0.00% value down to −10.00%.

The Varispeed display is shaded in orange. The tempo value turns orange, too, indicating that the song is no longer playing at its normal tempo due to the Varispeed feature. To the right of the Transport bar, the Varispeed button turns orange to indicate that the feature is turned on.

7   Listen to the project.

The entire project plays back 10 percent slower than its normal speed, but at the same pitch. This would be perfect for practicing a part with your instrument. You could even record your part at this speed, and then turn off Varispeed to play the whole song (including your new part) at the normal speed.

8   Double-click the Varispeed value, enter *10*, and press Return.

The Varispeed value is set to +10.00%.

9   Listen to the project.

The entire project plays 10 percent faster than its normal speed. This is a great way to audition your project at a different tempo. Now let's try the classic Varispeed mode that affects both the pitch and the speed of the project.

10 In the Varispeed display, click Speed Only.

A menu appears, in which you can choose one of the three Varispeed modes. At the bottom of the menu, you can choose one of four ways to display the speed variation.

11   Choose "Varispeed (Speed and Pitch)."

The pitch of the entire project is raised.

12   In the Varispeed display, click Varispeed to open the menu, and choose Resulting Tempo.

The speed variation is displayed as a tempo value rather than as a percentage. Now you know that your project is playing at 129.8 bpm.

13   In the Transport bar, click the Varispeed button to turn off Varispeed.

The Varispeed button, the display, and the tempo value are dimmed, and you can hear the project play at its normal speed and pitch. The Varispeed button allows you to toggle Varispeed on and off without changing the Varispeed value.

Time Stretching and Tempo Matching with Flex Time Editing

You were introduced to flex time editing in Lesson 3 when you used it to quantize a drums region and move a single hi-hat note within that region. In the next exercises, you will use flex time editing to stretch the waveform as you would a rubber band, and to match the tempo of an imported audio file to the project tempo.

Time Stretching with the Flex Tool

In this exercise, you will use the Flex tool to stretch the lead vocals, making a sustained note even longer than it was performed. You will then take a quick peek at Flex view, which shows you what is happening under the hood when you use the Flex tool.

1   On the Vox track (track 8), zoom in on the end of the Vox 2 region, making sure that you can still see the M3X Sansamp track above (track 7).

2   Drag a five-bar cycle from bar 49 to 54, and listen to that section.

You are listening to the end of a section. The singer sings, "Nothing, really," and then all the instruments stop at bar 52, where a drum fill announces the new section starting at bar 53. The goal is to stretch the singer's very last note to sustain it throughout the break.

3   Press Esc (Escape) to open the Tool menu.

4   At the bottom of the Tool menu, choose the Flex tool.

5   With the Flex tool, click anywhere on the Vox 2 region.

A dialog appears, to remind you that you must choose a flex mode before you can use the Flex tool. The advantage of using that dialog over selecting the Flex Mode parameter in the Inspector is that the dialog displays a bit more information about each of the flex modes.

6   In the Flex Mode dialog, click the disclosure triangle to view a description of the Rhythmic flex mode.

7 From the Flex Mode menu, choose Monophonic.

The description of the Monophonic mode says, "Good for solo vocals" so this should work great!

8 Click OK.

9 On the Vox 2 region, place the Flex tool pointer at the very end of the waveform, and drag to the end of the break (the downbeat of bar 53).

The region is lengthened and the waveform is stretched. Listen to the result. The vocal note sustains until the next section. Now let's look at what happened "under the hood."

10 In the Toolbar, click the Flex button to turn on Flex view.

In Flex view, light gray vertical lines represents the transients that Logic detected in the file—generally the notes' attacks. The bright vertical lines with an orange handle at the top are the flex markers, and they help you determine which parts of the waveform are stretched. Also, time-expanded sections of the waveform get an orange halo, while time-compressed ones get a green halo.

Transient marker   Flex marker

11 While in Flex view, press Command-Z (Undo), and then press Command-Shift-Z (Redo) to see what happened when you stretched the last note with the Flex tool.

Two flex markers were added around the last vocal note, which was time expanded (and therefore gets an orange halo).

To prepare for the next step, play the current section a few times to get really familiar with the waveform and which words it represents. You will now stretch the attack of the word *Really* to the left so that it starts a bit earlier.

12 In the lower half of the waveform, position the Flex tool over the attack of the word *Really*.

Pay close attention to the Flex tool. When positioned over a transient marker and in the lower half of the waveform, it should look like three little flex markers, as in the previous figure.

This symbol means that you're going to stretch the waveform using three flex markers:

▶ On the transient marker you're about to drag

▶ On the transient marker before (which will not move)

▶ On the transient marker after (which will not move)

13 Start dragging the Flex tool to the left.

You see the transient that you're dragging, the transients before, and the transients after all turn into flex markers. The time-compressed part of the waveform is high-lighted in green, and the time-expanded part is highlighted in orange. A mini-ruler appears at the top of the region to help you align transients to the grid.

14 Listen to your results.

You've shortened the *thing* part of the word *Nothing* and lengthened the word *Really*. Now the vocals seem to float in midair throughout the break. Cool!

15 Press Esc twice to return the Left-click tool to the Pointer tool.

16 In the Toolbar, click the Flex button to turn off Flex view.

While the Flex tool is the ideal tool to correct the placement of a note that may be a little too late or a little too early, it is equally powerful at stretching notes—lengthening some and shortening others—to rethink the groove of a musical phrase. Remember to use the Flex tool with moderation, as it can be quite addictive!

Make an Audio File Match the Project Tempo

At the beginning of this lesson, you imported a drum recording and used Logic to detect its tempo so that you could start a new song and match the project tempo to the drum recording tempo. You will now do the opposite: You will import a percussion recording and use a flex mode to make that recording match the tempo of your project.

1   Select the HH Sherman track (track 4).

2   At the top of the track list, click the New Tracks button, and create a new stereo audio track.

The new track (track 5) is added below the HH Sherman track.

3   In the Toolbar, click the Media button to open the Media area, and in the Media area, click the Browser tab (or press F).

4   Navigate to Logic 9 Files > Media > Additional Media, and drag **Tambourine.aif** to track 5 at bar 29.

5   Click "Play from Selection" (or press Shift-Enter).

The tambourine is playing more slowly than the rest of the song. You can use a flex mode to make it automatically match the project tempo.

6   Make sure that the Tambourine track is selected, and in the Inspector, set Flex Mode
to Rhythmic.

Logic analyzes the **Tambourine.aif** audio file to detect transients and automatically
time-stretches the file to match its tempo to your song tempo.

7   Click "Play from Selection" (or press Shift-Enter).

The tambourine plays perfectly in sync with the other tracks.

You can now copy the tambourine to the other choruses. First, use the Marquee tool and
the "Crop Regions outside Locators or Marquee Selection" key command (Control-C)
to crop a perfect eight-bar Tambourine region. Then drag one copy to bar 53 and
another copy to bar 81. Dragging the upper right corner of each region, you can use the
Loop tool to fill out each chorus. Finally, in the Inspector, turn down the level of the
Tambourine to about –5 dB and pan it slightly to the right to give it a place in the mix.

Creating a Turntable or Tape Slowdown Effect

When you stop a turntable with the stylus on the record or stop a tape machine with the
tape head in contact with the magnetic tape, the result is a signal that simultaneously
slows down and drops in pitch. Although tape machines and turntables are slowly disap-

pearing, this highly recognizable sound effect has regained popularity—along with its alternative, the tape or turntable that turns on and increases in speed while rising in pitch.

To re-create those effects in Logic, you apply a fade over an audio region, and then change that fade into a speed fade: speed up for a fade-in, slow down for a fade-out.

1   On the OutroTapeDelays track (track 11), zoom in on the last four or five bars.

2   Listen to the ending of the song from bar 100.

You are going to create a turntable slowdown effect from bar 101 to the end of the OutroTapeDelays region. First you need to create a fade-out. Remember, you can apply fades with the Pointer tool by holding down Shift-Control.

3   Shift-Control-drag the OutroTapeDelays region from bar 101 and over the right border of the region to apply a fade-out.

4   In the Inspector, click the Fade parameter and choose Slow Down.

TIP For a turntable start effect, add a fade-in to an audio region, and in the Inspector, click the Fade In parameter and choose Speed Up.

In the Arrange area, the OutroTapeDelays fade turns orange, indicating that it is a speed fade. Listen to your fade. It sounds just like a turntable stopping! You can adjust the length and curve of the speed fade just as you would a regular fade.

5   Shift-Control drag the fade slightly to the left to curve it.

The speed drops a bit faster at the beginning of the slowdown effect and a bit slower toward the end, and the result sounds more realistic.

While you just used a speed fade to create a realistic tape slowdown effect, you can also use speed fades for all kinds of effects. Try using short speed fades on rapid successions of short regions to create DJ scratching effects.

You now have a large repertoire of techniques you can use to ensure that any audio file recorded or imported in a project will play back at the project tempo. Mastering these techniques will give you the freedom to use almost any prerecorded material in your projects, so keep your ears tuned to interesting material that you could sample and loop for your future songs. Using Varispeed, turntable speed-up and slowdown effects, and time-stretching techniques, you have a new palette of special effects that can add ear candy to your productions.

Lesson Review

1. How can you change a project's key signature?
2. How do you match the project tempo to an audio file's tempo?
3. How do you make an audio region follow the project's tempo?
4. How do you insert tempo changes?
5. Which region types will always follow the project's tempo map?
6. How do you create an Apple Loops file from a region?
7. What are Apple Loops? Describe the difference between blue and green Apple Loops.
8. How do you apply speed fades on an audio region?

Answers

1. Open the global tracks, and double-click the key signature on the global Signature track. Choose a new key from the Key Signature window.
2. Select the region and choose Options > Tempo > "Adjust Tempo using Beat Detection."
3. In the Inspector's Track Parameter box, select a flex mode.
4. In the global Tempo track, double-click above or below the tempo line.
5. MIDI regions, Apple Loops, and audio regions with a flex mode selected.
6. Drag the region over the Loop Browser.
7. Apple Loops are AIFF or CAF audio files that automatically match the project's tempo and key. Unlike blue Apple Loops, green Apple Loops also contain the MIDI region and software instrument channel strips used to create them, and they can be used on software instrument tracks.
8. Create a fade-in or a fade-out, and in the region parameters, set the fade-in parameter to speed up, or the fade parameter to slow down.

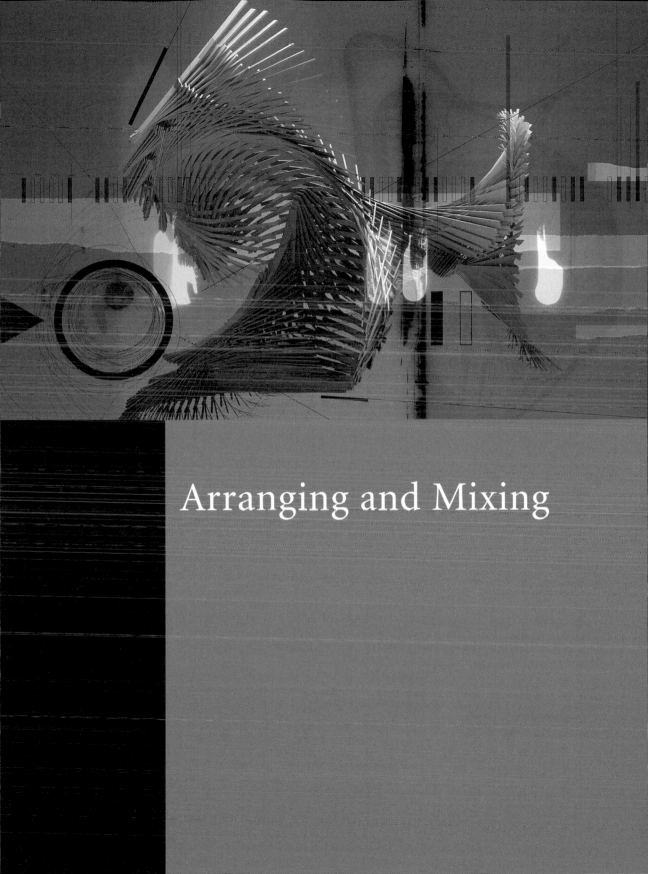

Arranging and Mixing

8

Lesson Files   Logic 9 Files > Lessons > 08 Darkside

Time   This lesson takes approximately 60 minutes to complete.

Goals   Experiment with the order of regions in Shuffle mode

Pack regions into folders

Cut and insert sections into a project

Divide a region into multiple slices

Clean up noisy recordings using Logic and Soundtrack Pro.

Lesson 8

Arranging and Preparing for the Mix

In previous lessons, you recorded and edited audio and MIDI regions of raw musical material. The next step is to arrange all that material into a song: copying and repeating some elements, removing others, and assembling only those elements that communicate the message of your song.

In this lesson, you will start with a song in which all the basic elements have been recorded, and you'll make that song come to life. You will use existing material to fill in missing elements, and employ clever editing to make a simple handclap sound more exciting. You will also suppress some musical elements when the arrangement sounds too busy, add an introduction, and clean up noisy recordings in preparation for the mixing stage.

Previewing the Song

Before you start arranging a song, you need to get to know its structure and instrumentation.

You can use markers in the global Marker track to visually identify different sections in a project. In this first exercise, you will listen to a song and navigate using existing markers to familiarize yourself with its structure. Using the Solo mode, you'll identify and audition the individual tracks.

1   Go to Logic 9 Files > Lessons and open **08 Darkside**.

At the top of the Arrange area, in the global Marker track, the markers identify the different sections of the song (Verse, Chorus, and Bridge). You will use the markers as visual aids as you copy, move, and loop regions.

TIP To create your own markers, choose the Pencil tool and click in the Marker track. To choose which global tracks are displayed, Control-click the Global Tracks header and choose from the shortcut menu.

2   Click the Global Tracks disclosure triangle (or press G) to close the global tracks.

The Marker track disappears, and the markers are now displayed in the lower half of the Bar ruler. The markers are translucent; but if you need to see the grid lines more clearly in the Bar ruler, you can reopen the Marker track.

TIP To toggle the global tracks, you don't have to precisely click the Global Tracks disclosure triangle. Clicking the words *Global Tracks* has the same effect.

3   Start playback.

Listen to the song and examine its structure. The song starts on bar 2, allowing space for guitar and clavinet pickup notes at the end of bar 1. The whole song is composed of eight-bar sections. It first alternates choruses and verses; then a bridge section starts on bar 42, followed by four choruses.

In popular music, it is common to work with eight-bar sections. This makes the Fast Forward and Fast Rewind key commands very useful for navigating a song, since they allow you to jump forward or back eight bars at a time.

4   As you listen to the song, press Shift-> (Fast Forward) to jump to the next eight-bar section and Shift-< (Fast Rewind) to jump to the previous one.

You can also press > (Forward) and < (Rewind) to jump ahead or back one bar at a time.

Use the key commands to listen to each verse, the different choruses, and the bridge. Except for the first chorus, the choruses feel empty. Later, you will add backup vocals in the choruses to give them substance.

To identify the material you are going to edit in the arrangement, you have to listen to individual instruments. You could use the Solo buttons on the track headers to keep a track selected as you edit any regions in the arrangement. However, soloing and unsoloing one instrument after another to preview them is inefficient. In the next steps, you'll use Solo mode as a faster alternative for soloing the selected region(s).

5   Click the Kick track header.

The Kick audio region is selected.

6   In the Transport bar, click the Solo button (or press S).

The Bar ruler is shaded yellow, indicating that you are in Solo mode. The selected
Kick region is outlined in yellow, indicating that it is soloed.

7   Start playback.

You are hearing the Kick audio region.

8   Click the Snare track header (or press the Down Arrow key).

The Snare region is selected, and after a little delay, you can hear the Snare region.

To avoid the delayed reaction of the Solo mode when changing the selection, you can
stop playback, select a new region, and restart playback. If you press the Spacebar to
toggle playback and press the Down Arrow to select the next track, you can become
very effective at quickly switching the soloed tracks.

9   Press the Spacebar.

Playback stops.

10   Press the Down Arrow twice to select the Hi Hat track.

The Hi Hat region is selected and soloed.

11   Press the Spacebar.

You can hear the Hi Hat region.

You can also select and listen to multiple regions.

12   Drag to select all of the backup vocal regions in the first chorus.

All selected regions are soloed.

13 In the Transport bar, click the "Play from Selection" button (or press Shift-Enter).

You hear all the backup vocals.

14 In the Transport bar, click the Solo button (or press S).

Solo mode is turned off.

By now, you should be a little more familiar with the song, and you're ready to start arranging it.

Using Existing Material to Fill In Parts

A good arrangement carefully balances between introducing new elements to keep listeners excited, and repeating sections to return listeners to familiar territory and motivate them to hum along.

Often the structure of the song is not set during the recording sessions. When you change the structure of the song during the arrangement process, you can use elements that were recorded only once and copy or repeat them to flesh out the arrangement.

Filling In the Bass Track

Two regions are present on the Bass track. You will work with the Bridge region shortly; but for now, you will use the first region to fill in the rest of the track and use the same bass line for verses and choruses.

1 Zoom in on the first Bass region on track 7.

2 Go to the beginning and start playback.

Listen to the bass. The bass player missed the first downbeat, so you can't use the bass recording in the first bar of the chorus. However, he played an extra bar at the beginning of the following verse. You can cut the Bass region to create a loop that starts on the second bar of the chorus (bar 3) and ends on the second bar of the verse (bar 11).

You can scroll down the Arrange area to bring the Bass region just below the Bar ruler, and use the markers and the Bar ruler as visual help.

At the top right of the Arrange area, look at the Tool menus: the Command-click tool is the Marquee tool.

3 Hold down Command to get the Marquee tool, and drag to select a section of the Bass region from bar 3 to bar 11.

The highlighted marquee selection includes all you need to fill in every chorus and verse in the song. You will now crop the marquee selection.

4   In the Toolbar, click the Crop button (or press Control-C).

The two regions outside the marquee selection are deleted, and a region corresponding to the marquee selection remains.

You will now copy the first bar of the verse (bar 10) to the beginning of the chorus (bar 2) to fill the missing first bar.

5   Using the Marquee tool, select the first bar of the verse.

6   Option-drag the marquee selection to the beginning of the chorus (bar 2).

The marquee selection is pasted as a new one-bar region at the beginning of the chorus. While it looks as if the first bar of the Verse is temporarily divided while you're copying it, the eight-bar Bass region you cropped earlier is automatically healed when you release the mouse button. (Make sure you release the mouse button first, and then release the Option key.) You can now loop the eight-bar Bass region until the bridge comes in.

7   Click the eight-bar Bass region outside of the Marquee selection to select it, and press L.

The eight-bar Bass region is looped until the next region on the track, the Bass Bridge region. Since the Bass region starts one bar after the beginning of the first chorus, all the repeats start one bar after the beginning of a section, and the last repeat is only seven bars long.

8   Option-Control-click anywhere in the Arrange area to zoom out.

9   Go to the beginning of the song and press the Spacebar.

The bass sounds good. You can now copy the Bass regions to the four choruses near the end of the song.

10   Select both Bass regions at the beginning of the song.

11   Hold down the mouse button on the first region and Option-drag the selection after the bridge (on bar 50).

Both regions are copied, and the second Bass region of the copy is looped like the original. You still need to adjust the number of repeats at the end of the song.

12 Scroll to the end of the song, at the end of the last chorus, and zoom in on the Bass track and the three tracks below.

When you Option-Control-drag the green selection rectangle to zoom in, make sure that the rectangle is high enough to cover the four tracks, but only about two or three bars wide. This will zoom in vertically so that you can see all four tracks, and horizontally so that you can see about three bars, allowing you to read the waveform and identify the bass notes.

Notice that the guitar and clavinet still play one final note on the downbeat of bar 82, after the last chorus. You want the bass to stop right after playing that last note along with the other instruments.

13 Click in the background of the Arrange area to deselect all regions (or press Command-Shift-A.)

This ensures that you will edit only one region when you zoom in on the end of the Bass region repeats, and not the two selected regions.

14 Position the pointer over the upper part of the Bass loop repeats so that the pointer turns into the Loop tool, and drag the Loop tool to stop the repeats after that last note.

15 Listen to the ending of the song, and make sure that the bass plays the last note along with the drums, the guitar, and the clavinet.

16 Option-Control-click anywhere in the Arrange area to zoom out.

Experimenting with the Order of Regions

Now you will experiment with the bass line in the bridge as you make an artistic decision. You will cut the Bass Bridge region into two four-bar regions and shuffle their order to determine which arrangement works best.

1 Position the playhead around bar 37, and listen to the transition from the chorus to the bridge.

The root note of the bass is changing when the bridge starts, making the transition strong.

Keep playing and listen to the transition from the bridge into the next chorus. The root note of the bass remains the same for the second half of the bridge and the first half of the next chorus, making the transition a little boring.

2   On the Bass track, zoom in on the Bass Bridge region.

You are going to cut the Bass Bridge region in two with the Scissors tool.

3   Press Esc (Escape) and choose the Scissors tool (or press Esc-5).

4   Drag the Scissors tool over the Bass Bridge region, and do not release the mouse button yet

As you drag, the region is selected, Solo mode is automatically turned on, and the Scissors tool allows you to scrub the audio region. When you locate the precise position (when the help tag reads 46 1 1 1) for your edit, release the mouse button. The region is cut at that position.

You now have two four-bar regions, Bass Bridge.1 and Bass Bridge.2. Next you will shuffle the order of those regions.

5   At the top right of the Arrange area, click the Drag pop-up menu and choose Shuffle R.

The shuffle modes allow you to swap the positions of regions by dragging one over the other. You don't have to be precise when dragging regions in a shuffle mode. Even if you barely drag a region over the other, the two will be shuffled.

NOTE ▶ In this situation, it doesn't matter whether you choose Shuffle R or Shuffle L. You will experience a different behavior between the two drag modes only when you delete a region or a marquee selection.

6   Press Esc twice.

The Left-click tool is reset to the Pointer tool.

7   Drag Bass Bridge.2 toward the left over Bass Bridge.1.

When you release the mouse, the two regions swap positions.

8   Zoom out to see the whole song again.

9   Position the playhead around bar 38, and listen to the transition from the chorus to the bridge.

The root note of the bass changes.

Then listen to the transition from the bridge to the chorus. The root note of the bass changes again, making the transition more exciting than it was before you swapped the regions.

10 At the top right of the Arrange area, from the Drag menu, choose Overlap.

Packing Regions into Folders

Folders are regions that can contain other regions. They are a powerful arrangement tool because once you pack multiple regions into a folder, you can edit the entire contents of the folder by editing the folder.

In this exercise, you will pack the backup vocal regions into folders and use those folders to flesh out the choruses that are lacking backup vocals. When folders are packed, a folder track is created above the selected track, so you must first select the desired track, depending on where you want your folder track to be placed.

1 Click the BU Mid L track header (the first backup vocal track).

The track is selected.

2 Select all backup vocal regions in the first chorus.

You are now ready to pack the selected regions into a folder.

3 From the Arrange area's local menu bar, choose Region > Folder > Pack Folder (or press Command-Shift-F).

A folder track is created above the selected track, and all the selected regions are packed into a folder.

NOTE ▸ You will navigate in and out of a folder later in this lesson.

Let's rename the folder track and the folder.

4   Double-click the folder track name, and enter *CHORUS BU*.

5   Press Esc to open the Tool menu, and then Command-click the Text tool.

The Text tool is now the Command-click tool.

6   Command-click the Backup Mid L folder and enter *Chorus Backups*.

Now let's copy that Chorus Backups folder to the other choruses.

NOTE ▸ Make sure that you changed the drag mode to Overlap in step 10 of the previous exercise. If the drag mode is still Shuffle R, the folder region will not be copied to the correct position.

7   Option-drag the Chorus Backups folder to copy it to the second chorus (bar 18).

8   Copy the folder to the third and fourth chorus (bar 34 and bar 50).

9   Use the Loop tool to repeat the last Chorus Backups folder once.

The repeat stops where the next backup vocal regions begin.

Let's pack the remaining backup vocal regions into a new folder and use it for the two last choruses. When a folder track is selected, packing a folder inserts the new folder region onto the selected folder track.

10 Select the remaining backup vocal regions in the chorus just before the final chorus.

11 From the Arrange area's local menu bar, choose Region > Folder > Pack Folder (or press Command-Shift-F).

The regions are packed into a new folder. The folder is inserted into the selected folder track.

12 Command-click the new folder and rename it *Chorus Hmm*.

13 Use the Loop tool to repeat the Chorus Hmm folder once.

All the choruses in the song now have backup vocals. Since all the backup vocal tracks are now empty, you can delete them and clean up the track list.

14 From the Arrange area's local menu bar, choose Track > Delete Unused.

All empty tracks are deleted.

Listen to the whole song, or use the Forward, Rewind, Fast Forward, and Fast Rewind key commands to jump to the choruses to hear the backup vocals.

You now have a sense of how useful folders can be. There are many more applications for folders, so try to keep them in mind when you organize your Arrange area. You can also divide folders and edit them the same way you edit a region. For example, a lot of producers pack an entire song into a folder, then cut the folder into sections to experiment with changing the section order.

Slicing and Doubling a Percussion Part

On the Claps track (track 6), you'll find a recording of a few handclaps. It works well, but you can make it more exciting. You will use that audio region to create a stereo handclap part for the entire song.

You will divide the region into single handclap hits and rearrange the handclaps on two tracks, panned left and right, to create a stereo effect. Slicing the handclaps will prepare you for the next exercise, in which you will shuffle the order of the individual slices.

1 Go to the beginning of the song and start playback.

Listen to the handclaps. The musician claps along with the snare, on the second and fourth beats of each bar.

First, you will slice the Claps region into two-beat regions, each containing one clap.

2 Press Esc and choose the Scissors tool.

3   Zoom in on the Claps region.

You'll use the Scissors tool to divide the region into multiple regions of equal length.

4   Position the Scissors tool after the first clap, and hold down Option.

The pointer turns into a scissors icon with a little plus sign, indicating that you are about to divide the region into multiple regions.

5   Option-drag the Scissors tool, and release the mouse button when the help tag reads 2 3 1 1.

Notice that as you Option-drag with the tool, the help tag reads Divide Multiple.

When you release the mouse button, the region is divided into 12 two-beat regions, each containing a single handclap.

You will now prepare to create a stereo effect from these regions by panning the existing Claps track hard left (all the way to the left), then creating another track and panning it hard right.

6 Select the Claps track header.

In the Inspector, the first channel strip on the left (Claps) controls the selected track.

7 Drag the Pan control down until it reads –64.

The audio signal on that track will now be heard only in the left speaker.

8 At the top left of the Arrange area, click the Duplicate Track button (or press Command-D).

The Duplicate Track button creates a new track with the same channel strip setting as the selected track's channel strip. In this case, there are no plug-ins on the Claps track's channel strip, but using that button is a quick way to create a new audio track.

9 Double-click the names in the track headers, and rename the tracks *Claps L* and *Claps R*.

10 With the Claps R track selected, drag the Pan control all the way up to pan the channel strip hard right.

Now let's move some of the Claps regions to the new track.

11 Press Esc twice.

The Left-click tool is reset to the Pointer tool.

12 In the Arrange area, select the last six Claps regions, and drag them below the first six Claps regions.

13 Go to the beginning and start playback.

You may want to solo the two Claps tracks to hear the results. You can now hear a nice stereo effect on the claps. It sounds like two musicians clapping their hands together, one on the left and the other on the right.

Let's fill in the whole song with claps.

14 Zoom out to see the whole song.

15 Select all Claps regions on both tracks and choose Region > Repeat Regions (or press Command-R). Set Number of Copies to *26* and click OK.

Copies of the selected regions fill the whole song. However, you will need to delete a few extra Claps regions at the end.

16 Zoom in on the last Claps regions, drag to select the last two Claps regions on both tracks, and press Delete.

You just took a simple six-bar mono recording of a few handclaps and turned it into a stereo handclap part spanning the whole song. Slicing the original region into single-hit Claps regions will allow you to rearrange the order of individual hits.

Humanizing a Percussion Part

In the previous exercise, you sliced the handclaps into regions of one handclap each. This allows you to swap the positions of individual handclaps, thereby randomizing the pattern to give the claps a more natural feel.

In this exercise, you will first pack all the handclap regions into a folder. Inside the folder, you will shuffle the regions to randomize them and to create accents by moving the louder handclaps to the beginning of verses and choruses.

1   Click the Claps L track header.

All the regions on the Claps L track are selected.

2   Shift-click the Claps R track header.

All Claps regions on both tracks are selected.

3   Choose Region > Folder > Pack Folder (or press Command-Shift-F).

All Claps regions are packed into a folder region.

4 From the Arrange area's local menu bar, choose Track > Delete Unused.

The two empty Claps tracks are deleted.

TIP ▶ To unpack the folder and display its contents at the top level of the Arrange area, choose Region > Folder > Unpack Folder (or press Command-Shift-U).

5 Double-click the new folder track header and enter *Claps*.

6 Double-click the folder to open it.

The folder opens, and the Arrange area displays the contents of the folder you double-clicked, which includes all the Claps regions.

Now you will shuffle the individual handclaps to randomize their positions.

7 At the top right of the Arrange area, set the drag mode to Shuffle R.

8 Zoom in on the first chorus.

Notice how some of the claps are louder than others (their waveforms show a taller transient). Try swapping the louder claps with the first regions in each eight-bar section.

9 Drag one of the louder Claps regions over a region at the beginning of a section to swap their positions.

Don't try to drag a region on the other track, or you will insert that region on the track you're dragging to, and you'll end up with an unequal number of regions on each track.

Take a few minutes and swap a few claps here and there, occasionally listening to your results. You only need to randomize a few claps for the part to sound more natural. You can experiment with the placements of louder claps to accent beats, and determine which placements work the best for the song.

As you prepared to drag a Claps region, you may have noticed that the Arrange area updated its content before you had a chance to drag the region. This is due to Catch mode, which is turned on by default when you start playback. Catch mode makes the visible part of the Arrange area (or other editors) update to follow the playhead position. The Catch button is blue when in Catch mode.

 Catch button

While the song is playing, when you see Claps regions that you want to shuffle, you can disable the Arrange area's Catch mode to stop it from following the playhead. This will allow you to keep the project playing as you work in a section of the Arrange area where the playhead is no longer visible.

10 Zoom in horizontally until about six Claps regions fill the Arrange area.

11 Start playback.

Verify that area's content Catch mode is on (the Catch button is blue). Each time the playhead reaches the end of the visible section, the Arrange area's content automatically jumps to the right to follow the playhead.

Wait to find a section where you would like to swap the positions of a couple of Claps regions.

12 At the top left of the Arrange area, click the Catch button.

Catch mode is turned off. Playback continues, but the Arrange area stops automatically updating its content to follow the playhead.

> **TIP** ▶ When you use the Zoom tool or scroll horizontally during playback, Catch mode is automatically turned off.

13 Drag one Claps region over another to swap their positions.

When you are done working in the visible section of the Arrange area, you can turn on Catch mode again to see the playhead position.

14 Click the Catch button.

Catch mode is on, and the Arrange area updates to display the playhead position.

Toggling Catch mode off and on, you were able to stop the Arrange area from following the playhead position automatically, perform your edit without interrupting playback, and finally catch up with the playhead position in the Arrange area.

When you are happy with the Claps part, it is time to close the folder.

15 Zoom out to see all the regions in the folder.

16 At the top left of the Arrange area, click the Hierarchy button.

The folder closes, and you can see the top-level Arrange area again.

TIP ▶ You can also close a folder by double-clicking the background of the Arrange area.

17 At the top right of the Arrange area, set the drag mode to Overlap.

Adding and Deleting Sections

Artists often get so involved in the creative process of writing a song that they may not see the big picture and arrive at an ideal structure for their song. Producers and A&R representatives may suggest adding an introduction or may want to shorten the song so that the chorus comes in earlier and the song's length is more suitable for radio play. Sometimes a shorter radio mix will be produced while a longer mix is produced for the album.

In the following exercises, you will insert and cut sections in the project to add an introduction and cut a chorus.

Adding an Introduction

To create an introduction, you will insert eight bars of silence at the top of the song and fill the new eight bars with the desired material. The position and length of the Cycle area determine where the silence will be inserted and how long it will be. For the introduction, you will insert eight bars.

1 In the Bar ruler, drag an 8-bar cycle area starting on bar 1.

2 In the Arrange area local menu, choose Edit > Cut/Insert Time > Insert Silence Between Locators.

An empty eight-bar section is added at 1 1 1 1.

You can now create your introduction. You will copy the Chorus Hmm folder to add backup vocals to the introduction, then add a lead vocal audio file that is stored in the project's Audio Bin.

3   In the Arrange area, click the background to deselect all the regions.

4   Scroll to the end of the song, and Option-drag the Chorus Hmm folder to 2 1 1 1.

Remember that when a region is looped, the loop repeats will end automatically at the beginning of the next region on that track. When copying the looped Chorus Hmm region, with the Snap mode set to Overlap, the repeats are automatically trimmed at the beginning of the Chorus Backups region after it.

Now let's add the lead vocal audio file, located in the Audio Bin.

5   In the Toolbar on the right, click Media (or press B).

The Media area opens and displays the Audio Bin.

In the Audio Bin, scroll all the way down to find the Intro Lead Vocal audio region.

6   Drag Intro Lead Vocal to the Lead Vocal track on 2 1 1 1.

7   In the Bar ruler, click the cycle area to turn off Cycle mode.

8   In the Toolbar, click the Media button (or press B) to close the Bin.

9   Listen to the new a capella introduction.

The introduction now commands your attention, pulls you into the first chorus, and sounds great!

Cutting a Section

Now you will cut a section from the song, first playing the song while skipping sections until you find which section you want to cut. To do this, you'll use a skip cycle area, which you define by dragging a cycle area, but from right to left.

1   In the upper half of the Bar ruler, drag right to left from bar 50 to bar 42.

A skip cycle area (represented by a green candy-striped area) is created that corresponds to the chorus before the bridge. Notice the help tag, which indicates that at bar 42, playback skips eight bars.

2   Start playback a few bars before the skip cycle area.

When the playhead reaches the skip cycle area, it jumps to the bridge, skipping the whole eight-bar chorus.

The new transition from the verse to the bridge is not very pleasing. Let's try something else.

3   Drag the skip cycle area to the next chorus, just after the bridge.

4   Start playback in the middle of the bridge.

Skipping the chorus right after the bridge sounds great, and it allows you to shorten the ending of the song, reach the Chorus Hmm regions faster, and introduce that new element before the listener has a chance to get bored.

The locators define both the length and position of the section to cut.

5   From the Arrange area local menu, choose Edit > Cut/Insert Time > Snip: Cut Section Between Locators.

The regions below the skip cycle area are cut, and all the regions to the right of the skip cycle area are moved eight bars to the left to eliminate the gap. The four-chorus ending is turned into a shorter three-chorus ending.

6   Click the skip cycle area to turn it off.

7   Listen to the bridge and the new, shorter ending section.

Muting Elements

Arranging is not always about layering instruments and adding elements to a project. Sometimes the creative process can lead to too many tracks, or an improvising musician can play too many notes. When you recognize those situations, you'll find that removing elements from a song improves the final results.

Muting Sections of an Instrument

You will work on the Moog keyboard track in this exercise, listening to how the performance of the keyboardist affects the vocal tracks. You will mute sections of the Moog where it overlaps the vocals, allowing space in the mix for the vocals to naturally stand out.

1   In the first chorus and first verse, zoom in on the Moog and Lead Vocal tracks.

2   Start playback at the beginning of the first chorus.

Listen to the Moog, the vocals, and the backup vocals. You will notice that sometimes the Moog complements the vocals nicely, answering them by playing a little melody, but sometimes it clearly overlaps the vocal performance.

This happens in bar 15, where the Moog plays a busy rhythm while the vocals and backup vocals are already singing intricate parts.

You will use the Marquee tool to select portions of the Moog region to mute.

3   Press Esc and Command-click the Marquee tool.

4   On the Moog track, Command-drag the Marquee tool over the whole musical phrase starting before bar 15 and ending after bar 16.

Don't bother looking at the help tag. For this exercise, you will rely solely on your waveform-reading skills and your ears.

5   Press M (Mute).

The marquee selection is divided into a new region, and the region is muted.

TIP ▶ You can also click a marquee selection with the Mute tool to divide it into a new region and mute it.

6   Start playback at the beginning of the chorus.

Listen to the vocals and backup vocals where the Moog region is muted. Muting that melodic phrase really opened space in the mix and gave more importance to the vocals. You can press the M key to toggle the mute status of the selected region and listen again to compare the section with and without the Moog.

The next melodic phrase played by the Moog sounds good and really answers the vocals that conclude the chorus; but in bar 18, the first note at the beginning of the verse jumps out and steals attention from the lead vocals. Let's mute that note.

7   Command-drag the Marquee tool over the Moog note in bar 18.

8   Press M.

The Marquee selection is divided into a region and the region is muted.

Continue listening to the entire Moog track, and mute all the sections of the Moog track that in your judgment are taking away from the vocals. You may find that you want to mute a large amount of the Moog performance, starting with all the repeated notes between bars 19 and 22.

Developing the rare skill of knowing what to mute and when to mute it will help make your song breathe and later make the mixing process easier. While you acquire that skill, you'll also learn to listen to the ways instruments interact with each other, making sure they aren't fighting for a listener's attention.

Cleaning Up Noisy Recordings

At the end of the arranging process, you have to make sure that your song is ready for the next step, the mixing stage. You want to avoid unnecessary noises that could blur the mix. You already learned how to clean up edit points and avoid audible clicks in Lesson 3. You will now clean up the Kick track and the Guitar track using two additional techniques.

Removing Snare Leakage from the Kick Track

To prepare your song for mixing, you will edit the Kick track to cut the leakage from the snare drum sound into the kick drum microphone. Instead of performing the edit manually, you will use a feature called Strip Silence that automatically cuts out portions of a recording that fall below a specific volume threshold.

It is easier to use Strip Silence on a shorter audio region, so you will first cut a small portion from the Kick region.

1   Zoom out to see the whole song, and zoom in on the Kick track to see the first chorus.

2   Command-drag the Marquee tool over the first half of the first chorus, from before the Kick region starts to just after the first downbeat of bar 14.

3   Using the Pointer tool, click the marquee selection to divide it into a new region.

4   In the Transport bar, click the Solo button (or press S).

   The selected Kick region is soloed.

5   In the Transport bar, click the "Play from Selection" button (or press Shift-Enter).

Listen to the soloed Kick region and pay attention to the snare drum in the background. Count the number of kick drum hits in the region, using both your ears and your eyes to read the waveform. You should count 16 hits.

You will use Strip Silence to cut the selected region into 16 regions, each containing one kick drum hit, and in so doing, remove the snare drum hits.

6   From the Arrange area's local menu bar, choose Audio > Strip Silence (or press Control-X).

The Strip Silence window opens, showing you how the region will be edited.

Strip Silence parameters   Number of regions created by Strip Silence

You can see the number of regions that Strip Silence will create displayed near the bottom right of the waveform. Using the default parameter settings, Strip Silence will create 24 regions. Looking at the waveform, you can see that some of the resulting regions (for example, the first and third regions) consist of snare drum hits.

Snare drum hits

Kick drum hit

You will need to adjust the parameters at the bottom left of the Strip Silence window until Strip Silence creates only 16 regions containing the kick drums.

The Threshold parameter adjusts the minimum volume that Strip Silence detects to create a region. You need to raise the threshold so that the snare drum hits don't create regions.

7   Drag the Threshold value up to 5.0%.

Strip Silence now creates 16 regions, and all the regions are kick drum hits.

Leave the default settings for the other parameters, but notice that the Pre Attack-Time is set to 0.0060 sec. This makes sure that each region starts 6 ms (milliseconds) before the attack detected by Strip Silence.

8   Click OK (or press Return).

In the Arrange area, the selected region is replaced by the 16 individual kick drum regions created by Strip Silence.

Since the regions are selected and Solo mode is still turned on, the regions are soloed and you can listen to your results.

9   Start playback just before the first chorus.

You can hear all the kick drums, but you no longer hear any snare drums on the Kick track.

The regions are so short that you can barely see a waveform. Let's zoom in on one of the kick drums.

10 Zoom in on the first kick drum region.

Notice the black vertical line that indicates the position of the anchor in the audio region. Although Strip Silence places the region start 6 ms before the attack, it automatically positions the anchor on the attack of the sound. This is helpful if you need to reposition the audio region on the grid.

11 Zoom out and turn off Solo mode.

Take a moment to use Strip Silence on another portion of the Kick track, or on the whole track, if you want. It is easier to use Strip Silence on smaller regions because you can count the kicks and check your work as you progress through the track.

Reducing a Wah Noise from the Guitar Track

Next, you will use a processing plug-in called Denoiser to reduce the noise of the guitarist's wah-wah effect pedal on the Guitar track.

1 On the Guitar track header, click the Solo button.

2 Start playback anywhere in the song.

You can clearly hear the noise of the guitarist's wah-wah pedal. In fact, you can hear the wah modulate the frequency of the noise when the guitar is not playing.

You can use the Denoiser plug-in to reduce that noise.

3 Click the Guitar track header.

The Guitar track is selected, and the Guitar channel strip is displayed in the Inspector.

4 Click the first Insert slot on the Audio 8 channel strip and choose Specialized > Denoiser.

The Denoiser plug-in window opens.

5   At the top right of the Denoiser plug-in window, click the Settings field and choose Effect Wah-Wah Denoiser.

Settings field

6   Close the plug-in window (or press Command-W).

7   As you listen to the soloed Guitar track, Option-click the Denoiser plug-in insert on the channel strip to toggle it on and off.

Denoiser   Denoiser
  on   bypassed

Compare the sound of the Guitar track with the Denoiser on (blue Insert slot) and with the Denoiser bypassed (gray Insert slot). The Denoiser is efficient at reducing the noise from the wah-wah pedal, so leave it on.

8   On the Guitar track header, click the Solo button to turn it off.

Reducing Noise Destructively Using Soundtrack Pro

In the previous exercises, you explored two ways to clean up noisy tracks using Logic. Included with the Logic Studio suite of music production software is Soundtrack Pro, an audio editing application that excels at the challenging art of removing noise in an audio file. In this exercise, you'll edit the clavinet recording to harness the power of Soundtrack Pro as an external audio editor.

> **LOGIC EXPRESS ▶** Logic Express does not include Soundtrack Pro. Express users can reduce the noise of the Clavinet track using the same Denoiser plug-in applied to the guitar in the previous exercise.

1 Select the Clavinet track (track 9).

The Clavinet audio region of the track is also selected.

2 Click the Clavinet track's solo button.

3 In the Inspector, Option-click the Clavinet's volume fader.

The fader jumps to 0 dB.

4 Listen to the clavinet.

You can hear some kind of electrical noise. You can remove that noise by editing the clavinet audio file in Soundtrack Pro.

5 Choose Options > Audio > Open in Soundtrack Pro (or press Shift-W).

The Clavinet audio file opens in Soundtrack Pro's waveform editor.

For Soundtrack Pro to efficiently remove noise from the audio file, it needs to analyze a section where only noise is present and create a *Noise Print*. Notice the gap in the waveform a little after 0:01:00. The clavinet player wasn't playing in that small section, which makes it perfect for the Noise Print.

6 Click the waveform in the middle of the gap.

The playhead moves to that location.

7 At the lower left of the waveform editor, drag the zoom slider toward the left.

As you're zooming in on the playhead position, make that sure you can clearly see the gap section.

8 Drag on the waveform to select a section that contains only noise.

9 Choose Process > Noise Reduction > Set Noise Print.

While it may seem like nothing happened, Soundtrack Pro now knows what the noise in the clavinet file sounds like.

10 Click anywhere on the waveform.

The entire waveform is deselected. In Soundtrack Pro, when no section of an audio file is selected, processes are applied to the entire file.

11 Choose Process > Noise Reduction > Reduce Noise.

The Reduce Noise window opens.

12 In the Reduce Noise window, click the preview button.

You'll hear that the noise has disappeared!

13 In the Reduce Noise window, click the Preview Bypass Effect button.

The Noise Reduction process is bypassed, and you can hear the original clavinet audio file. The difference is quite dramatic.

14 At the lower right of the Noise Reduction window, click Apply.

The entire clavinet audio file is processed, and the noise is removed. Up to this point, all editing you performed in Soundtrack Pro was non-destructive, so you could still undo the noise reduction. To finalize the round trip to Logic Pro, you will need to apply those edits destructively to the audio file by flattening your actions and saving the processed audio file.

15 Choose Process > Flatten All Actions.

In the Action tab on the left of the audio editor, a progress bar shows the progress as the Clavinet.aif file is updated.

16 Choose File > Save (or press Command-S).

The updated Clavinet.aif file is saved.

17 Press Command-Tab to return to Logic.

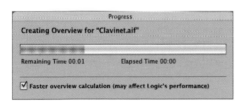

In Logic, the Clavinet file is updated and the new overview is created.

18 In Logic, listen to the clavinet.

You can verify that the file was correctly updated and the noise removed.

19 Unsolo the Clavinet track and return its level to −10.2 dB.

You now have a few tools and techniques in your arsenal to arrange a song in Logic. Remember that a successful arrangement balances repeated elements and new elements. Repeating melodies and grooves gives the listener a chance to get familiar with the song, sometimes to the point of singing along or dancing. The new elements are like ear candy that keep the listener excited and curious to hear what's coming up.

As you produce more music, you will become increasingly acute in determining what makes a good arrangement. Try to analyze the arrangements of the songs you love, and incorporate some of those ideas into your own compositions.

Lesson Review

1.   How do you use the Solo mode?

2.   How can you swap the positions of regions?

3.   How do you pack regions into a folder?

4.   How do you open and close a folder?

5.   How do you slice a region into regions of equal length?

6.   How do you insert a new section into a project?

7.   How do you skip a section when playing back a project?

8.   How can you remove background noises on a track?

Answers

1.   In the Transport bar, click the Solo button (or press S), and then select the region(s) you want to solo.

2.   At the top right of the Arrange area, set the Drag menu to one of the shuffle modes, then drag a region over another one..

3.   Select the regions to pack, and choose Region > Folder > Pack Folder (or press Command-Shift-F).

4. Double-click a folder to open it. Double-click the background of the Arrange area, or click the Hierarchy button, to close a folder.

5. Hold down Option as you cut the first slice with the Scissors tool.

6. Adjust the cycle area to identify the length and position of the section to insert, and from the Arrange area local menu, choose Edit > Cut/Insert Time > Insert Silence Between Locators.

7. Create a skip cycle area by dragging in the upper half of the Bar ruler from right to left.

8. You can use Strip Silence to remove all the portions of a region that fall below a specific level threshold. You can use the Denoiser plug in to reduce the noise level of a track.

9

Lesson Files Logic 9 Files > Lessons > 09 Mitral Valve Prolapse

Media Logic 9 Files > Media > Mitral Valve Prolapse

Logic 9 Files > Lessons

Time This lesson takes approximately 90 minutes to complete.

Goals Navigate the Mixer and use effect plug-ins

Adjust volume levels and use groups

Adjust pan positions

Filter frequencies with the Channel EQ plug-in

Process with aux sends and aux channel strips

Add depth with delay and reverberation plug-ins

Volume ② Panning ③ Dynamics ④ EQ ⑤ Specialty ⑥ Grouping

Delay Based effects → Depth in mix

Lesson **9**

Mixing

Mixing is the art of blending all the instruments and sounds in a stereo sound field. A good mix can make the difference between an amateur demo and a professional production. Mixing should carefully balance two goals: blending all the elements into a cohesive whole and, at the same time, keeping them sufficiently defined so that listeners can distinguish between them. In other words, make the musicians sound as if they are playing in the same room, while ensuring that they don't mask each other and muddy the mix. A good mix is like a completed puzzle, in which all the pieces (all the instruments) fill their proper places in the sound field without overlapping each other.

With those goals in mind, you can adjust four parameters of an instrument to define its space in the stereo sound field. You can adjust the instrument's volume, its position in the stereo field (from left to right), its distance and depth, and its frequency spectrum. Those parameters are interrelated, and changing one often means that you will need to readjust the others.

In mixing, it is also fundamental to be consistent with the genre of the song. In the previous lesson, you worked with a mix that was really dry because the song genre didn't call for many effects, and the simple instrumentation didn't require much processing to get the desired results. In this lesson, you will work with a modern pop rock song that will benefit from a variety of processing effects. A more complex arrangement with more layered instruments also means that more attention must be paid to each instrument's place in the mix.

Previewing the Final Mix

Before you open the project and start mixing the song, watch a QuickTime clip of the music video to get familiar with the song and its final mix.

1   Go to Logic 9 Files > Lessons and open **09 MVP Video.mp4**.

The music video opens in QuickTime.

2   At the bottom of the QuickTime Player window, click the Play button (or press the Spacebar).

Watch the whole music video and listen to the mix, trying to identify the effects it uses and the position of each instrument in the stereo sound field.

In the following exercises, you will open a project file that has been partially mixed, but it requires that some of the instruments receive additional polish. You will use techniques that will help you achieve a mix like the one you just heard.

Using the Amp Designer

You can use effects-processing plug-ins to sculpt the sound of the instruments and help them find their places in the mix. These plug-ins will also give those instruments a different timbre and, later, influence the way you adjust their levels or EQs (equalization).

The Amp Designer is a plug-in that emulates the sound of a guitar amp, its speaker cabinet, and the microphone used to pick up that sound. It offers several amp models that resemble famous vintage to modern guitar amps that produce sounds ranging from clean to devastating high gain distortion, and every nuance in between.

Choosing an Amp Model

In this song, the electric guitar on track 22 was recorded direct, without using a guitar amp. To start your mix, you'll apply Logic's Amp Designer plug-in to give the guitar a vintage low gain distortion tone. Throughout this exercise, take the time to experiment with various models, and tweak the amp knobs to get a feel for the different sounds that the Amp Designer can produce.

1   Open Logic 9 Files > Lessons > **09 Mitral Valve Prolapse**.

2   Listen to the beginning of the song.

When you reach the middle of verse 2, you can hear that the electric guitar plays a few harmonics, and then plays rhythm starting in the pre-chorus on bar 25. You will focus on that pre-chorus as you adjust the sound of the guitar, so let's create a cycle area.

3   In the ruler, Command-drag the PRE CHORUS marker to the upper half of the ruler.

A cycle area corresponding to the pre-chorus is created. Now, pressing the Spacebar will always start playback at the beginning of the pre-chorus.

4   Click the E Guitar's solo button.

You can hear the dry sound of the electric guitar recorded "direct."

5   Select track 22.

The electric guitar's empty channel strip is displayed in the Inspector.

6   In the Inspector, on the left channel strip, click the first insert, and choose Amps and
Pedals > Amp Designer.

The Amp Designer plug-in opens. In the graphic interface you can see the amp and
its parameters (Gain, EQ, Reverb, and so on), and to the right, the cabinet and the
microphone. At the bottom, menus allow you to choose a model, and to customize
the model by selecting the desired amp, cabinet, and microphone.

7   From the Model menu, choose British Blues Combo.

The character of the sound and the picture of the amp change to reflect the sound
characteristic of an early British combo amp. First, you'll dial in the desired distortion
level. A great way to get a warm and thick distortion from early British amps is to use

the power amp's distortion by raising the master volume. On real amps, this creates the challenge of dealing with huge levels of sound. But on a modeled amp, you simply bring down the output!

8   At the bottom right of the Amp Designer, turn the Output down to –9.0 dB.

9   On the amp, turn the Master volume all the way up!

You can now dial in more distortion with the Gain knob from the preamp.

10   On the amp, turn the Gain to about 9.

Inserting an Amp Designer plug-in on your dry guitar track and choosing the desired amp model gives you a sound that is very close to the sound of a mic'ed guitar amp cabinet. The modeled amp gives you the sound you want without the hassle of dealing with high acoustic sound levels, and with great flexibility. However, don't restrict this plug-in to dry guitar tracks! It can work wonders to add sizzle to a drum track or give an edge to a vocal track.

Customizing an Amp Model

A great way to personalize the sound of a guitar amp is to pair it with a specific speaker cabinet and microphone. As you customize and fine-tune your guitar amp, don't forget to unsolo the guitar occasionally to see how your changes affect the guitar within the mix of the entire song.

1   From the Cabinet menu, choose Modern British 4x12.

You'll now see a bigger cabinet sporting four 12-inch speakers, and the guitar sounds bigger. In fact, it's a bit too bassy. Choosing a different microphone will help you get a more focused tone.

2   From the Mic menu, choose Dynamic.

Before you start using the EQ to sculpt your sound further, you can customize the type of EQ you'll be using. In this exercise, you will use an amp with the EQ section of another amp!

3   On the amp, click the EQ label and choose British Bright.

The sound is fuller and the EQ label now reads "CUSTOM EQ." Notice how changing the EQ model drastically alters the character of the amp.

To get electric guitar that cuts nicely through this busy pop mix, you will use the EQ to make some space for the bass guitar, and give the electric guitar a brighter sound.

4   Turn down the Bass a bit, and slightly turn up the Treble.

For even more sparkling brightness, you can use the Presence knob.

5   Turn up the Presence.

The guitar's sound is now nice and bright. You will explore one final way to sculpt the sound of the guitar by carefully positioning the microphone in front of one of the cabinet's speakers.

6   Place the pointer over the speaker cabinet.

A graphic appears that displays the position of the microphone in front of the speaker (represented as a white dot).

7   Drag the white dot over the graphic while listening to the effect on the guitar sound.

The mic position strongly influences which frequencies generated by the cabinet will be picked up by the mic. When the mic is aligned with the center axis of the speaker, you'll hear the maximum level of high frequencies, and the guitar will sound brighter and more present. Moving the mic off-axis tends to *scoop* the frequency spectrum, lowering the mids while emphasizing the lows. Moving the mic closer to the speaker also tends to accentuate the speaker's bass response.

Try to place your mic slightly off the speaker's axis and not too close to the speaker, as seen in the preceding figure.

TIP ▶ When you have chosen a speaker cabinet and a mic, and positioned the microphone, you can click the disclosure triangle in front of the Mic menu to work with a smaller Amp Designer window.

You will now add subtle amp designer effects to give dimension to your guitar sound.

8   Click the Reverb's On/Off switch to turn it on.

As with the EQ section, you can click the Reverb label to choose another reverb model.

9   Click the Reverb label and try different reverb models.

When choosing a reverb, consider how you intend to place the guitar in the mix. In this case, you only want to add a bit of dimension to the sound, while keeping the guitar up front. Pay close attention to how each reverb affects the low-frequency content of your sound. Your mix can get muddy quickly when too much bass content fights for attention.

10 Choose the Mellow Spring reverb model.

The best way to judge how a reverb affects the guitar sound is to toggle the reverb's on/off switch and compare the two sounds. This particular type of reverb creates too much low-tone rumbling, which can be challenging when you later try to mix the guitar with the bass and the kick drum.

TIP ▶ To revert to the original EQ or Reverb model used by the current amp model, Option click the EQ or Reverb label.

11 Choose the Boutique Spring reverb model. This model is nicely bright and sparkling; however, you're going for a subtler effect.

12 Turn down the Reverb Level so that its effect is barely noticeable.

You will now add more dimension with a slight vibrato effect.

13 Turn on the Effects section.

The default effect is a tremolo (rapid variations in volume), which is a more obvious effect than the vibrato. This will allow you to clearly hear and adjust the speed of the effect.

14 Raise the Depth so that you can clearly hear the effect, and adjust the Speed to suit yourself.

TIP▶ You can click the Sync button when you want the speed parameter to snap to divisions of the song tempo.

15 Click Vib to set the effect to Vibrato.

The vibrato effect is less pronounced than the tremolo, and you may have to toggle the Effect section's On/Off switch to hear what the vibrato is adding to the sound.

16 Close the Amp Designer plug-in window.

17 Turn off the Cycle mode and listen to the guitar from bar 21.

You can clearly hear the vibrato effect when the guitar is playing single note harmonics in the second half of Verse 2.

Your guitar now has a sparkling, crunchy sound that faithfully emulates the famous tone of early low-gain British amps. It has just enough distortion to thicken the tone without muddying the harmony of the chords.

When customizing and adjusting the settings of an amp, remember that all settings interact, and the quest for the ultimate guitar tone is rarely a sequential process. Trying a different mic probably means you'll have to correct its position. Experiment with a new speaker cabinet to find the perfect cabinet/microphone pairing, and then readjust the Gain and EQ.

Using the Pedalboard

Electric guitarists love to collect and manipulate effect pedals that personalize their sound by creating unique effect combinations. After all, who would recognize The Edge (U2's guitarist) without his signature delay pedals? How interesting would Nirvana's "Come As You Are" guitar riff be if Kurt Cobain wasn't using his favorite chorus pedal?

Electric guitars usually present a challenge, as they produce sounds in the same frequency range as the lead vocals, which you normally want to keep intelligible so that listeners don't have to strain to decipher the lyrics. Adding a modulating effect to a guitar can help make it noticeable even when you turn down its volume, leaving more space for the vocals to sit comfortably in the mix. In this exercise, you will add a rotor cabinet effect to the guitar, then set it to a reasonable level in the mix.

1   In the Inspector, click the insert below the Amp Designer, and choose Amps and Pedals > Pedalboard.

The Pedalboard plug-in window opens. The large dark area on the left is the pedal area, which is currently an empty canvas where you can drag the desired pedals from the pedal browser on the right.

While in the real world you would typically process your guitar signal with effect pedals *before* it reached the guitar amp, in the virtual world you are free to insert the Pedalboard and Amp Designer plug-ins in the order you want. Different orders will produce quite different results, and in this case placing the modulation effect after the amp's distortion gives a better result.

2   At the top left of the Pedal Browser, click the Show All menu and choose Modulation.

Only the modulation effect pedals are displayed in the Pedal Browser.

3   Drag the Spinbox pedal to the Pedal area.

4   In the Bar ruler, click the cycle area above the PRE CHORUS marker to turn on Cycle mode.

5   Listen to the guitar with the Spinbox effect turned on.

Once again, take a minute to try other pedals and tweak their knobs to explore the sound palette that the Pedalboard has to offer. After you've experimented for a while, return to a single Spinbox pedal with the default settings to continue this exercise. (To remove pedals from the pedal area, drag them out of the plug-in window.)

6   On the Spinbox pedal, set the Cabinet knob to Single.

7   Click the Bright switch to turn it on.

The effect is now a rotating speaker; however, it almost hides the guitar tone that you worked on in the previous exercise. Wouldn't it be nice if you could use the Spinbox modulation effect without mangling your crunchy guitar tone? Well, there's an easy solution. You can use the Pedalboard's signal routing capabilities to mix dry signal and effect, dialing in just the amount of effect you need.

8   Move your pointer over the routing area at the top of the Pedal area.

The routing area's lid opens, and you can see a rectangle representing your effect (called Cabinet, as the Spinbox emulates the sound of a rotating speaker cabinet).

9 In the Routing area, click the Cabinet label.

The guitar signal is now divided into two busses, and the cabinet effect jumps to the upper bus. A Mixer pedal is automatically inserted after the cabinet so that you can mix the signal from both busses:

• Bus A (lower bus) is your dry, crunchy guitar tone

• Bus B (upper bus) is the wet tone modulated by the Spinbox

10 On the Mixer pedal, drag the mix fader down toward A, about halfway between A and the middle position.

The crunchy guitar tone you worked on in the previous exercise is now coming through clearly, mixed with just a dash of the rotating speaker effect. Let's compare the results with the sound you had previously.

11 At the bottom of the Mixer pedal, set the Mix switch to B.

You can hear Bus B, the 100 percent wet tone. It's heavily modulated, and the nice crunch from the Amp Designer is muffled.

12 Set the Mix switch to A.

You can hear Bus A, the 100 percent dry tone without the modulation.

13 Set the Mix switch to Mix. Close the Pedalboard plug-in window.

You have the best of both worlds! You can clearly hear the Amp Designer's crunchy distortion mixed with the Spinbox's modulation effect. Now you can lower the level of the guitar to make it sit in the mix.

14 In the Inspector, make sure the E Guitar is no longer soloed, and drag its volume fader down to −11.8 dB.

NOTE ▶ When the volume fader is set to values equal or lower than −10.0 dB, the minus sign is no longer displayed in the fader's handle.

When you spend a lot of time adjusting the sound of an instrument, it can be difficult to detach yourself from that specific instrument and shift your focus to the song as a whole. To find the right level for the guitar, it may help to turn it all the way down, listen to the whole mix (without the electric guitar) for a while, then slowly raise the level of the electric guitar. (Closing your eyes makes sure that you use your ears, and not any preconceived notion of what value the fader should be.) When you feel that the electric guitar adds texture to the song without taking away from the other instruments (especially the lead vocals), you've found the right level.

The flexibility of the Pedalboard gives you an extended palette of sound to play with. Spend some time experimenting with more pedals and more complex routings. When using multiple pedals, you can reorder them by dragging them left or right in the Pedal area. In the Routing area, you can make them jump from one bus to the other by clicking their labels. At the top left of the Pedal browser, when you choose the Utility category, you'll see a Splitter pedal that you can use to send the high frequencies, or your guitar signal, to one bus and send the lows to another. This allows you to use different effects for the different frequency ranges of your guitar!

Adjusting Levels

Adjusting the level of each instrument may seem like the most obvious part of the mixing process. You will usually start setting levels while you build the song. However, the perception of an instrument's loudness will change during the mixing process, and you will often have to readjust the level of an instrument after you change its pan position or EQ settings, or as you mix other instruments that influence the perception of the first instrument.

Another consideration when adjusting levels is to avoid distortion. If an instrument is too loud, it will start clipping the signal (the clip detector indicates this by turning red), and you may hear distortion. Although clipping a channel does not always result in audible distortion, it is usually best to follow good mixing practice and ensure that all track level meters stay below 0 dBFS and the clip detectors don't turn red.

Adjusting the Levels of the Drum Tracks

In this exercise, you will solo all the drum tracks and adjust their levels to get a good balance among all the drums in the drum kit.

1   At the bottom of the Arrange area, click the Mixer button (or press X).

The Mixer opens, and you can see the channel strips for all the tracks you have in the Arrange area.

NOTE ▶ If you have a small screen resolution, the Mixer area may not show the entire height of the channel strips and may be hiding the Arrange area. To perform the exercises in this lesson, you may need to resize the Mixer area to see a few tracks in the Arrange area, and you may need to scroll the Mixer area vertically to see the channel strip names at the bottom, or Setting button and EQ display at the top.

The first nine channel strips from Kick to Room are the drum channel strips. (You may have to scroll to the left to see them.) You should solo all the drum channel strips to focus on them while adjusting their levels. In the Mixer, selecting multiple channel strips will temporarily link their settings, allowing you to solo all nine channel strips at once.

2   Starting with the Kick channel strip, drag across the bottom of the first nine channel strip labels.

All nine channel strips are highlighted, indicating that they are selected.

3   On one of the selected channel strips, click the Solo button.

All selected channel strips are soloed.

A good way to find the right level for each drum is to use the kick as a reference, setting it at 0 dB, turning the other drums all the way down, and then slowly raising each drum individually, stopping when you find the level you prefer.

4   On one of the selected channel strips, drag the volume fader all the way down.

All the faders in the drum channel strips are turned all the way down.

Now you need to deselect the channel strips to unlink their parameters, so that you can adjust their volume levels independently.

5   At the bottom of the Kick channel strip, click the Kick label.

The Kick channel strip remains selected, and all other channel strips are deselected. Although you could click anywhere in the background of a channel strip to select it, clicking its label is the best way to ensure that you're not going to change one of its settings accidentally.

6   Option-click the Kick volume fader to set it to 0 dB.

You can keep looping the pre-chorus section as you mix the drums.

7   In the Arrange area, make sure that the cycle area above the PRE CHORUS marker is still on.

8   Start playback.

You are now ready to adjust the level of the drum channel strips in relation to the Kick.

9   Slowly drag the Snare volume fader until you find the appropriate level. Set the Snare fader to −11.0 dB.

Before you can adjust the levels of the other drums, you should find the right level for the overhead microphones (the stereo pair of microphones placed above the kick to pick up the sound of the cymbals) and the room microphones (a pair of microphones placed farther away from the kick to pick up the sound of the whole drum kit in the room).

10 Slowly raise the Overhead fader to −11.0 dB.

11 Slowly raise the Room fader to −27.0 dB.

You can experiment with the Room fader by raising it a little higher if you want your drums to have a roomier sound.

12 Continue adjusting the drum track levels as follows:

▶ Set Snare B (the microphone placed at the bottom of the snare) to −13.0 dB.

▶ Set Hats to −13.0 dB.

You now need to find a section of the song in which the drummer hits the toms. Since the drummer plays the toms only a few times in the song, you need to loop one of those sections as you adjust the toms' volume levels.

One way to adjust the cycle area is to use the Marquee tool to select a section and set the cycle area to match the marquee selection.

13 Zoom in on the three tom hits in the second chorus, around bar 41.

14 Drag the Marquee tool (your current Command-click tool) over the three tom hits to select them.

15 In the Toolbar, click the Set Locators button.

The cycle area matches your marquee selection, encompassing the three tom hits.

TIP ► For a faster workflow, you can hold down the Cycle button in the Transport bar and select Auto Set Locators. Selecting a region or an area with the Marquee tool will automatically set locators around that region or area.

16 Start playback.

17 Adjust the three toms' track levels as follows:

▶ Set the Tom1 fader to –7.8 dB.

▶ Set the Tom2 fader to –7.2 dB.

▶ Set the Tom3 fader to –7.2 dB.

You now have a good balance between all the drum tracks. In the next exercise, you will make sure the whole drum kit is at the right level when you listen to it in the context of the song.

18 Turn off Cycle mode, and click in the background of the Arrange area to undo your marquee selection.

Grouping Tracks

Some channel strips are closely related to each other, such as all the drum channel strips that make up the drum kit. When you're mixing, it is useful to group those tracks and link some of their parameters, so that you can adjust parameters for the whole group at once.

You'll try this by grouping all the drum tracks, then adjusting the volume level of the entire drum kit while listening to the rest of the instruments in the song, all the time preserving the relative level of each individual drum track.

1 Starting with the Kick channel strip on the left, drag across the labels of the first nine channel strips.

All nine channel strips are selected and temporarily grouped.

2 On the Kick channel strip, click the Group slot, and choose Group 1 from the pop-up menu.

The number "1" appears in the Group slot of the selected channel strips, indicating that they are assigned to Group 1.

NOTE ▶ The first time you use a group in a project, the Group Settings window opens automatically. In this project, Group 1 was used before the project was saved, so you must manually open the Group Settings window.

3   In one of the grouped channel strips, click the Group slot, and choose Open Group Settings.

The Group Settings window opens.

All the parameters selected in the Group Settings window are linked for the whole group. The Volume parameter is selected by default, so you don't need to change any settings. You can, however, name the group to easily identify it.

4   Double-click in the Name column for the first group, type *Drums* and press Return.

The name "1: Drums" appears in the Group slots on all the drum track channel strips.

You will also need to quickly toggle the solo status of the Drums group.

5   In the Group Settings window, make sure your Drums group is selected, and select the Solo parameter.

6   Click the Kick Channel Strip label to deselect the other channel strips.

7   In the Mixer or in the Arrange area, click the Solo button of one of the drum tracks.

All the tracks in the Drums group are unsoloed.

8   Close the Group Settings window.

9   Start playback at the beginning of verse 2.

The drums are now too low, so you will raise their level.

10 Drag the Kick fader up to about +4.5 dB.

All the drum channel strip volume faders are raised by the same amount, raising the level of the whole drum kit while preserving each drum's relative level.

Choosing Pan Positions

Positioning instruments to the left or to the right of the stereo mix is a good way to separate them and make it easier for the listener to distinguish between the instruments. Panning instruments and positioning them at different places in the stereo field can also result in a wider stereo mix.

Continuing with your drum kit, you will use the Pan control knobs to reproduce the real positions of the individual drums, from the drummer's perspective. Then you will spread the guitar tracks throughout the stereo field.

First, imagine that you are the drummer, and visualize the pieces of the drum kit in front of you. The hi-hat is slightly to your left, and the toms are spread out left to right. You will re-create those positions using the Pan control knobs on the drum channel strips.

1   In the Mixer, click the solo button of one of the drum channel strips.

The entire drum kit is soloed.

2   Start playback at the beginning of the second pre-chorus (around bar 55).

TIP ▶ When mixing, you often need to repeatedly start playback from the same position. You can use the Marquee tool to indicate a playback position. First zoom in on a section, and click the Marquee tool (your current Command-click tool) in the Arrange area to create a thin vertical white line. Then use the Spacebar to toggle playback from that position. To clear the Marquee playback position, click the background of the Arrange area with the Pointer tool.

Marquee playback position

3   On the Hats channel strip, set the Pan control to –24.

To pan the toms, you need to find a playback position in the Arrange area where the drummer plays a tom fill—for example, toward the beginning of the last chorus. You will exaggerate the toms' panning to make the drum kit sound wider than it really is.

4   On the tom channel strips, set the Pan controls to the following values:

▶   Tom1: –57

▶   Tom2: +24

▶   Tom3: +49

Listen again to a section where the drummer hits the toms. They sound spread out in the stereo field, widening the sound of the tom fills.

5   Click one of the soloed channel strips' Solo button to unsolo them all.

To spread the guitars in the stereo field, you will pan them left and right. First, solo all the guitar channel strips.

6   In the Mixer, scroll toward the right, and drag across the six acoustic guitar channel strip labels, from channel strip 16 to channel strip 21.

All six channel strips are selected, and their settings are temporarily linked.

7   On one of the selected channel strips, click the Solo button.

All six channel strips are soloed. You need to deselect the channel strips to unlink their parameters.

8   Select a currently deselected channel strip to deselect the six guitar channel strips.

Notice that the six acoustic guitars were recorded in pairs: two guitars during the verses (V Acous 1 and V Acous 2), two guitars during the choruses (Acoustic 1 and Acoustic 2), and two 12-string guitars. Focusing on one pair of guitar channel strips at a time, you will pan the first guitar to the left and the second to the right. However, on each side of the stereo field, you don't want to end up with four guitars overlapping each other in the same position. So, you will vary the amount of panning for each pair of guitars.

You may want to scroll down in the Arrange area to see all the guitar regions, so that you can easily navigate to a section where the guitars you are adjusting are playing.

9   Play a verse, and pan V Acous 1 to –24 and V Acous 2 to +23.

10 Play a chorus, and pan Acoustic 1 to –53 and Acoustic 2 to +50.

MORE INFO ▶ While mono channel strips include a Pan control (which determines the position of the mono signal in the stereo field), stereo channel strips include a Balance control (which determines the relative levels of the left and right signals). In other words, a stereo channel strip always sends the left signal to the left speaker and the right signal to the right speaker, but turning the Balance control to one side turns down the level of the signal sent to the speaker on the other side.

For true stereo panning, you can use the Direction Mixer plug-in (in the Imaging category).

11 Pan 12 String 1 to –64 and 12 String 2 to +46.

Now the guitars are spread out and you have achieved better stereo separation, making it easier for the listener to distinguish each individual guitar.

TIP ▶ To unsolo all the channel strips in a project, you can Option-click the Solo button of a soloed channel strip.

12 On one of the guitar channel strips, Option-click the Solo button.

The mix sounds much wider with an ensemble of six acoustic guitar players placed at different positions in a room, rather than a single guitar player who layered six acoustic guitar tracks.

Choosing EQ Settings

The sound of an instrument is composed of several frequencies mixed together in various amounts. By using an EQ plug-in to attenuate or boost certain ranges of frequency, you can alter the timbre of the sound, much as you would change the sound of your stereo by tweaking the bass or treble knobs.

EQ plug-ins can shape the sound of your instruments, focusing the sound in a specific frequency range and helping that instrument cut through the mix without boosting the overall level of its channel strip. Equalizing (EQing) an instrument can also decrease unwanted frequencies in its recording and keep it from masking another instrument in the same frequency range.

To shape the frequency spectrum of your snare, you will use the Channel EQ plug-in to attenuate some of its low rumbling while boosting the high frequencies to make it sound snappier.

1   In the Bar ruler, click the cycle area above the PRE CHORUS marker to turn it on, and click the background of the Arrange area to clear any marquee selection you may still have.

To equalize the snare, you need to solo its channel strip. However, the snare belongs to the Drums group. To solo only one channel strip from a group, Option-click its solo button.

2   In the Mixer, scroll to the left and Option-click the solo button of the Snare channel strip (channel strip 2).

3   On the Snare channel strip, double-click the EQ area.

A Channel EQ plug-in is inserted in the first available Insert slot below the compressor, and the Channel EQ window opens.

The Channel EQ plug-in allows you to adjust eight bands of EQ. You can toggle a band on and off by clicking the button at the top of the band. By default, the first and last bands are turned off, and all of the other bands are turned on. Each band's settings are shown below the graphic display in the parameter section.

Clicking the Analyzer button turns on the frequency analyzer, which displays the frequency spectrum curve of the sound on the graphic display when the track is playing.

TIP ▶ By default, the frequency analyzer displays the frequency spectrum of the sound at the output of the Channel EQ plug-in. You can click the Pre/Post EQ button below the Analyzer button to switch the frequency analyzer to pre EQ. It will then display the frequency spectrum of the sound at the input of the Channel EQ, before being adjusted by the Channel EQ.

4   Click the Analyzer button.

5   Start playback.

A curve appears in the graphic display, showing the sound's frequency spectrum curve in real time. Every time the kick hits, notice the pulsating movement in the very low range of frequencies (to the left).

You will filter out those very low frequencies to attenuate the low frequencies of the kick drum in the snare audio signal.

6   On the left, click the first Band On/Off button to turn that EQ band on.

The first EQ band's shape appears on the graphic display, and you can see that the low frequencies are attenuated below 30 Hz.

7 In the parameter section below the graphic display, drag the Frequency parameter of the first band up to 70 Hz.

The EQ band shape updates in the graphic display. In the frequency curve displayed by the Analyzer, you can watch the low-frequency content disappear from the snare signal. Not all speakers reproduce very low frequencies, and you may not hear the result, but it will make an audible difference in a system that accurately reproduces very low frequencies.

Now you will attenuate the low-mid frequencies to get the mud out of the snare sound. Instead of adjusting the numerical settings in the parameter section, you can drag the pointer in the graphic display to adjust the shape of individual bands.

8 Position the pointer over the graphic display, and move the pointer from left to right.

Pivot point

As you move the pointer horizontally, you can see the settings for the EQ band highlighted in the parameter section.

You can shape the selected EQ band by dragging in the graphic display.

▶ To adjust the gain, drag vertically in the area of the EQ band.

▶ To adjust the frequency, drag horizontally in the area of the EQ band.

▶ To adjust the Q (or width, or resonance), drag the pivot point (which appears at that band's frequency) vertically.

You first need to adjust the gain of the band to see its shape on the graphic display.

9 Position the pointer to select the fourth band, which is currently set to a frequency of 500 Hz.

10 Drag down so that the Gain parameter below reads –10.0dB.

The shape of the selected EQ band appears on the graphic display, and the settings below are adjusted according to your mouse movements.

Now, while listening to the snare, you will adjust both the Q and the frequency of the EQ band you are attenuating.

11 Drag the pivot point all the way down to get a wide band of EQ.

12 Drag the band to the left to set the frequency to 455 Hz.

13 Drag down in the area of the band to set the gain to −11 dB.

The snare sounds less muddy already. Remember to click the Bypass button to compare the snare sound before and after the EQ.

Now you can boost a high-frequency EQ band to make the snare sound snappier and have it more easily cut through the mix.

14 Adjust the sixth EQ band's parameters:

▶ Set the frequency to 5700 Hz.

▶ Set the gain to +7.5 dB.

▶ Set the Q to 0.12.

Now the snare sounds clearer and will cut through the mix.

15 Close the Channel EQ window (or press Command-W).

16 Unsolo the Snare channel strip.

17 Keep playing the song, and Option-click the Channel EQ plug-in to toggle it on and off, comparing the sound with and without the Channel EQ.

With the Channel EQ turned on, the snare volume is lower, so you need to raise its volume fader to bring it back up in the mix. First you need to temporarily disable the drums group so that you can adjust the snare volume level without adjusting the whole drum kit.

18 From the Mixer's local menu bar, choose Options > Group Clutch (or press Command-G).

In the drum channel strips' Group slot, the Drums group is dimmed.

19 Drag the Snare fader up to –3.1 dB.

20 Press Command-G again to turn the drums group back on.

21 In the Bar ruler, click the Cycle area to turn off Cycle mode.

By applying an EQ plug-in to the snare, you shaped its frequency spectrum to make it sound clearer and snappier, giving the snare its appropriate place in the frequency spectrum of the mix.

Using Delay and Reverberation

In a natural environment, an instrument's sound is reflected by the floor, walls, and ceiling of a room. The sounds of those reflections, combined with the direct sound of the instrument, allow listeners to determine the distance from the instrument to their ears and understand the nature of the acoustic space.

When recording instruments, you can choose to record in an absorbent studio to primarily record the direct sound of each instrument. You then use delay and reverberation plug-ins to create artificial reflections, giving you total control over the apparent placement and depth of the instruments.

Adding Delay to the Vocals

By adding delay and reverberation to vocals, you'll give them more depth. Since you are now working with a single channel strip, you can close the Mixer to get a better view of your arrangement.

1   Close the Mixer.

2   Select the Lead Vocal track (track 24).

3   Start playback at the beginning of the first verse.

Notice how dry the vocals sound. They were recorded in an absorbent studio, and you can't hear much reverberation.

First, you will add a delay plug-in to add dimension to the vocals.

4   On the left Arrange Channel Strip, click the first available Insert slot (below the DeEsser), and choose Delay > Tape Delay.

The Tape Delay plug-in is inserted and its window opens. You can hear the reflections on the vocals as an echo. By default, the tape delay is automatically synchronized to the project tempo so that the reflections are produced every quarter note. That sounds fine for this song.

In the Tape Delay window, you can use the two Output sliders to the right to adjust the level balance between Dry (the sound not affected by the plug-in) and Wet (the reflections generated by the plug-in). You will bring the Dry signal all the way up to its maximum level, so that you have the same level of direct sound as you had before inserting the plug-in.

5   Drag the Dry slider up to 100%.

At the lower left of the Tape Delay window, you can adjust the Low Cut and High Cut sliders to filter the sound of the reflections. Narrowing the frequency range of the reflections gives them a more rounded sound, so they are not as sharp as the dry sound. This allows you to make the echo effect less perceptible and more natural sounding.

6   Drag the Low Cut slider toward the right to 160 Hz.

7   Drag the High Cut slider toward the left to 10,000 Hz.

The reflections are now softer and don't steal attention from the dry vocal sound.

Adding Reverb Using Aux Sends

You could insert a reverb plug-in directly in the channel strip the same way you inserted a delay plug-in in the previous exercise. However, when you use reverb to place the instruments in an artificial room, using an individual reverb plug-in for each instrument would require a lot of processing power. You would also have to readjust the parameters of every reverb plug-in each time you wanted to change the sound of your artificial room.

Instead, you can use aux sends to route some of the signal from a channel strip to a new channel strip, called an *aux* (auxiliary channel). Once you have set up an aux channel strip with the desired reverb plug-in, you can add reverberation to any instrument by sending some of its signal to that aux for processing.

In this exercise, you will use an aux send to send the lead vocal to an aux, and insert the reverberation plug-in on the aux channel strip.

1   Make sure the Lead Vocal track (track 24) is still selected, and solo it.

2   On the left Arrange channel strip, click the first Send slot and choose Bus > Bus 2.

When you click a Send slot and choose an available bus, a new aux channel strip is automatically created and added to the Mixer. In the Inspector, the right channel strip automatically shows the Aux 2 channel strip, so you can see the signal path from the lead vocal channel strip to the aux channel strip. In the I/O section of the Aux 2 channel strip, the input is set to Bus 2.

A bus is a virtual audio cable that allows you to route the audio signal from one channel strip to another—in this case, from the lead vocal channel strip to a new aux channel strip. By default, an aux send is positioned in the signal flow of the channel strip after the volume fader but before the pan. For routing vocals to a reverb, that position is perfect, as the balance between dry and wet will be preserved if you adjust the level of the vocal.

3   On the left channel strip, Option-click the Send level knob next to Bus 2.

The Bus 2 send level is set to 0.0 dB, and the Aux 2 channel strip meter displays the same signal level as the left channel strip.

By default, choosing a new bus in the Send slot of a mono channel strip creates a mono Aux channel strip. In this case, you want to make that Aux stereo have a wider stereo reverb effect, where different reflections have different positions in the stereo field. You can toggle the mono/stereo status of a channel strip by clicking its Format button below the meter.

4   Below the Aux 1 channel strip's meter, click the Format button.

The Format button now displays two interleaved circles, indicating that the channel strip is stereo. Notice that the channel strip now has a stereo meter.

MORE INFO ▶ You can also hold down the Format button to choose other channel strip formats such as Left, Right, or Surround (Logic Pro only).

Now you will insert a reverb plug-in.

5 On the aux channel strip, click the first Insert slot and choose Reverb > Space Designer.

You will now choose a preset for the Space Designer plug-in.

LOGIC EXPRESS ▶ Instead of Space Designer, choose Reverb > GoldVerb, and in the following step, choose the Medium Room setting.

6 In the Space Designer plug-in header, click the Settings menu and choose 01 Large Spaces > 01 Rooms > 02.1s_Big Drums.

You can hear the reverb's effect on the vocals. When you solo a channel strip, any channel strip included in its signal flow is not muted. In this case, Output 1-2 and Aux 2 are not muted, so you can hear the vocals and their reverb.

At the upper right of the Space Designer plug-in window, notice the two Output sliders, Dry and Rev. When a plug-in is inserted on an aux channel strip, the Dry slider is automatically set to 0, so the aux channel strip processes 100 percent of the signal that is sent to that aux. You can adjust the balance between dry and wet signals on the left channel strip. The volume fader adjusts the dry signal, and the Bus 2 Send level knob adjusts the amount of reverb.

7 Drag the Bus 2 Send level knob down to –7.2 dB.

You can now send any channel strip to Bus 2 to route it to that aux channel strip and add the same reverb effect to its sound. Let's add some reverb to one of the guitar tracks.

8 Unsolo the vocals.

9 Select the V Acous 1 track (track 16).

10 Solo the V Acous 1 channel strip.

Make sure that you start playback in a verse to hear the sound of the V Acous 1 guitar.

11 On the V Acous 1 channel strip, click the first aux Send slot and choose Bus > Bus 2 (Aux 2).

12 Slowly raise the Bus 1 Send level knob to adjust the amount of reverb in the acoustic guitar.

13 Unsolo the guitar.

14 Close the Space Designer and Tape Delay plug-in windows.

Using Dynamic Processing Plug-ins

The dynamic range of a recording is the difference between the softest and loudest parts of the recording. Sometimes too much dynamic range in a recording can be a problem, as the loudest parts become too loud, and the softest parts are barely audible. You can use dynamic processing plug-ins such as a compressor or a limiter to control the dynamic range of an audio signal, usually to make the audio signal level more consistent over time.

Dynamic processing can be applied to a single channel strip or to the entire mix.

Using the Compressor

When recording an instrument, the musician rarely plays all the notes at the same volume. This can become a challenge when mixing, as some of the notes stick out and others are buried in the mix.

A compressor attenuates a signal when its level reaches a specific threshold. You can use it to attenuate notes that are too loud and then raise the overall level of the instrument to bring up the softer notes.

You will use a compressor plug-in to make the dynamic range of the acoustic guitar in your intro more consistent, making sure that you can hear all the notes at the same level.

1   Drag a cycle area from bar 4 to bar 9.

2   Start playback.

Listen to the acoustic guitar. The first few notes are nice and loud, but the two notes around bar 7 are too soft and get buried behind the bass and the vocals.

3   On the V Acous 1 channel strip, click the first Insert slot below the Channel EQ, and choose Dynamics > Compressor.

While the song is playing, look at the Gain Reduction meter. It becomes active when the compressor is triggered. Some of the guitar notes barely trigger the compressor (you can see the meter react).

Below the Compressor Threshold slider, two buttons let you choose between peak and RMS methods to analyze the incoming audio signal and determine how it should trigger the compressor. The acoustic guitar notes have strong attacks, and you want the attacks to be attenuated by the compressor, so you'll choose Peak.

4   Below the Compressor Threshold slider, click the Peak button.

On the Gain Reduction meter, you can see the attack of the notes being attenuated a little more than when RMS was selected.

You will now adjust the threshold so that all the notes trigger the compressor.

5   Drag the Compressor Threshold slider down to –19.5 dB.

On the Gain Reduction meter, you can see the compressor being triggered by all the notes. The gain reduction slowly decreases as the notes sustain, and you can hear the notes sustain longer.

You can adjust the amount of compression with the Ratio slider, which adjusts the ratio by which the signal is reduced when it exceeds the threshold.

6   Drag the Ratio slider to 3.3:1.

TIP ▶ If you want to make the compression really obvious, you can experiment with more extreme settings by turning the threshold down further and raising the ratio.

Notice that the Gain slider is set to 4.0 dB, raising the overall level of the guitar signal. The compressor attenuates the parts of the signal that go above the threshold, then raises the overall level to compensate for that attenuation.

The guitar sound is now more consistent. The attacks are softened, and the notes sustain longer. All the notes are closer to being the same level, and you don't hear the guitar drop in volume around bar 7 as much as you did before compressing it. Don't hesitate to solo the guitar track and toggle the compressor's bypass button to compare the sound with and without compression.

7   Close the Compressor window.

8   In the Bar ruler, click the cycle area to turn off Cycle mode.

Using a Compressor and a Limiter on the Master Channel Strip

On a professional project, you would usually send your final mix to a mastering engineer, who would put a final polish on the stereo audio file using subtle amounts of EQ, compression, reverb, or other processing.

When you don't have the budget to hire a mastering engineer, you can master your own mix, inserting plug-ins on the Stereo Out channel strip, as in this exercise. You will start by using a compressor to make the mix level consistent throughout the song, and then apply a limiter to make sure you're not clipping the Stereo Out channel strip audio.

1   Start playback at the beginning of the song.

When you choose a bus in the Send slot of the left Arrange channel strip, the right Arrange channel strip automatically updates to display the Aux corresponding to that bus. You can choose to display any channel strip in the signal flow of the left Arrange channel strip by clicking the desired send or output slot.

2   On the left Arrange channel strip, click the Output slot.

The right Arrange channel strip now displays the Stereo Out channel strip.

3   On the Stereo Out channel strip, click the first Insert slot and choose Dynamics > Compressor.

The compressor is inserted and its window opens. This time you will use a setting designed to emulate the soft, warm compression of analog tape recorders.

4   Click the Setting menu and choose 05 Compressor Tools > Platinum Analog Tape.

Try playing different sections of the song. In the intro, the bass barely triggers the compressor. In the first verse, the compressor attenuates the mix by 1 or 2 dB. In the loudest parts of the song, like the choruses, the compressor attenuates the mix by 3 to 5 dB. Since the Gain parameter raises the overall gain at the output of the compressor, you end up with a louder mix with more consistent levels from section to section.

You can see the clip detector on the Stereo Out channel strip going into the red.

You will now insert a limiter after the compressor to ensure that you don't clip the output. A limiter works in a manner similar to a compressor; but when the signal reaches a certain threshold, the limiter attenuates the signal so that the output signal never exceeds a specific ceiling.

5 Click the Insert slot below the compressor and choose Dynamics > Adaptive Limiter.

LOGIC EXPRESS ▶ Choose Dynamics > Limiter and keep the default settings.

At the bottom of the Adaptive Limiter plug-in window, the Out Ceiling is set to 0.0 dB, ensuring that the audio signal will never go over 0 dBFS on the Stereo Out channel strip. The meters on the left display the signal level at the input of the plug-in; the meters on the right display the signal level at the output of the plug-in.

When adjusting the Adaptive Limiter, you should adjust the Input Scale knob to avoid having red *overs* warnings on the input meters. However, sometimes a few red overs can be OK. When in doubt, trust your ears!

6 Drag the Input Scale down to -3.4 dB.

7 At the top of the input meters, click both red "over" warnings to reset them.

The overs are dimmed. Keep playing the song, and make sure that the overs don't turn red all the time.

You can now adjust the Gain knob in the middle of the plug-in window to raise the perceived level of the mix. This is when you need to pay close attention to what you are hearing. Although it is tempting to raise the Gain to produce a louder mix, high gain settings will introduce distortion.

8 Drag the Gain knob up to 10.0 dB.

You can clearly hear the distortion introduced by the Adaptive Limiter, even though the signal is not clipping on the Stereo Out channel strip meters.

NOTE ▶ During playback and after you stop playback, the clip detector keeps displaying the last maximum peak value. When you start playback again, the clip detector is automatically reset. If you have not stopped playback since you inserted the Adaptive Limiter plug-in, remember to click the clip detector on the Stereo Out channel strip to reset it.

TIP ▶ When you are not sure how a specific plug-in parameter affects the sound, don't hesitate to turn it all the way up and all the way down. The results are most probably not going to be good, but you will hear how that setting affects the sound, and you will know what to focus on in the sound as you adjust the parameter to a more reasonable setting.

9 Drag the Gain down to 5.9 dB.

Even though the Adaptive Limiter's output meters still display "over" warnings, the audible distortion disappears, and the Adaptive Limiter still gives you a nice gain boost on the whole mix.

10 Close the plug-in windows, and on the Stereo Out channel strip, Option-click the plug-in inserts to turn both plug-ins on and off, comparing the mix with and without the compressor and limiter.

The compressor and limiter plug-ins make your mix sound more consistent.

You have finished your mix using effect plug-ins and adjusting the four main parameters of the instrument sounds (volume levels, pan position, frequency, and depth) to give each sound its own place in the stereo sound field.

To study and listen to one possible version of this final mix, go to Logic 9 Files > Media > Mitral Valve Prolapse and, depending on your version of Logic 9, open one of these Logic projects:

▶ Mitral Valve Prolapse Logic Express 9

▶ Mitral Valve Prolapse Logic Pro 9

The final mix is more complete, with additional tracks and more processing plug-ins applied. It also includes a lot of track automation, which will be the topic of the next lesson.

A Few Tips and Tricks

Like any other art, mixing requires a combination of skill, experience, and talent. It takes practice to learn how to apply mixing techniques efficiently, and even more practice to learn to listen. Here are a few tips and tricks that will help you perfect your craft and become better at mixing your projects.

Take a Break

After you mix for while and listen to the same song for the hundredth time, you can lose your objectivity and experience ear fatigue. Take frequent breaks while mixing, and return to the mix with rested ears. You will then be able to better judge your results.

Listen to Your Mix Outside the Studio

When you feel your mix is pretty advanced and you are happy with the way it sounds in your studio, burn it on a CD and listen to it in a boombox in another room or, even better, in your car while driving. You will probably hear things you didn't notice in your studio, and miss things you could hear clearly in your studio. You can take notes and go back to your studio to rework the mix. Obviously, the mix will never sound the same in the studio and in the car, but it's the mixing engineer's job to make sure that all the instruments can be heard in most situations.

Compare Your Mix with Commercial Mixes

Compare your mix with the commercial mixes you like. Build a small library of good-sounding mixes in the same genre of music as the songs you are mixing. You can open a new Logic project, and place your mix on one track and a professional mix on another track so that you can solo them and compare them one after the other.

Lesson Review

1. Identify the four main instrument sound components that you can adjust to give each instrument its place in a mix.
2. For what purpose do you use an aux send?
3. How can you temporarily link the parameters of several channel strips?
4. How can you permanently link the parameters of several channel strips?
5. How can you adjust the level of an individual channel strip assigned to a group?
6. Where is an aux send positioned in the signal flow of a channel strip?
7. What does a compressor do?
8. What does a limiter do?
9. How can you choose which channel strip is displayed in the right Arrange channel strip?
10. How do you change the mono or stereo status of a channel strip?

Answers

1. Volume level, pan position, frequency spectrum, and depth.
2. You use an aux send to route some of the signal from a channel strip to an aux channel strip, usually to be processed by plug-ins.
3. Select multiple channel strips in the Mixer to temporarily link their parameters.

4. By using groups. Click the Group slot on a channel strip to choose a group to assign that channel strip to.

5. Choose Options > Group Clutch to toggle the groups on and off.

6. By default, aux sends are positioned after the volume fader but before the pan.

7. It attenuates the level of a signal after that signal goes over a certain threshold, giving the signal a more consistent level.

8. It works in a similar fashion to a compressor, but it makes sure that the signal is attenuated so it never goes over a certain output ceiling.

9. On the left Arrange channel strip, click any send slot or the output slot to display the corresponding channel strip on the right.

10. Click the format button below the meter.

10

Lesson Files   Logic 9 Files > Lessons > 10 LVL-Home

Time   This lesson takes approximately 40 minutes to complete.

Goals   Edit automation offline

Record live automation

Record live automation using a control surface

Export the final mix

Automating the Mix and Using Control Surfaces

When multitrack recorders first appeared in recording studios, they forever changed the way artists produced music. Having separate recordings of individual instruments opened the door for experimentation, and soon artists and producers alike placed their hands on the mixing board during the final mixdown, panning an instrument from left to right or riding a volume fader to change the level of a track throughout a song. Soon enough, two or three pairs of hands weren't enough to perform all the changes needed throughout a mix, and a solution was needed.

Eventually, mixing consoles were designed so that moving a fader also generated a data stream. By recording those data streams onto a separate track of the multitrack tape, the console could automatically re-create the fader movements during playback. This started the era of automated consoles. Today, professional computerized mixing boards and digital audio workstations are fully automated.

In Logic, you can automate almost all the controls on a channel strip, including volume, pan, and all plug-in parameters. In this lesson, you will draw and edit offline automation to play a snare at different volume levels in verses and choruses, create a decrescendo on a pair of grouped guitars, and pan a sound effect from left to right. You will then record live automation using the mouse, bypassing a plug-in and tweaking its parameters remotely using the knobs on a control surface.

Creating and Editing Offline Automation

In Logic, the techniques used to create and edit track-based automation closely resemble Hyper Draw, the graphic editing of MIDI continuous controller events that you explored in Lesson 5, "Programming and Editing MIDI." While Hyper Draw allows you to automate MIDI CC parameters in a region, track automation lets you automate almost any channel strip controls (including all plug-in sliders, knobs, and bypasses) and to do so independently of the regions on the track.

Drawing automation graphically is also known as *offline automation*, because it is independent of the playhead position and can be performed while Logic is stopped.

Creating Automation to Adjust the Volume of a Section

When you need accurate control over the volume of an instrument in specific sections of the song, drawing offline automation over the waveform gives you surgical precision without the pressure of performing fader movements in real time.

You will now create offline volume automation on the snare track so that it plays softer during the verses.

1   Go to Logic 9 Files > Lessons and open **10 LVL-Home**.

2   Play the song.

Throughout this lesson, you may want to use the Track Solo buttons or Solo mode to listen to a track before automating it.

Listen to the snare. It is really sharp and sounds great in busier sections such as the choruses, but it is a little too loud and distracting during the verses. You will automate the snare volume to remedy this.

3   In the Toolbar, click the Automation button.

In the Arrange area, tracks need to be tall enough to display their automation data, so the Arrange area is automatically zoomed in vertically. In the Automation Parameter menu on the track header, you can choose the parameter to be displayed in the *automation track,* a transparent gray area overlaid on the track.

While it can be useful in some cases to view the automation tracks for all the tracks, in this case you need to automate only the snare track. You can use Auto Track Zoom to automatically expand the height of the selected track, thereby displaying the automation data only on the selected track.

4   In the Toolbar, click the Automation button to hide the automation tracks.

The Arrange area returns to its previous vertical zoom level.

5   In the Toolbar, click the Auto Zoom button (or press Control-Z).

The selected track (Main Loop, track 1) expands vertically, and all other tracks retain their original vertical zoom levels.

6   In the Toolbar, click the Automation button (or press A).

The automation track is displayed for the selected track only.

7   Click the Snare track header (track 6).

The Snare track is selected and zoomed in vertically, and the previously selected track returns to its original zoom level. You can see the snare's volume automation track and its Automation Parameter menu in the Snare track header. In the automation track, a horizontal black line indicates the current volume level of the track (−11.2 dB).

8   Option-Control-drag to zoom in on the Snare track around the Verse 1 section.

TIP ▶ If you need more horizontal space in your Arrange area, you can close the Inspector by clicking the Inspector button in the Toolbar (or by pressing I).

9   Zoom in on the first few snare hits at the beginning of the verse.

Using your waveform-reading skills, you'll notice that the last snare before the verse is a reversed snare. You will drop the snare volume level after that reversed snare plays.

You can edit track-based automation using the same drawing techniques you learned when creating Hyper Draw automation of MIDI CC events in Lesson 5.

10 Just after the reversed snare that leads into the verse, click the black line to create a node at the current volume level (−11.2 dB).

Automation mode

The node is created and the yellow volume automation line appears.

When you create the first automation node on a track, the automation mode automatically switches from Off to Read, so that the next time you play the project, the volume automation you create will be read by the level fader. You can see the automation mode of the selected track on its channel strip and track header.

11 Hold down the mouse button slightly below the yellow automation line and to the right of the node you just created—but before the first snare in the verse—and then drag the new node to −16.4 dB.

You have reduced the volume just before the verse. Now you need to create two more nodes at the end of the verse to return the volume to its original level for the following chorus.

12 Option-Control-click in the background to return to the previous zoom level.

You should now be able to see the entire Verse 1 section. Depending on your screen resolution, you may need to zoom in to perform the following steps, but if you can clearly see the individual snare hits on the waveform, try to create the automation without zooming in.

13 After the last snare in the verse (at bar 119), click the yellow automation line to create a node at −16.4 dB.

14 Place your pointer slightly above and to the right of the node you just created, and drag up to position the new node at a value of −11.2 dB.

When trying to create a node close to an existing node, you may accidentally click the existing node and delete it. If this happens, hold down the mouse button a little farther to the right of the existing node, and then drag the new node to the desired position.

You have changed the level of the snare so that it drops to −16.4 dB during Verse 1 and then returns to −11.2 dB at the beginning of Chorus 1. You will now create the same automation in Verse 2.

15 Scroll to the right until you can see the entire Verse 2.

This time, you will use a new technique with the Marquee tool to quickly set a different volume for a section of the song. Remember to press Command to use the Marquee tool.

16 In Verse 2, drag the Marquee tool from just before the first snare to after the last snare.

You can now adjust the volume of the section by vertically dragging the horizontal line within the Marquee selection.

17 Drag down the horizontal line within the Marquee selection to –16.4 dB.

As you drag the line down, you can see two nodes created on each end of the Marquee selection, so dragging the automation line adjusts the volume only for the selected section.

18 Option-Control-click the background area to zoom out.

19 Start playback just before the first verse.

On the left Arrange channel strip, watch the level fader "read" the automation you just created, and notice the softer snare in the verses.

Creating a Decrescendo with Volume Automation

In this exercise, you will create a slow decrescendo on the Heavy Guitars track to evolve the timbre of the Guitar Drop section. It will start with an assault of aggressively distorted guitars; then the guitars will slowly fade out throughout the section, leaving some space in the mix for the synths that start playing a melody and, later, a chord progression.

1 Select the Heavy Guitars track (track 10).

The Heavy Guitars track expands vertically, and you can see its volume automation track.

2 Listen to the Guitar Drop section (starting around bar 69).

When the guitars come in at the beginning of the Guitar Drop section, they are supported by two more guitar tracks playing an octave lower (in tracks 11 and 12), which creates a strong impact. The mix is very sparse at that point, so the guitars fill the entire sound field. Then the drumbeat and the synths return at bar 79. At bar 87, the synth starts playing a melodic riff and is joined by a dreamy high-pitched synth. You can hear an evolution from the very aggressive guitars at the beginning of the section to the more musical synths at the end. However, the guitars play the same rhythm at the same volume throughout the section, fighting with the melodic synths at the end of the section.

You will now create a decrescendo on the Heavy Guitars to slowly make space for the dreamier synth melodies at the end of the section.

3 Click the black horizontal line at the beginning of the first Heavy Guitars region to create a node at the current volume (−5.3 dB).

The node is created, and the Heavy Guitars automation mode is set to Read.

Before you create the decrescendo, you will create another node at the current volume level before the next Heavy Guitars region on the track. This will ensure that the next regions on that track play at −5.3 dB.

4   Click the yellow volume automation line after the end of the first Heavy Guitars region, but before the next region on the track.

You can now draw the decrescendo over the first Heavy Guitars region without worrying about changing the volume automation of the remaining regions to the right.

5   Create a node at the end of the first Heavy Guitars region, before the last node you created, and drag it all the way down.

You can now add a curve to the decrescendo to make it a little slower at the beginning and faster toward the end of the Guitar Drop section.

6   Shift-Control-drag the sloped automation line in the Guitar Drop section upward to create a convex curve.

7   Listen to the Guitar Drop section.

Listen to the way the section evolves as you see the level fader slowly move down on the left Arrange channel strip. It starts with the guitars playing loudly; then they slowly fade out as the synths start playing. Later in the section, the guitars slowly disappear as the synths play melodic lines. The Guitar Drop section evolves from an aggressive rhythm guitar pattern to a melodic synth part that leads into the first verse.

Creating Pan Automation

Pan automation can be a fun way to create movement in your mix, moving a sound from one side of the stereo field to the other. It is a powerful effect that calls attention to the automated sound but, when used in moderation, can add life to a sound effect.

You will now draw offline pan automation on the first sound effect after the intro, making it move from the left speaker to a position slightly right of center.

1 Select the Perc FX track (track 7).

Automation
Parameter
menu

You can use the Automation Parameter menu in the track header to choose the parameter you want to automate.

2 In the Perc FX track header, click the Automation Parameter menu and choose Pan.

The Perc FX track now displays the pan automation track.

3   Zoom in on the first Perc FX region.

The black horizontal line at the top of the pan automation track indicates the current pan position (−64) which is all the way left.

4   Create a node on the black horizontal line (−64) at the beginning of the region.

The node is created, and the green pan automation line appears. The Perc FX automation mode is automatically set to Read.

5   Create a node around the middle of the region, and drag it down to +20.

Your new pan automation will move the sound effect from the left speaker to its new pan position, slightly to the right (+20).

6   Start playback before the first Perc FX region to listen to your pan automation.

The pan automation is a little slow, but you can make it happen quickly so that the effect will be more obvious.

7   Drag the second node (+20) to the left.

Listen while you adjust the position of the second node, or create a curve shape until you get the desired pan automation. For a more pronounced effect, try dragging the second node all the way down to +63.

8   Zoom out.

Recording Live Automation

While offline automation is a good option when you know in advance what automation movements you want to achieve, you sometimes want to hear the song playing as you adjust the controls of a channel strip (or in a plug-in window) in real time.

To record live automation, you need to choose a live automation mode for the track(s) you want to automate, start playback, and tweak the desired controls on the channel strip.

Recording Automation in Touch Mode

In Touch mode, any existing automation on the track will be read as in Read mode. As soon as you hold down the mouse button on a knob or slider, its automation is recorded. When you release the mouse button, Touch mode behaves like Read mode again, and the automation parameter returns to its original value or reproduces any existing automation on the track.

In this exercise, you will slowly fade in a synth in the DropKick section, returning it to its original value when the snare enters.

1   Select the Virus 747 A track (track 13).

2   Listen to the beginning of the DropKick section (starting at bar 29).

The Virus synth comes in suddenly at bar 33. You will create a slow crescendo so that the synth fades in slowly, reaching full volume as the snare starts on bar 41.

3   In the Virus 747 A track header, set the automation mode to Touch.

You are ready to record live automation. You don't need to put Logic in record mode to record live automation. You only need to put the track in one of the live automation modes (Touch, Latch, or Write) and start playback.

When you record automation in Touch mode, hold down the mouse button until you want the parameter to return to its original level (in this case, after you hear the first reversed snare).

4   Zoom in on the group of Virus regions in the DropKick section (bar 33 to bar 49).

Since you will now record live automation as the song is playing back, you may want to first read steps 5 through 9 before starting.

5   Start playback at the beginning of the DropKick section.

6   On the left Arrange channel strip, drag the volume fader all the way down, but don't release the mouse button.

You can see volume fader movements being recorded in the Virus 747 volume automation track.

7   When the playhead reaches the beginning of the first Virus region, slowly drag the volume fader up to create the crescendo.

Try to time your crescendo so that the level is almost back to the original level (–7.0 dB) at the beginning of the snare region.

8   When you hear the first reversed snare in bar 40, release the mouse button.

The automation line jumps back to its original level (–7.0 dB).

9   Stop playback.

At the end of the crescendo, where you released the mouse button, you can see the volume automation jump back to the original level on the track (–7.0 dB).

If you are not entirely happy with the crescendo or with a particular section of the crescendo, you can stay in Touch mode and correct your automation. Let's correct it now to start the crescendo a little later in the section.

10   Start playback before the first automation node on the track.

As long as you don't touch it, the level fader reproduces the volume automation on the track.

11   When the level fader is all the way down (–∞), position the pointer over it and hold down the mouse button.

As soon as you start holding down the mouse button, a node is created, and the position of the fader (–∞) overwrites the existing volume automation.

12 A little later in the section, slowly start raising the level fader.

The new fader movements continue to overwrite the existing automation.

13 Continue raising the fader a little faster, trying to catch up with the level of the existing automation in the middle of the crescendo, and then release the mouse button.

When you release the mouse button, the fader reproduces the movements of the existing volume automation on the track.

When you are done automating the track, make sure that you return its automation mode to Read, or you could accidentally record automation if you adjust any channel strip or plug-in setting while the project is playing.

14 Set the automation mode to Read.

15 Start playback at the beginning of the DropKick section to listen to the automation you created.

The Virus synth should come in slowly and jump to its original level right after the reversed snare.

Recording Automation in Latch Mode

Latch mode works the same way as Touch mode, except that when you release the mouse button, the automation continues to be recorded and the parameter stays at the same value. If automation is already present for that parameter on that track, the automation is overwritten until you stop playback.

You will now use the Latch mode to record pan automation on the Virus 747 A synth without the need to hold down the mouse button.

1 Start playback at the beginning of the DropKick section.

Listen to the Virus 747 A track. It repeats the same four-bar melody four times (although the new crescendo makes the first four-bar melody barely audible). You will try to time your Pan control movements to place each successive four-bar melody on opposite sides of the stereo sound field.

Even though you don't need to display automation tracks to record live automation, you will now display the Virus 747 A track's pan automation track to look at the pan automation as you record it.

Rather than choose Pan from the Automation Parameter menu, you can open a second automation track for the same track. That way, you can still watch your volume automation as you record the pan automation.

2   In the lower-left corner of the Virus 747 A track header, click the disclosure triangle.

A separate automation sub-track opens below the track.

3   From the sub-track header's Automation Parameter menu, choose Pan.

4   In the Virus 747 A track header, choose Latch from the Automation Mode menu.

5   On the left Arrange channel strip, set the Balance control to –20 in order to pan the synth to the left.

> **NOTE** ▸ The Pan automation parameter allows you to automate the Pan control of a mono channel strip or the Balance control of a stereo channel strip.

In the automation track, notice that the black horizontal line indicating the current pan position moves up to –20.

6   Start playback at the beginning of the DropKick section.

7   When you hear the synth start to fade in, wait for the end of a four-bar melody, and quickly drag up the Pan control to about +20; then release the mouse button.

The pan automation is recorded, and the pan remains at the position it was in when you release the mouse button.

8   Wait for the end of that new four-bar melody, and drag the Pan control down to about –20; then release the mouse button.

Continue panning each four-bar melody to the opposite side of the stereo field.

9   When you have entered the last pan automation, stop playback.

10 Listen to your result.

The synth slowly fades in during the DropKick section, reaching its full volume when the snare comes in, and the four-bar melodies alternate their pan positions from left to right.

11 In the lower-left corner of the Virus 747 A track header, click the disclosure triangle to close the pan automation sub-track.

12 Set the automation mode back to Read.

13 Zoom out.

NOTE ▶ The Write automation mode is rarely used. It erases *all* automation data as the playhead passes it and records any new movements you make on the channel strip. It can be quite dangerous, as it even erases automation not currently displayed in the automation track.

Recording Plug-in Bypass Automation

Like a guitar player engaging a distortion pedal to play a solo, you'll sometimes want to use an effect plug-in for only specific sections of a song. Automating the plug-in bypass allows you to turn the effect on and off at particular positions in the song.

You will now automate the bypass of a distortion plug-in on a synth track, turning off the plug-in when the vocals enter to give them some space in the mix.

1   Select the V 2 String track (track 18).

2   Zoom in on the group of regions at the end of Verse 2.

3   Start playback before the group of regions, around bar 145.

The first small region at the end of bar 146 sounds good as it punctuates the drum and guitar fills. Then, after bar 147, that synth starts fighting for attention with the vocals. You will bypass the Bitcrusher plug-in on the channel strip right after the first region at the end of bar 146, to bypass the distortion when the vocals enter.

4   On the left Arrange channel strip, set the automation mode to Latch.

> **NOTE ▶** Remember that it is not necessary to choose a parameter from the track header's automation menu to record live automation.

Get ready to Option-click the Bitcrusher plug-in as soon as you've heard the distorted synth punctuating the drum fill at the end of bar 146.

5   Start playback around bar 145.

6   When you hear the end of the drum fill, Option-click the Bitcrusher plug-in to bypass it.

On the V 2 String track, the Insert#1 bypass automation is automatically displayed (Bitcrusher is the first insert on the channel strip).

The bypass automation should occur on the first downbeat of bar 147, but it's OK if it's a little later, as long as you don't hear the distortion on the synth when the vocals come in.

7   On the left Arrange channel strip, set the automation mode back to Read.

8   Zoom out and listen to the result.

You still have the punctuating effect of the first synth hit at the end of the drum and guitar fill, but now the synth is not distorted during the verse, letting the vocals shine through.

Using Control Surfaces

Recording live automation by dragging onscreen sliders and knobs with the mouse can be a powerful means of expression, but nothing beats the feel of a real fader or knob under your fingers. Adding a control surface to your Logic setup allows you to map different knobs to the desired channel strip or plug-in parameters, and to remote-control those parameters while you record live automation.

Many supported control surfaces (such as the Mackie Control Universal) can be detected automatically by Logic, which also will automatically assign their faders and knobs.

MORE INFO ▶ To learn more about supported control surfaces, choose Help > Logic Pro Support.

When the controls are not automatically mapped—for example, when control knobs are used on a MIDI keyboard that isn't a supported device—you can manually assign the physical knobs to the parameters you want to automate.

> **NOTE** ▶ If your only control surface is a MIDI keyboard that does not have a controller knob of any kind, you can use the pitch bend and modulation wheels as controller sliders to perform the following exercises. Any device sending MIDI CC events can be assigned to any channel strip or plug-in parameter.

Using Automation Quick Access

Automation Quick Access allows you to assign a single controller knob to the automation parameter that is currently displayed on the selected track. You need to assign the controller knob only once, and you can then use it to control any parameter on any track. You just select a track and choose the desired parameter from the Automation Parameter menu.

> **NOTE** ▶If you're not getting the expected behavior during this exercise, your control surface preferences may be corrupt. Close Logic, then in the Finder, navigate to Home Folder > Library > Preferences. Locate the file named com.apple.logic.pro.cs and drag it to the trash. Open Logic again and start over.

1 Select the ES 2 track (track 20).

2 Start playback at the beginning of the first ES 2 region (bar 79).

You may want to solo the ES 2 track to clearly hear the results of your automation.

You will use a controller knob to create wide pan automation on the ES 2 track, creating drastic movements of the synth in the stereo field to add frenzy to this aggressive part of the song.

First, you need to set up a controller knob using Automation Quick Access.

3 From the Arrange area local menu, choose Track > Track Automation > Automation Quick Access (or press Command-Option-Control-A).

An alert message appears asking you to assign a controller to Automation Quick Access.

NOTE ▶ If a controller has already been assigned to Automation Quick Access, this alert does not appear, and choosing Track > Track Automation > Automation Quick Access will toggle Automation Quick Access on and off. To reassign Automation Quick Access to a new controller knob, choose Logic Pro > Preferences > Automation, make sure that Automation Quick Access is turned on, click Learn Message and continue with step 5 of this exercise.

4   Click Assign.

The Automation Preferences window opens, Automation Quick Access is turned on, and you can assign the controller knob that you want to use.

5   Move a knob or slider on your control surface.

A help tag appears to indicate that the controller has been assigned.

6   In the Automation Preferences window, click Done.

7   Close the Automation Preferences window (or press Command-W).

8   Move the controller knob, giving it a wide swing to cover its entire range from the minimum to the maximum positions.

In the Inspector, the volume fader of the ES 2 should follow the movements of the knob. On the ES 2 automation track, the black line representing the current volume value moves in the same way.

Since Automation Quick Access controls the displayed automation parameter, you need to display the pan parameter. First, make sure that the ES 2 returns to its original volume.

9   Set the ES 2 volume back to –12 dB.

10   In the ES 2 track header, choose Pan from the Automation Parameter menu.

11   Move the controller knob until you see the pan control move on the left Arrange channel strip.

The controller knob now remotely controls the panning of the selected track, and you can use it to record live pan automation.

12   From the Automation Mode menu, choose Touch.

13   Start playback before the Guitar Drop section.

14   When the ES 2 starts, move the knob left and right to generate wide pan automation.

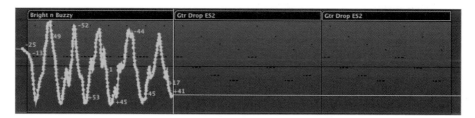

The pan automation is recorded on the track.

Feel free to go crazy with the pan automation in the first few bars, and then gradually narrow the range of your controller movement to decrease the width of the pan automation, finally settling back to a center position around the middle of the Guitar Drop section. Remember, that section evolves from frantic to melodic, and you want to respect that mood progression in the panning of the ES 2 synth.

15   Set the automation mode back to Read, and listen to your results.

Now that you have assigned a controller to Automation Quick Access, you can use that same controller for any parameter on any track. Try selecting another track, choosing a parameter from the Automation Parameter menu, and automating that parameter using the same controller.

16 From the Arrange area local menu, choose Track > Track Automation > Automation Quick Access to turn it off.

Using knobs on a control surface to tweak plug-in parameters in real time can be a lot of fun as you discover new ways to "play" the plug-ins as musical instruments. Make sure that you keep this technique in mind when you feel an instrument or a section of a song is a little static or repetitive and could benefit from automation.

Exporting the Mix

When you finish mixing and automating a project, you need to export it—to a CD or an MP3 file, for example—so that you can share it with other listeners.

You can use the cycle area to select the section of the project you are going to bounce. In this exercise, you will export the mix to an uncompressed audio file. First, you will zoom out so that you can see the entire song in the Arrange area.

1 In the Arrange area, click the background (or press Command-Shift-A).

All regions are deselected.

2 Press Z, the keyboard shortcut for "Toggle Zoom to fit Selection or All Contents."

You can see the entire song.

3 In the Arrange area, click the background to deselect all regions and marquee selections.

4 Make sure Cycle mode is turned off.

5 In the Toolbar, click the Bounce button.

The Bounce window opens.

6   Name the bounce file *LVL-Home* and save it to the desktop.

In the Destination area, make sure that PCM is selected, so your mix is saved as an uncompressed digital audio file. At the lower right of the Bounce window, you can change the PCM file parameters.

The sample rate is set by default to the sample rate of the project, 44,100 Hz in this case, so don't change it unless you need to convert the bounced audio file to a new sample rate.

However, this project was recorded mainly with 24-bit audio files. If you intend to send the bounced file to a mastering engineer so that he can put the final touches on the master before it is sent to the CD production plant, you will want to export your mix with the full dynamic range offered by 24-bit audio files.

7   In the Resolution menu, make sure that 24 Bit is selected.

8   Click Bounce. A progress indicator shows that your project is bouncing. This process may take a few minutes.

9   Press Command-Tab to open the Finder, and press Command-Option-H to hide all other applications.

10   On the desktop, Control-click **LVL-Home.aif** and choose Open With > iTunes (or QuickTime Player) to preview your final mix.

Using automation, you have taken your song to a new level, fading instruments in and out to evolve the instrumentation and mood of a section in time. You have used offline automation to draw automation on the track, and you have recorded live automation using both the mouse and a control surface. Let your imagination run wild, and try to think of other applications to automate your own projects.

To hear a more complete version of the finished automated mix, go to Logic 9 Files > Media > LVL-Home and, depending on your version of Logic, open one of the following files:

▶   LVL-Home Logic Pro 9

▶   LVL-Home Logic Express 9

Lesson Review

1.   How can you view the automation track on the current track only?

2.   Describe the steps needed to record live automation.

3.   Compare the similarities and differences of the Touch and Latch modes.

4.   When using Automation Quick Access, how many parameters can you control, and how many controller knobs can you use?

Answers

1.   In the Toolbar, click the Auto Zoom button to automatically zoom in vertically on the selected track; then click the Automation button to display the selected track's auto-mation track.

2.   Choose the desired automation mode (Touch, Latch, or Write); then start playback and adjust the desired parameters.

3.   In both modes, recording automation begins when you first touch a controller slider or knob (or hold down the mouse button over a slider or knob on the interface). When you release the controller knob (or the mouse button), Touch mode returns the automation to the original parameter value or existing automation on the track, whereas Latch mode continues recording at the current parameter level.

4.   You can use only one controller knob and control only one parameter at a time, but you can easily choose the desired parameter by displaying it on the selected automation track.

11

Lesson Files   Logic 9 Files > Lessons > 11 New Day

Logic 9 Files > Lessons > 11 Testing MIDI

Time   This lesson takes approximately 60 minutes to complete.

Goals   Learn good backup practices

Understand the principles of troubleshooting

Learn basic troubleshooting steps

Lesson 11
Troubleshooting and Optimization

As an Apple Certified Pro, you will find yourself in situations where you are responsible for the proper functioning of several Logic systems. Whether maintaining your home studio or a professional studio, teaching in a classroom with student computer stations, or working as a technical consultant, you will often need to safely and quickly solve problems.

Problems can generally be attributed to one of three causes.

► Human errors: The user forgot to press a button, didn't connect devices properly, didn't install the proper driver, or made another mistake.

► Hardware limitations: The user reached the limitations of the computer, was trying to use too many plug-ins, or asked the system to play back more tracks than it could handle.

► Software- and hardware-related problems: Incompatible devices, corrupted preferences or project files, and other defects can result in unexpected behaviors.

In this lesson, you will explore the most common issues you may run into and will develop a sense for general troubleshooting techniques that you can apply to many situations.

Making Backups

Before starting to troubleshoot, you should make sure that you have current backups of all your critical projects. Now is a good time to learn responsible backup practices.

The importance of backing up cannot be overstressed. Backing up data is a precautionary measure that guarantees you will always have a properly working copy of your Logic projects, no matter what system problems you might encounter.

While some Logic problems can be fixed using the troubleshooting techniques described in this lesson, many problems—such as human error, data corruption, power failure, and hard drive failure—can result in data loss. The most reliable way to recover lost or corrupted data is to revert to a backup copy. Obviously, that means you must follow a strict backup routine.

Saving a Project and Making Automatic Backups

In Lesson 1, you learned the importance of saving your project at regular intervals. Now is a good time to further understand Logic's behavior when saving a project, and the way automatic backups are created.

When you open a Logic project, the project file is transferred from the hard disk to the computer's random-access memory, or RAM. RAM has a much faster access speed than hard disk storage and allows most operations to occur instantaneously. However, RAM is also volatile. In the event of a power failure, a computer crash, or unexpected program termination, your project is erased from RAM without giving you a chance to save it to the hard disk.

When you save your project, you are copying it from RAM to the hard disk. If an incident causes the project to disappear from RAM, you can always open it again from the hard disk in the same state that it was in the last time you saved it. Therefore it is important to save it frequently, or at least after any important operation has been performed. Each time you save a project, the previously saved version of the project is backed up automatically, as in the next exercise.

When switching between Logic and the Finder, remember that you can use Command-H
to hide the application with key focus, and Command-Tab to switch between applications.
You will first save the project to your desktop to have easy access to the project folder and
clearly see its contents.

1   Go to Logic 9 Files > Lessons, and open **11 New Day**.

2   Choose File > Save As.

A Save dialog appears.

3   If a file browser is not open, click the disclosure triangle next to the Save As field.

A file browser opens.

4   Click the desktop icon in the sidebar (or press Command-D), make sure that Include
Assets is selected, and click Save.

The whole project is saved on the desktop, and a few progress indicators show the audio files being copied to the new project.

TIP To save all the audio files along with the project file in the project folder, always make sure that "Include Assets" and "Copy external audio files to project folder" are selected in the Save window.

5 In the Finder, double-click the 11 New Day project folder to look at its contents.

The project folder contains the 11 New Day project file and an Audio Files folder.

6   Click the Audio Files folder to view its contents.

All the audio files used in the project have been copied to the Audio Files folder inside your new Project folder.

7   Leave the Finder window open, switch back to Logic, and look at the Arrange window's title bar.

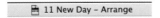

In the title bar, notice the plain Logic project icon in front of the project name. That plain icon indicates that the open project is identical to the one on the hard disk.

8   In the Arrange area, drag a region to move it by a few bars.

Now notice the Logic project icon. It is dimmed, indicating that the current project exists only in RAM and is different from the version on the hard disk.

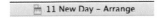

9   Choose File > Save (or press Command-S).

Your project is saved to the hard disk, and the icon returns to its previous state to indicate that the versions onscreen and on the hard disk are identical.

10   Switch to the Finder.

The project folder now includes a Project File Backups folder, which contains a backup of the project file. That backup corresponds to the previously saved version of the project file, which was made before you last saved. In this case, the 11 New Day.00 file in the Project File Backups is the file you first saved in step 4, before moving the region, while 11 New Day (at the root of the project folder) is the new project file you saved in step 8, after moving the region.

Each time you save a project, the previously saved version is moved to the Project File Backups folder and assigned a sequential number. By default, the Project File Backups folder contains up to ten saved versions of your project, numbered 00 through 09. The file numbered 00 is the most recent and 09 is the oldest. If you ever save your project by mistake, you can close the project and open an earlier backup.

NOTE ▶ You can change the number of project files that Logic keeps in the backup folder by changing the value in Preferences > General > Project Handling.

Backing Up Project Files

Like any other computer file, a Logic project file can become corrupted. This usually results in unexpected behaviors when you work with a project, behaviors not present when you work with other project files.

When a project file is corrupt, the only solution is to rebuild the project (see next exercise). Of course, a proper backup regimen may avoid the need for a rebuild.

You should save copies of your project file at regular intervals, or after you've made any significant changes. For example, if you save a copy every 20 minutes, and your project is corrupted, the worst that can happen is that you have to return to the previous version and will lose the past 20 minutes of work.

1   Choose File > Save As (or press Command-Shift-S).

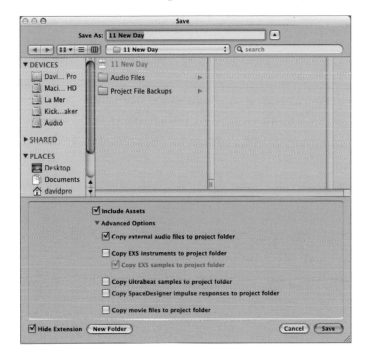

The Save As dialog opens, and you can see the contents of the project folder. You don't have to change the location of the file you are about to save—it will be saved in the project folder. However, you don't need to copy all the audio files again. The new project file will use the same audio files as the current file.

2   Deselect Include Assets.

3 Name the new project file *11 New Day_2*, and press Enter.

A copy of the project file is saved on the hard disk as *11 New Day_2*, and that is the version you are now working with. You can verify the name in the title bar of the Arrange window.

You will now save one more backup version of the project file.

4 Choose File > Save As (or press Command-Shift-S).

You can see the contents of the project folder, which now contains two project files: 11 New Day and 11 New Day_2.

5 Name the copy *11 New Day_3* and save it.

6 Close the project.

This saving technique ensures that you have an earlier backup to go to in case of project file corruption. It also offers an easy means to revert to a previous version of your project, should you decide that you are no longer happy with the artistic direction you have taken in the last saved version(s).

Rebuilding a Project File

When your project seems to be corrupted and you don't have access to a recent backup, you can create a new empty project and import all the data from the corrupted project.

1 Choose File > New and create an Empty Project.

The Empty Project's Arrange window opens, and the New Track dialog appears.

2 Create one audio track.

You will now locate the old project file to import its data.

3 Make sure the Media area is open.

4 At the top of the Media area, click the Browser button (or press F).

5 Click the Home button.

6 Navigate to Desktop > 11 New Day > 11 New Day, and select the Project file.

7   At the bottom of the File browser, click the Import button.

The File browser now displays a list of all the tracks in the old project. To completely rebuild the project, you will also import all the Global tracks. This will ensure that the new project has the same tempo track, marker track, and so on.

8   At the top of the File browser, click the Global button.

The File browser now also shows the global Marker, Signature, and Tempo tracks.

9   Choose Edit > Select All (or press Command-A).

All the tracks in the File browser are selected.

In this instance, you want to import the content of all the tracks, the plug-ins of their corresponding channel strips, and their input/output settings. Because you selected all the tracks, you need to select only one checkbox in each of those columns.

10 Select one checkbox in the Content column, one in the Plug-ins column, and one in the I/O column.

All checkboxes in those three columns are selected.

11 At the bottom of the File browser, click the Add button.

TIP If you have customized settings in the old projects, you can import them to the new project by clicking the Import Project Settings at the bottom of the File Browser.

All the tracks from the old project are added to the Arrange area. You can now delete the empty track you created at the beginning of this exercise to start this project.

12 In the Arrange area, click the first track's track header, and choose Track > Delete.

This new project now contains the same tracks with the same regions as the old project. You've also successfully imported the tempo, plug-ins, and I/O settings of the old project.

13 Save and close your project.

Backing Up Project Folders to External Devices

Until now, you saved your project file to the hard disk and made backup copies inside the project folder. But one day your hard disk will die, and you can't know when that day will be. It could be the very first day you use the hard disk, or it could be years from now.

To protect yourself against human error or hard disk failure, you have to back up the entire project folder to another hard disk. An easy solution is to purchase an external hard disk dedicated to backing up your project folders. You can also back up to another computer's hard disk over a network, or even to online storage (such as a MobileMe account). Having a backup in a remote location adds protection in case of burglary or fire.

When your project folder contains only one project file, you can choose File > Save As, make sure that Include Assets is selected, and choose a location on your external hard disk. However, if you use the technique described in the earlier exercise, "Backing Up Project Files," your project folder will have several project files, and a Save As won't work. In that case, use the Finder to copy the whole project folder to the new location.

Solving Audio and MIDI Routing Problems

A music production system built around Logic can quickly grow into a complex network of interconnected devices. When a problem occurs, finding its cause can become a high-tech scavenger hunt.

Troubleshooting requires one part logical reasoning and one part experimentation. When troubleshooting a signal chain comprising several devices, you can systematically bypass each device in turn, or substitute one device for another, to find the culprit. By carefully examining which device combinations work and which don't, you can often isolate the offending device.

Whether the problem is due to human error (such as an improper setup) or to component failure (such as a bad connection), the techniques to identify the point of failure are the same.

Restoring Your Audio Output

The greatest frustration of working with music equipment occurs when the equipment does not produce any sound. When troubleshooting the solution, you can easily rule out your audio interface and monitoring system by making sure that Logic can play Apple Loops from the Loop Browser.

1 Open an empty project and create an audio track.

2 In the Media area, click the Loops tab (or press O).

3 Click any category.

4 Select the first loop in the search results list.

The loop icon turns into a speaker, and its signal is displayed in the Inspector on the Stereo Out channel strip's level meter.

If the loop icon doesn't change when you click it and no signal is displayed on the Stereo Out channel strip, check your audio driver settings.

5   In the Toolbar, click the Preferences button, and choose Audio from the pop-up menu.

Make sure that the Enabled checkbox is selected and the correct audio interfaces are chosen in the Output Device and Input Device menus. If those settings are correct, you can try to restart the Core Audio driver.

6   If the settings that you checked in step 5 appear to be correct, deselect Enabled.

The audio driver is disabled.

7   Select Enabled again, and click Apply Changes.

After a moment, a progress indicator appears, showing the initialization progress of the Core Audio engine.

If the loop icon still doesn't change when you click it, try bypassing your audio interface as described in the next section.

When a signal appears on the Stereo Out channel strip, you know that Logic is producing sound. If you still can't hear the sound, you should suspect the monitoring chain (drivers, audio interface, cables, monitors, and headphones).

Any level meter on your interface, mixer, or even speakers can help you figure out where the signal is being lost. Plugging headphones into your audio interface can help determine if the problem occurs between the computer and the audio interface (no sound in the headphones), or between the audio interface and the monitors (sound in the headphones but not in the monitors).

A few things to check:

▶   If you are using your Mac's built-in audio interface, click the speaker icon on the right side of the main menu bar and make sure that the volume slider is up.

▶   Make sure that you have installed the latest audio interface drivers.

▶   If the audio interface has additional software installed, open that software and make sure that the signal routing is correct and no volume fader handle is down or mute button is on.

▶   Check the audio interface's manual for a reset procedure.

▶   Check the fuse or temporary protection on the monitors.

▶   Check all cables between the computer, the audio interface, and the monitors.

Bypassing Your Audio Interface

Many audio problems and data errors (such as sample rate errors, or audio and MIDI synchronization errors) can be traced to the audio interface and its drivers. The easiest way to determine if the audio interface is at fault is to bypass it and use the Mac's built-in interface and speakers.

1   From the main menu, choose Logic Pro > Preferences > Audio; or, in the Toolbar, click the Preferences button and choose Audio from the pop-up menu.

2   From the Output Devices menu, choose Built-in Audio (or Built-in Output).

3 Click Apply Changes.

4 From the Apple menu, choose System Preferences.

5 In the Hardware area, click the Sound button.

TIP ▶ To quickly access your Mac's Sound preferences, skip steps 4 and 5, and while holding down Option, click any of the speaker keys (Volume Up, Volume Down, or Mute).

6   Click the Output button.

7   Select Internal Speakers, or Headphones.

8   Make sure that the Output volume slider is positioned toward the right and Mute is deselected.

If the problem goes away when you're using the Mac's built-in interface, then you can suspect your external audio interface or your speakers. After you've made sure that the speakers work, check the audio interface's manufacturer's website to be sure that you're using the most current drivers for your system. Check the audio interface manual for a way to implement a reset procedure. If all else fails, contact the manufacturer to get help troubleshooting the audio interface and its accompanying software.

Checking Audio Input

If no sound is produced when you're recording or monitoring an audio source in Logic, you should first verify that you are getting sound out, as described in the previous exercises. In other words, before troubleshooting your microphones, make sure that your speakers work!

If your interface has input meters, check that the meters display a level when the artists perform. If they don't, the problem lies ahead of Logic's inputs. Try replacing the instrument or microphone, switch to another cable, or use the built-in audio interface.

If your interface does display an input level and you still can't hear incoming sound in Logic, chances are you are dealing with human error. Check that your audio interface settings are correct and your incoming audio signal is properly routed.

First look at the channel strip. Does the level meter display a signal? If it doesn't, you might be attempting to monitor the wrong device or the wrong input on the correct device.

1   In the Arrange area, record-enable the audio track.

    A Save As dialog opens.

2   Name your project *Audio Test* and save it to the desktop.

3   In the Toolbar, click the Preferences button and choose Audio from the pop-up menu.

4   Make sure that the correct device is chosen.

5   Verify that Software Monitoring is selected, and close the Preferences window.

NOTE ▶ Some audio interfaces offer near-zero latency monitoring, usually accessible through the software accompanying the interface. Other configurations use a hardware mixer to route live instruments directly to the headphones or monitors. In those situations, Software Monitoring should be deselected so that Logic no longer routes incoming audio to its outputs.

6   On the audio channel strip, see that the correct input from the Input menu is chosen.

Sometimes audio interfaces don't label inputs in the same way as Logic, and what appears to be Input 1 on the audio interface could be labeled Input 3 in Logic. In that case, you can use the driver labels.

7   Open the Mixer, and choose Options > I/O Labels.

The I/O Labels window opens.

8 For all input channels, select the options in the "Provided by Driver" column.

NOTE ► The number of channels and their labels depend on the audio device you use. Some drivers do not provide labels. You can select the User labels and enter your own custom labels.

9 On the audio channel strip, check the Input menu again, this time looking at the driver labels.

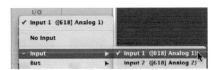

10 Make sure the Record Enable button is turned on in the channel strip.

If the record-enabled channel strip displays a signal and the Stereo Out channel strip still doesn't display a signal, you need to check for proper routing of the signal.

11 Make sure the output of the channel strip is set to Stereo Out.

12 Make sure the Level fader is up.

13 Make sure the Mute button is not on.

14 Make sure the Mute button is not blinking.

Blinking Mute button

A blinking Mute button indicates that the channel strip is temporarily muted, even though its Mute button is not on. This situation happens when another channel strip is soloed.

TIP ▶ When you realize that one or more tracks are soloed, it can be cumbersome to open the Mixer and unsolo them all, especially in larger sessions featuring many tracks. Instead, click to turn on the Solo button of the current channel strip, and then Option-click that same Solo button again. This will take all tracks out of Solo mode.

15 Close the project, and don't save it.

Once the Stereo Out channel strip meters display a signal, you should hear that signal through your monitors. If you don't, take another look at "Restoring Your Audio Output," earlier in this lesson.

Getting MIDI Out

When trying to play MIDI regions on external MIDI instrument tracks, first make sure that the track is assigned to the correct MIDI instrument, as explained in the appendix "Using External MIDI Devices."

When troubleshooting MIDI Out routing, it is important to isolate the MIDI Out signal routing from the audio routing of your MIDI device. If the MIDI device has a MIDI input activity monitor, you can check it to verify that the MIDI device is receiving the MIDI data sent by Logic. You can also plug a headphone directly into the MIDI device to verify that the device properly responds to the MIDI events it receives. If it does, then use the techniques described in the previous exercises to check the audio input routing (from the MIDI device into Logic) and the audio output routing (from Logic to your speakers).

The MIDI Activity (In/Out) display in the Transport bar is a great tool for troubleshooting MIDI problems. It displays incoming (upper line) and outgoing (lower line) MIDI events in real time.

If you do not see any outgoing MIDI activity in the display, check for muting at the track, region, and note levels.

1 Open 11 Testing MIDI.

2 Start playback.

Watch the MIDI Out display: It doesn't show any activity.

3 On track 1, click the Mute button to unmute the track.

You still can't see any activity in the Transport bar's MIDI Out display.

4 With the Mute tool chosen, click the MIDI region (or select it and press M), and start playback.

The MIDI Out display still doesn't show any outgoing MIDI activity.

5   Double-click the MIDI region.

MIDI notes are displayed in the Piano Roll Editor, but they are dimmed, indicating that they are muted.

6   Select all the notes, click them with the Mute tool (or press M), and start playback.

The notes are unmuted, and the MIDI Out display shows activity.

If Logic's MIDI Out display shows note events and you still can't hear anything, then the problem lies somewhere else. Check your MIDI routing, as explained in Appendix A. To temporarily bypass all audio routing, plug your headphones directly into the receiving MIDI device's headphone output. Make sure that you have installed the latest drivers for your MIDI interface or MIDI device.

> **MORE INFO ▶** To monitor all incoming and outgoing MIDI events at the computer level, you can use a free third-party utility, MIDI Monitor, available from Snoize (http://www.snoize.com/MIDIMonitor/).

Getting MIDI In

In Logic, all incoming MIDI events are routed by default to the record-enabled MIDI or software instrument track. Incoming MIDI events are also shown in the Transport bar in the MIDI In display.

If no MIDI activity is displayed when you play a MIDI controller, check all the MIDI devices in the chain *before* Logic.

1   Check your MIDI controller's MIDI output activity display, if present.

2   Check your MIDI interface's MIDI input activity display, if present.

3   Power-cycle the MIDI controller. Turn it off, and then turn it on.

4   Power-cycle the MIDI interface.

5   Disconnect and reconnect the cable connecting the MIDI device or MIDI interface to your computer.

6   If you are using a USB MIDI device, try using another USB port on your computer.

7   Try unplugging other USB devices from your computer, aside from the keyboard and mouse.

8   In the Toolbar, click the Preferences button, then choose MIDI from the pop-up menu.

9   In the General tab, click "Reset All MIDI Drivers."

After these steps, if Logic still does not show any incoming MIDI activity when you play your MIDI controller, close the current project and open a factory template. If the template shows activity on the Transport bar's MIDI In display, then the problem lies with your project file. Reopen your project.

In Logic, the Environment contains all the objects you can assign to a track in the Arrange area, such as audio and instrument channel strips and external MIDI devices. It also contains several MIDI objects that control MIDI input and output.

When a MIDI input issue has been isolated to a specific project file, you need to check the default MIDI input cabling of objects in the Environment.

In this project file, the default cabling was broken. Now, you will fix it.

10   Create a new software instrument track, and choose a channel strip setting from the Library.

11   Play a few notes on your MIDI controller.

In the Transport bar, the MIDI In display does not show any activity, and you can't hear the piano.

12   Choose Window > Environment (or press Command-8).

The Environment window opens. The Layer menu at the upper left allows you to view different layers or sections of the Environment. The Click & Ports layer is where incoming MIDI is connected to Logic's sequencer input.

13 Next to the Layer menu, click the arrow button and choose Click & Ports.

The Click & Ports layer appears. A default Click & Ports layer should show a Physical Input object. The SUM output of the Physical Input is cabled into a keyboard named Input Notes. The keyboard is cabled to a monitor named Input View. That monitor is cabled into the Sequencer Input. Make sure that those objects are properly connected. If a cable is missing, cable the objects according to the picture.

In this project file, you can see that a cable is missing between the Input View object and the Sequencer Input object. Now, you will reconnect the two objects. To cable objects, click the output triangle at the top right of the source object, and drag the connector to the destination object.

14 Hold down the Input View output triangle and drag the cable onto the Sequencer Input object.

Output triangle

When the proper default cabling is restored, incoming MIDI events should be displayed in the Transport bar on the MIDI Activity display, and you can hear sound when playing notes on your MIDI controller.

 MIDI in display

15 Close the project but don't save it.

Optimizing Hardware Performance

To get the most performance out of your system, you need to understand how Logic uses and balances hardware resources.

The computer consists of three main components:

▶ Random access memory, or RAM

▶ The hard disk

▶ The CPU

The hard disk stores the applications and files. When the computer starts, Mac OS X is loaded from the hard disk into RAM. When an application is opened, it is also loaded into RAM. Then the CPU can process the files as requested by an application.

When a Logic project is opened, the project file is loaded into RAM along with all the samples (including impulse responses used by Space Designer), Apple Loops, audio files set to follow tempo, and plug-ins used in the project. The amount of RAM influences the number of Apple Loops, samples, and audio files set to follow tempo that can be used in a project.

When playback starts, the audio files and samples used by the project are streamed from the hard disk. The hard disk influences how fast the computer starts, how fast applications are opened, and how many simultaneous audio tracks and samples can be played or recorded.

> **NOTE** ▸ By default, the EXS24 mkII sampler loads only the attack section of longer samples. When those samples are played, the rest of the sample is then streamed from the hard disk, and each sample also uses hard disk bandwidth.

The CPU influences the amount of processing power that Logic can use in real time while playing back a project. All plug-in and summing calculations require real-time processing. Certain plug-ins (like Amp Designer or Space Designer) require a lot of processing, while others (like Channel EQ) require very little.

When any of the three main components overload, Logic will stop, or display an alert message, or both. Logic doesn't always know precisely why the problem arises but usually tries to point you toward the source.

Other times, Logic will alert you to a problem without giving you any hint as to the source. For example, a loss of synchronization between audio and MIDI can be triggered by many events, including too much stress being placed on the hard drive or the CPU.

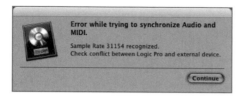

When you have a problem or feel Logic's performance is sluggish, monitor the CPU and HD (hard drive) meters in the Transport bar. Once you know which component is responsible, you can take the necessary measures to fix or work around the issue.

Optimizing CPU Resources

When the CPU meter goes into the red, it indicates that you are reaching the limits of the computer's processing power. Effects and software instrument plug-ins all use processing power, some more than others. With a little experience, you will get a sense of which plug-ins need the most processing power. Try to locate the more demanding channel strips on the Mixer, and freeze their corresponding tracks. Freezing a track bounces it to an audio file, thereby eliminating all the real-time CPU calculations needed by the software instrument and effects plug-ins on that track.

When all the calculations required by a project cannot be processed in real time, the CPU overloads and you usually get the following message:

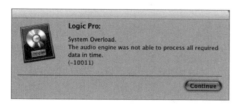

When you get this alert or another indication that you might be reaching the limits of the CPU, look at the CPU load meter.

If the meter goes into the red, it's time to freeze some tracks.

TIP ▶ You can double-click the CPU and HD meter to open a more detailed meter in a floating window.

1   Open **11 New Day**.

2   Control-click a track header and choose Freeze from the pop-up menu.

The track headers display the Freeze button.

3   Click the Freeze buttons for the tracks you want to bounce to an audio file.

The buttons turn green, indicating that those tracks will be frozen.

When deciding which tracks to freeze, find the tracks that include the most CPU-intensive plug-ins and that you don't intend to tweak any further, at least for now. Plug-in settings cannot be modified on a frozen track.

4   Adjust the project end marker's position to bar 23.

Project start marker   Project end marker

The project end marker is in the Bar ruler. When freezing, Logic bounces individual tracks between the project start and end markers. If your project end marker is located beyond the actual end of the project, you are wasting precious time bouncing silence!

NOTE ▶ Logic bounces freeze files in 32-bit floating point, which is the internal resolution of its audio engine. The audio quality of the freeze file is exactly the same as for the unfrozen track.

5   Press the Spacebar.

Logic starts the freezing process and displays a progress indicator. Wait until the process ends.

6   Start playback.

The CPU load meter should now be at a lower level. Note that the HD load meter will reach a little higher, since Logic has to stream the freeze files from the hard disk. When a track is frozen, you can't edit the regions on that track, and you can't change the plug-in settings on its channel strip. If you need to access a track's plug-ins or regions, click its freeze button to unfreeze it.

TIP ▶ When no signal is routed to a channel strip, the plug ins on that channel strip have nothing to process and do not use any CPU cycles. You can temporarily relieve the CPU by muting all the regions on a few tracks.

Addressing Unexpected Behaviors

While issues related to signal routing and hardware limitations can be easy to identify, sometimes you may experience unexpected behaviors for no apparent reason. It can be hard to trace the exact cause of those problems; however, you can try a few safe and fast methods that will solve most of them.

First Steps

When facing unexpected behaviors, the first step you should take is to return the system to its normal condition or initial state.

▶ Restart Logic, or

▶ Restart the computer

Initializing Preferences

A common cause of application error is corrupt preferences files. When an application opens, its preferences file is loaded into RAM. When you quit the application, the preferences file is saved to the hard disk. If the application quits unexpectedly or the computer crashes, an application may not properly write the preferences file to the hard disk, which results in a corrupted preferences file. This often is responsible for unexpected application behaviors.

Keep in mind that after initializing your preferences, you will have to reset them manually.

1   From the main menu, choose Logic Pro > Preferences > Initialize All Except Key Commands.

A confirmation alert appears.

2   Click Initialize.

NOTE ▶ You can also delete the preferences files manually from the Finder. Your main preferences file is ~/Library/Preferences/com.apple.logic.pro.plist, and your control surface preferences file is ~/Library/Preferences/com.apple.logic.pro.cs. (Logic Express preferences are named com.apple.logic.express.plist and com.apple.logic.express.cs.)

To avoid manually resetting your preferences every time you troubleshoot, you should make a backup of your preferences file. Locate the file ~/Library/Preferences/com.apple.logic.pro.plist, and copy it to another drive or storage device.

Restoring Preferences

If you have a backup preferences file, and you suspect the current one might be corrupt, you can replace your current file with the backup.

1   Quit Logic.

2   Locate your backup preferences file, and drag it to ~/Library/Preferences/.

A dialog appears, asking if you want to replace the current file with your backup.

3   Click Replace.

4   Open Logic again.

Project File Corruption

When a project file is corrupted, you may experience unexpected behaviors, and some functions may stop working altogether.

When experiencing unexpected behaviors even after restarting and initializing the preferences, open a brand-new template and try to reproduce the problem. If after experimenting for a while you notice that a particular problem or behavior occurs only in a specific project file, chances are the file is corrupt.

Although you won't be able to repair the file, identifying project corruption can help you decide on what direction to take: revert to an earlier backup, rebuild the project by importing the audio and MIDI regions in a new template, or attempt to finish the project with the limited functionality.

Monitoring Problems

Input/output buffers were explained in Lesson 2, "Recording Audio." The smaller their size, the more pressure on the CPU. This generally results in clicks and pops in the monitoring, or in extreme cases a complete loss of monitoring. If you experience monitoring problems, increase the I/O buffer size.

Disabling Audio Drivers at Startup

When Logic freezes at startup, the problem usually lies with the Core Audio engine. Often an incompatible or corrupted third-party plug-in contained in a template or song that opens at startup is the cause of freezing. You can disable the audio drivers at startup by holding down Control immediately after clicking Logic in your Dock. A dialog will open, allowing you to open Logic without launching the Core Audio engine. You can then look at the template or song, uninstantiate any suspicious third-party plug-ins, and re-enable the Core Audio devices in your Audio Preferences window.

When a problem occurs, it can be difficult to decide where to start. In this lesson, you learned typical troubleshooting steps you can take depending on the issue at hand. As you gain more experience and a better understanding of how your system works, you will get faster at diagnosing issues you may have when you work in Logic, and finding a solution to fix them.

Lesson Review

1. When are automatic backups created, and where are they saved?
2. Describe an easy way to have Logic produce an audio signal in Logic when troubleshooting audio output.
3. When you are reaching the limits of your CPU, how can you quickly reduce the load on it?
4. How can you avoid reaching the limits of your hard disk's bandwidth?
5. When a project file isn't receiving incoming MIDI events, even though other project files are, what should you do?
6. How can you determine if your audio interface is causing a playback problem?

Answers

1. Each time you save a project file, Logic moves the previously saved project file into the Project File Backups folder inside the project folder.
2. Preview an Apple Loops file from the Loops Browser.
3. Freeze CPU-intensive tracks.
4. Unfreeze tracks, submix several tracks together, or load audio regions into RAM using Follow Tempo.
5. Open that project file's Environment window and check for proper default Click & Ports layer cabling.
6. Bypass the external audio interface by playing a project through your Mac's built-in audio interface. If the project plays properly, the problem probably lies in the interface.

A

Using External MIDI Devices

Although Logic comes with a wide array of software instruments and supports third-party Audio Units software instruments, sometimes you may want to use Logic to trigger a hardware synthesizer or sampler, or even a software instrument in another software application.

In the following exercises, you will set up hardware instruments so that you can access them from Logic, and use external MIDI tracks to route the MIDI events to a MIDI instrument outside of Logic. You can then record on external MIDI tracks with the same techniques you used to record on software instrument tracks. An external MIDI track can be routed to a hardware MIDI device, a ReWire application (such as Ableton Live or Propellerhead Software's Reason), or to any other MIDI-compatible application on your computer or network.

Configuring MIDI Hardware

Logic can access any device configured in Audio MIDI Setup, a Mac OS X configuration tool. Audio MIDI Setup automatically detects USB or FireWire MIDI devices connected directly to the computer, provided that the necessary drivers have been properly installed. The MIDI synthesizers connected to that MIDI interface would not be detected, however. Setting up those synths in Audio MIDI Setup will allow you to access them by name in Logic, so that you don't have to remember which device is connected to which port on the MIDI interface.

For the purposes of this exercise, you will set up two external synthesizers in Audio MIDI Setup, a Korg Triton and a Yamaha Motif.

1   Open a Finder window.

The Finder is the active application, and its name is displayed to the right of the Apple menu in the main menu bar.

2   Choose Go > Utilities (or press Command-Shift-U).

The Utilities folder opens.

3   Double-click Audio MIDI Setup.

The Audio MIDI Setup utility opens.

4   If you're using Mac OS X Snow Leopard, choose Window > Show MIDI Window. If you're using Mac OS X 10.5.x or earlier, click the MIDI Devices tab at the top of the Audio MIDI Setup window.

You should see an IAC Driver button, a Network button, and buttons for MIDI devices connected directly to your computer.

NOTE ► If a device is connected to your computer but does not appear in Audio MIDI Setup, make sure you properly install the most recent driver for that device.

You can double-click the Network button to create network MIDI ports. Network MIDI ports are virtual MIDI cables that allow you to connect applications over a wired or wireless network. Existing network MIDI ports are displayed in Logic's Library when an external MIDI track is selected.

You can double-click the IAC Driver button to create Inter-Application Communication buses. IAC buses are virtual MIDI cables that allow you to connect applications on your computer. Existing IAC buses are displayed in Logic's Library when an external MIDI track is selected.

5   Click the Add Device button.

A new external device is created.

6   Click the Add Device button again.

A second new external device is created.

7   Double-click the first new device.

A Properties floating window appears.

8   In the Device Name field, enter *Triton*.

9   Click Apply.

The device is renamed.

10 Close the Triton Properties window.

11 In the Audio MIDI Setup window, double-click the second device.

A new Properties floating window appears.

12 In the Device Name field, enter *Motif*.

13 Click Apply and close the Properties window.

Now you need to identify the physical connections between the MIDI interface and the synthesizers in Audio MIDI Setup. Since Logic routes all incoming MIDI events to the record-enabled track, you only need to route outgoing MIDI events. For this exercise, let's assume you have an MT4 MIDI interface with the following physical MIDI connections:

▶ MT4 MIDI Out port 1 connects to the Triton MIDI In port.

▶ MT4 MIDI Out port 2 connects to the Motif MIDI In port.

You will now enter these connections in Audio MIDI Setup.

14 Click the MIDI Out port 1 of the MT4 interface, and drag the cable to the MIDI In port of the Triton.

15 Click the MIDI Out port 2 of the MT4 interface, and connect it to the MIDI In port of the Motif.

16 Choose Audio MIDI Setup > Quit Audio MIDI Setup (or press Command-Q).

Now Audio MIDI Setup knows which MIDI Out port is connected to which device, and Logic's Library will display *Triton* and *Motif* instead of MT4 Port 1 and MT4 Port 2.

> **MORE INFO** ▶ If you want to record or monitor the audio outputs from the hardware synthesizers in Logic, you also need to connect the synthesizers' audio outputs to audio inputs on your audio interface. In Logic, record-enable an audio track to record or monitor those audio inputs (make sure you have chosen the desired setting in the input slot of the I/O section on the audio track's channel strip).

Routing External MIDI Tracks

When using external MIDI tracks, you use the Library to route the MIDI events on the track. All the devices set up in Audio MIDI Setup are displayed in the Library (including IAC buses and network MIDI ports). All the ReWire applications installed on your computer are also displayed in the Library.

In the next exercise, you will use the Library to choose a destination for an external MIDI track.

1   Open a new Empty Project template, and in the New Tracks dialog, leave 1 in the Number field, choose External MIDI as the Type, select the Open Library checkbox, and click Create.

A new external MIDI track is created.

The Library opens and displays available MIDI destinations for the external MIDI track (the available destinations depend on your studio setup).

General MIDI Device

MIDI Devices configured in Audio MIDI Setup

▶ The GM (General MIDI) device is a multi-timbral instrument that always sends to all existing MIDI Out ports. A *multi-timbral* instrument is one that can respond to more than one MIDI channel at a time to play several sounds (more commonly called *patches* or *programs*) simultaneously. A single MIDI port can transmit 16 MIDI channels simultaneously, and each MIDI channel can play one program. The 16 MIDI channels of the GM device are displayed in the right column.

▶ The Motif and Triton MIDI synthesizers you configured in Audio MIDI Setup are displayed in the list of available MIDI destinations.

▶ All ReWire applications on your computer are displayed in the Library. You can double-click a ReWire application in the left column to open it, and all available ReWire instruments will be displayed in the right column.

You will now assign the selected track to MIDI channel 1 of the Motif synthesizer.

MORE INFO ▶ If you do not have an external MIDI synthesizer or sampler, in the next step choose GM Device instead of Motif, then follow along with the steps, but keep in mind that, since no external instrument is connected, you won't hear any sound.

2 In the Library, click Motif.

3 In the right column, click Channel 1.

The track is assigned to MIDI channel 1 of the Motif. Any MIDI events on that track will be routed to that destination. While the track is record-enabled, any incoming MIDI events will be routed to the track, and from the track to MIDI channel 1 of the Motif.

The track header displays the name of the program or patch currently used on that track's MIDI Channel.

In the Inspector, the Arrange channel strip appears unlike the audio and software instrument channel strips. Since the external MIDI channel strip generates MIDI events, it does not have processing plug-in inserts or audio routing settings.

External MIDI channel strip

The volume fader and the knobs on the external MIDI channel strip send MIDI continuous controller events to the external MIDI instrument, allowing you to remotely control the external instrument's volume, pan position, reverberation, and chorus of the program on that MIDI channel.

Choosing a Program Remotely

Logic allows you to remotely choose a program or patch on your external MIDI device. This avoids interrupting your workflow to choose the program on the MIDI device itself and also allows you to save the programs used on each track in your project.

1   On the track header, double-click the track name.

The Motif's Multi Instrument window appears.

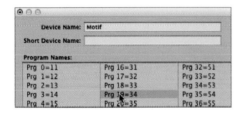

NOTE ▸ The GM Device Multi-Instrument window contains the General MIDI program names.

2   Click a program name.

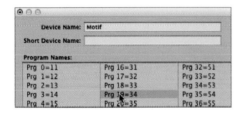

The corresponding program-change MIDI event is sent to the external MIDI instrument. (You can see the program-change event on the Transport bar's MIDI Out display.) When you play your MIDI keyboard, you can hear the new sound.

Most instruments have more than 128 programs. To access additional programs, you need to switch to another bank of programs.

3   Click the Bank menu, and choose 1.

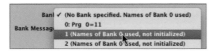

An alert message appears, asking if you want to initialize the bank.

4   Click Initialize.

Choosing a bank in the Bank menu sends a bank select MIDI event to the external MIDI instrument, instructing it to switch to the new bank. If your instrument does not react to the bank select event, try choosing another type of bank select event for that instrument in the Bank Message menu (right below the Bank menu).

You can name all the programs for your instruments and save the project as a template so that you can choose programs by name, rather than by number.

5   Double-click the first program number.

A text field appears.

6   Type a name for the first program, and press Enter.

The text field focus moves to the second program, ready to be renamed.

TIP You could repeat this process until you've named all the programs in all the banks, but that could take a while! To save time, search a website devoted to Logic users for a Logic template where the desired hardware instruments have already been configured.

If you can't find a Logic template, look online for an electronic voice list, usually in PDF format (sometimes part of the electronic manual). Start your search by searching the instrument manufacturer's website. Copy and paste the list of program names for your MIDI device into a text editor (such as Apple TextEdit) and edit it so that you have a list of 128 names, one name per line. Select all 128 names and choose Edit > Copy. In Logic, at the upper right of the Multi-Instrument window, click Options and choose Paste All Names. Repeat the process for each program bank.

When you are done entering program names for all the instruments, save that project as a template. Program names are saved in the project file, not as a general preference; so, unless you save the project, all your program names will be lost.

7 Choose File > Save As Template.

A Save As dialog appears, and the location is already set to the Project Templates folder. All you need to do is name your template.

8 Name and save your template.

Your new template is available in the Templates dialog that appears when choosing File > New, in the My Templates collection folder.

B

Keyboard Shortcuts (U.S. Preset)

Transport Controls

Keyboard Shortcut	Action
R	Record
Command-Option-Control-R	Capture as recording
Shift-R	Toggle record (for punching on the fly)
Enter	Stop recording or playback and go to last locate position
Shift-Enter	Move playhead to start of selected region or event and begin playback
Control-Home	Move playhead to start of first selected region or event in active window
Return	Stop (or return to beginning when stopped)
Option-Return	Pause playback
Return-Return	Stop recording or playback and go to beginning
Shift-Return	Play
Shift-Control-Return	Play from left window edge
Spacebar	Play/stop
/ (on main keypad)	Open "Go to Position" dialog

Transport Controls *(continued)*

Keyboard Shortcut	Action
< (left angle bracket)	Rewind
Shift-<	Fast Rewind
> (right angle bracket)	Forward
Shift->	Fast Forward

Zooming

Keyboard Shortcut	Action
Z	Toggle Zoom to Fit Selection or All Content
Option–Control–Down Arrow	Zoom in vertically
Option–Control–Left Arrow	Zoom out horizontally
Option–Control–Right Arrow	Zoom in horizontally
Option–Control–Up Arrow	Zoom out vertically
Control–Option-drag	Zoom tool

Tools

Keyboard Shortcut	Action
Control–Option–any tool	Turn current tool into Zoom tool
Control–Shift–drag	Apply fade
Control-click	Opens shortcut menu

Tools *(continued)*

Keyboard Shortcut	Action
Esc	Opens Tool menu at pointer position
Esc-Esc	Make Pointer tool the default (Left-click) tool
Option–drag Pointer tool	Copy
Shift-Option-drag	Adjusts parameter to same value
Shift–Pencil tool	Import audio file at clicked location
Option–click Crossfade tool	Delete crossfade
Option–Resize tool	Time-stretch region when resizing

Channel Strip, Track, and Region Operations

Keyboard Shortcut	Action
Command-A	Select all
Command-Shift-A	Deselect all
Control-C	Crop regions outside marquee selection
Command-Shift-F	Pack selected regions into a folder
Command-G	Toggle group clutch
L	Toggle looping of selected region
Control-L	Convert loop to a real copy of selected original region
M	Mute/unmute selected notes, regions, or folders
Control-M	Mute/unmute selected Arrange area track
Command-Option-N	Create new tracks

Channel Strip, Track, and Region Operations *(continued)*

Keyboard Shortcut	Action
Shift-Option-N	Assign name of selected track to its regions
Command-R	Repeat regions/events
S	Toggle Solo mode
Command-S	Save
Command-Option-S	Save selection as new audio file (Sample Editor)
Option-S	Lock the Solo status of selected regions
Command-Option-T	Match project tempo to that of selected audio region, using beat detection
Command-Shift-U	Unpack regions from folder
Shift-U	Select unused (Audio Bin)
Command-Z	Undo
Command-Shift-Z	Redo
= (equal sign)	Set locators by regions/events/marquee
Shift-=	Set locators by rounded regions/events/marquee
Shift-[(left bracket)	Load previous channel strip setting
Shift-] (right bracket)	Load next channel strip setting
Command-click Track Mute button	Mute/unmute all tracks
Option-click fader or knob	Reset parameter to default value
Option-click Insert	Bypass plug-in

Views

Keyboard Shortcut	Action
B	Show/hide Audio Bin
Option-C	Open Color palette
E	Show/hide Event List
G	Show/hide global tracks
Option-G	Open Configure Global Tracks dialog
Control-H	Hide current track and select next track
Shift-Control-H	Unhide (show) all tracks
I	Show/hide Inspector
Command-K	Open controller assignment window
Option-K	Open Key Commands window
Command-Shift-L	Lock/unlock current screenset
N	Show/hide Score Editor
Command-Option-O	Open QuickTime movie
P	Show/hide Piano Roll Editor
Option-P	Open project settings
X	Show/hide Mixer
Control-X	Open Strip Silence window
Y	Show/hide Hyper Editor
V	Show/hide all open plug-in windows
Option-V	Open Video project settings

Views *(continued)*

Keyboard Shortcut	Action
Command-Option-W	Close active project
Option-Y	Open Synchronization project settings
Control-Z	Auto track zoom
Option-Z	Open Undo History window
Caps Lock	Use computer keyboard as virtual MIDI keyboard
Tab	Cycle key focus forward through Arrange window areas
Shift-Tab	Cycle key focus backward through Arrange window areas
Command-1	Open Arrange window
Command-2	Open Mixer
Command-3	Open Score Editor
Command-4	Open Transform window
Command-5	Open Hyper Editor
Command-6	Open Piano Roll Editor
Command-8	Open Environment window
Double-click MIDI region	Open default editor (in Arrange area)

Automation

Keyboard Shortcut	Action
A	Show/hide track automation
Command-Option-Control-A	Toggle Automation Quick Access

Automation *(continued)*

Keyboard Shortcut	Action
Option-A	Open Automation preferences
Command-Shift-Control-O	Turn automation mode off for all tracks
Command-Shift-Control-R	Set automation mode to Read for all tracks
Command-Shift-Control-T	Set automation mode to Touch for all tracks
Command-Shift-Control-L	Set automation mode to Latch for all tracks
Command-Control-Backspace	Delete currently visible automation data of current track
Command-Shift-Control-Backspace	Delete all automation data of current track
Shift–drag Pointer tool	Select nodes while dragging around them in automation track
Shift–Control–Pointer tool	Adjust curves in automation track

Finder

Keyboard Shortcut	Action
Command-H	Hide active application
Command-Option-H	Hide other applications
Command-Tab	Switch to next application
Command-Shift-Tab	Switch to previous application

Glossary

5.1 A common surround sound format, typically comprising five full-frequency speakers, which are fed by five independent channels, plus one dedicated low-frequency subwoofer.

aftertouch MIDI data type generated by pressure on keys after they have been struck. Aftertouch is also known as *pressure*.

AIFF Audio Interchange File Format. A cross-platform file format supported by a large number of digital video and audio editing applications. AIFF audio can use a variety of bit depths, but the two most common are 16-bit and 24-bit.

alias A region in the Arrange area that mirrors a MIDI region someplace else. You cannot edit an alias, only a real region, but any change to the region will be reflected in the alias. To create an alias, Shift-Option-drag the original MIDI region to a new location.

anchor A temporal reference point, or the point that Logic Pro uses to snap a region to the Arrange area's time grid. In the Audio Bin window and Sample Editor, the anchor is represented by a small triangle under the starting point of a region.

Apple Loops An audio file format in which recurring rhythmic musical elements or elements suitable for repetition are recorded. Apple Loops have tags that allow Logic to perform time stretching and pitch shifting. These tags also allow you to locate files by instrument, genre, or mood in the Loop Browser.

arming Enabling a track to be recorded.

Arrange area The primary working space of the application, where audio and MIDI regions are edited and moved to create a project.

Arrange window The primary working window of the application. It shows the Arrange area (see above) and can incorporate all other working areas and editors.

Audio Bin A window, or a tab in the Media area, used to add audio files from your hard disk to your project. You can use the Audio Bin to manage the project's audio files.

audio file Any digital audio recording stored on your hard disk. The default storage format for audio files in Logic Pro is AIFF, but you can store audio files in the CAF, Sound Designer II, and WAV formats as well.

audio interface A device that provides audio inputs and outputs to your computer.

audio region An area of an audio file registered in the Audio Bin for use in the project. It can be placed on audio tracks in the Arrange area, just as a MIDI region can be placed on MIDI tracks. Audio regions are pointers to portions of audio files.

audio track A track in the Arrange area used for the playback, recording, and editing of audio regions.

automation The ability to record, edit, and play back the movements of all knobs and switches, including volume faders and pan, EQ, and aux send controls.

Automation Quick Access A Logic Pro feature that assigns a slider or knob on your hardware MIDI controller keyboard to modify track automation data.

aux An auxiliary channel strip, either mono or stereo, in the Mixer.

B

bar A measure of music, containing a specified number of beats, that establishes the rhythmic structure of the composition.

Bar ruler The timeline that runs the length of the project, divided into bars, beats, and even finer divisions. It contains the playhead, the cycle and autopunch areas, and markers. It is found at the top of the Arrange area, Piano Roll Editor, Hyper Editor, and Score Editor.

bit depth The resolution (number of 0s and 1s) of a digital audio sample, which influences the dynamic range of a digital audio recording.

bounce To combine several tracks of audio into one file.

bus A virtual audio cable to route audio between channel strips, for processing or submixing tasks.

bypass To temporarily deactivate a plug-in.

Caps Lock Keyboard A small MIDI controller on your screen, activated by pressing the Caps Lock key on your computer keyboard.

C

Catch A mode that continuously updates the contents of a window to show the position of the playhead. The Catch button shows a person running.

CD Audio Short for Compact Disc–Audio; the current standard for stereo music CDs is a 44.1 kHz sampling rate and a 16-bit depth.

channel A path used to transport a signal.

channel strip A virtual representation of a channel strip on a mixing console. Each channel strip contains a number of controls, such as Solo and Mute buttons, a volume fader, a pan/balance knob, Input and Output slots, Send slots, and Insert slots.

channel strip settings A combination of plug-ins and their settings that make a certain sound.

clip To feed too much signal through a channel, producing a distorted sound. Audio channel strips have a clip detector.

continuous control number (cc#) The number assigned by the MIDI specification regarding audio events or software functions such as volume, modulation, or sustain.

Core Audio The standardized audio driver for a computer running Mac OS X 10.2 or higher. Allows the connection of all audio interfaces that are Core Audio compatible.

Core MIDI The standardized MIDI driver for a computer running Mac OS X 10.2 or higher. Allows the connection of all MIDI devices that are Core MIDI compatible.

cross-fade To bring the volume of one audio file up while simultaneously lowering the volume of another file in a smooth transition.

Crossfade tool One of the tools in the Arrange area Tool menu. The tool creates a cross-fade when you drag across a section where two audio regions meet. You can also drag the tool over the beginning or end of a region to create a fade-in or fade-out, respectively.

Cycle mode A mode in Logic Pro in which you can repeat a section of a project. To turn on Cycle mode, click the Cycle button in the Transport bar or click the top part of the Bar rule (on the gray locators stripe). Two locators define a cycle region.

D

dB Short for *decibels*, a measurement that relates the relative change in the volume of audio.

digital audio workstation (DAW) A computer that records, mixes, and produces audio files.

Digital Factory A suite of digital signal processors in the Sample Editor. It can time-compress or time-stretch an audio region, change its pitch, add groove or swing to a machinelike audio loop, or alter a sampling rate. The Digital Factory functions are destructive, permanently changing the source audio file.

digital signal processing (DSP) In Logic Pro, the mathematical process of manipulating digital information to modify sound. An example is the Insert slot of a channel strip, which assigns DSP effects such as dynamic range compression and delay to a channel's sound.

dithering A process of reducing an audio signal from a higher-bit resolution to a lower one.

driver A software program that allows your computer to communicate with another piece of hardware.

editor In Logic Pro, one of a multitude of editors to help you compose music. All of them alter the raw input in some way. The primary MIDI editors are the Piano Roll, the Hyper and Score editors, and the Event List. You can edit audio regions in the Arrange area, Audio Bin window, and Sample Editor.

E

Environment A window that graphically reflects the relationship between hardware devices outside your computer and virtual devices within your computer.

Environment layer A place to organize the objects in the Environment for easy access. As a general rule, objects of the same type are usually placed on the same layer.

Eraser tool A tool for deleting items. When you click a selected item, all other currently selected items are also deleted.

event A MIDI message. The main events in Logic Pro are note, control-change, pitch bend, aftertouch, and SysEx events. MIDI events can be edited in a number of ways.

Event List A list of events and regions that gives you access to all recorded event data. Thus, you can directly manipulate events and regions and make precise alterations.

F

fader Generally thought of as a volume control found on audio channels.

Finger tool A tool that looks like a hand with an extended index finger. The selection tool changes from the Pointer tool to the Finger tool to enable you to manipulate events or change window parameters. Different mouse and key commands activate the Finger tool in different windows.

floating A term that describes a window that's always visible on your desktop.

folder A container in Logic Pro's Arrange area for MIDI regions, audio regions, or other folders.

Freeze function A function that bounces a track and its plug-ins into an audio file and then plays back that audio file instead of the original one, saving your computer's processing power.

G

General MIDI (GM) A specification designed to increase compatibility between MIDI devices. A musical sequence generated by a GM instrument should trigger the same sounds on any other GM synthesizer or sound module.

global Tempo track A track in which you can view and edit all the tempo changes of a project. The track displays tempo changes as nodes.

global Video track A track displaying frames of a QuickTime movie as "thumbnails" that are perfectly synchronized with the music, making it ideal for film scoring. Cuts in the movie can be automatically detected and marked.

Glue tool A dedicated tool for merging regions or events.

grid Vertical lines used to map the positions of measures, beats, and sub-beats in various editors.

H

Hand tool A tool that appears when you click and hold an event or region with the Pointer tool. It is used to move regions or events in the editors.

headroom Refers to the available dynamic range before clipping, or distortion, occurs.

help tag A small yellow text window that appears when the pointer is placed over an interface element, indicating its name, value, or other information.

Hyper Draw A function that lets you create and edit MIDI CC automation in a region by graphically inserting a set of points or nodes, which are automatically connected.

Hyper Editor A MIDI editor, used mainly for creating and editing drum sequences and control-change data.

hyper set A layer in the Hyper Editor containing a user-defined collection of MIDI events

input filtering Preventing MIDI information such as pitch bend or aftertouch events from reaching a track. The Input Filter tab is in the MIDI Project Settings window.

Insert slot A slot on channel strips where you can insert an audio processing plug-in.

Inspector The pane at the left edge of the Arrange area and editors containing the Parameter boxes and Arrange channel strips of the selected track.

instrument object An object in Logic Pro's Environment that represents a physical or virtual device that reacts to MIDI information.

I/O buffer size How big a bite a computer tries to chew at one time when working with audio. Larger buffers give you more CPU power, but also more latency when monitoring record-enabled tracks. The buffer size is set in the Audio Hardware & Drivers preferences.

I

key command An instruction to Logic Pro that triggers an action, done by pressing a key or a combination of keys. All of Logic Pro's main functions can be activated by key commands.

K

L   **latency** The delay between, say, playing your keyboard and hearing the sound. One factor contributing to latency is the I/O buffer size.

Link mode A mode that determines the relationship of one window to another. Clicking the Link button toggles Link mode.

local menu bar The place where the functions of the currently active window can be found.

locators The two positions defining the edges of the cycle area. The locators are displayed in the Transport bar, directly to the right of the playhead position.

Loop A region parameter allowing a region to repeat.

M   **marker** Used for indicating and quickly moving to sections of your project.

Marquee tool A crosshair-shaped tool in the Arrange area with which you can select and edit regions, or even portions of regions.

menu bar The bar extending along the top of the computer screen that gives options for global functions such as opening windows and saving and loading projects. The local menu bars in the individual editing windows provide access to most of Logic Pro's functions.

metronome In Logic Pro, a component that produces a sound measuring the beat. It can be set with a button in the Transport bar.

MIDI Musical Instrument Digital Interface. It's an industry standard that allows devices like synthesizers and computers to communicate with each other. It controls a musical note's pitch, length, and volume, among other characteristics.

MIDI channel A conduit for MIDI data. MIDI data flows through MIDI ports in channels, and up to 16 MIDI channels can pass through each port at the same time.

MIDI region Data container for MIDI events, shown in the Arrange area as a named horizontal beam. It does not contain sounds, but rather contains MIDI events that tell a synthesizer how to produce sounds. In earlier Logic versions, MIDI regions were called *sequences*.

Mixer A virtual mixing console used to position Logic Pro's tracks. It mirrors the number and order of tracks in the Arrange area. In the Mixer you can also change a channel strip's volume or panorama (pan) position, insert DSP effects, or mute and solo channels.

mixing The process of shaping the overall sound of a project by adjusting the volume levels and pan positions, adding EQ and other effects, and using automation to dynamically alter aspects of the project.

MP3 A digital coding standard used to compress audio files and distribute them over the Internet.

multi-instrument An object in the Environment that represents a multitimbral device.

multitimbral Describes an instrument or other device that can use several MIDI channels simultaneously.

mute To silence the output of a region or track.

Mute tool A tool that stops a region or event from playing when you click with it.

nodes Dots in Hyper Draw and automation tracks that mark the positions where data manipulation begins or ends. Occasionally referred to as *points*. **N**

nondestructive Said of an audio editor that does not change the source audio files in the course of editing.

object In Logic Pro, a general term that refers to the graphical representations of elements in the Environment. Each connection between Logic Pro and the studio's MIDI devices is represented by an object, and objects can be used to create and process MIDI and audio data. **O**

O   **Object Parameter box** A box that displays the properties of an object in the Environment.

output channel strip Channel strip type in the Mixer that controls the output level and pan or balance for each physical output of your audio interface.

P   **PCM** Pulse-code modulated audio. This is simply uncompressed digital audio, including AIFF, WAV, and SDII files.

Pencil tool A tool used to draw various types of information in an editor.

Piano Roll Editor The main MIDI editor in Logic Pro. It displays note events as horizontal beams. Events can be cut, copied, moved, and resized in a similar fashion to regions in the Arrange area.

playhead A vertical white line in the Arrange area and in other horizontal time-based windows that indicates where you are in a project. In Play mode, the project begins playing from the playhead position. You can position the playhead with the mouse, by clicking the Bar ruler, or by entering bar numbers in a dialog.

plug-in A small software application that adds functions to a main program (in this case, Logic Pro). Logic Pro's plug-ins are typically audio effects processors.

Pointer tool The default selection tool, shaped like an arrow. It is in every window's toolbox.

preferences User settings that are applied to all Logic Pro projects.

programs Synthesizer sounds.

proxy movie A low-resolution and tightly compressed version of a high-resolution movie that places less strain on your computer as you score.

punch in, punch out A technique that allows you to interrupt playback and record audio as the sound is playing. It can be automated in Logic Pro.

quantize To correct the position of notes so that they conform to a specific time grid.

Q

QuickTime Apple's cross-platform standard for digitized media. You can run QuickTime movies in a Logic Pro window or on a global Video track, in sync with the project. Whenever you move the playhead, the video follows, and vice versa.

region A rectangular beam that represents a container for audio or MIDI data. Regions can be found in the tracks of the Arrange area. There are three types: audio regions, MIDI regions, and folders.

R

Region Parameter box A pane in the upper left corner of the Arrange window, used to nondestructively set the individual regions' playback parameters, including quantization, transposition, velocity, and delay. These parameters do not alter the stored data. Rather, they affect how the events are played back.

Replace mode An operating state you can activate in the Transport bar. The Replace button is next to the Cycle and Autodrop buttons. In Replace mode, newly recorded information takes the place of the old information.

sample accurate Describes editors (such as the Sample Editor or Arrange area) that display or allow you to edit individual samples in an audio region.

S

Sample Editor An editor in Logic Pro where stereo or mono audio files are destructively cut, reversed, shortened, changed in gain, and processed in a number of other ways. The Sample Editor allows sample-accurate editing of an audio file.

sampling rate Refers to the number of times per second a digital audio file is sampled. When audio comes in through your sound card, analog-to-digital converters sample the signal's voltage level. Logic Pro can record and edit audio at sampling rates ranging from 44.1 kHz (44,100 times per second) to 192 kHz.

Scissors tool A tool with which you divide regions. It offers different options for dividing audio regions from those for MIDI regions.

Score Editor A MIDI editor that displays notes in standard musical notation.

screenset An onscreen layout of windows that you can save. Each window retains its position, size, and zoom settings.

Scroll in Play A function similar to the Catch function, but instead of the playhead's playing across the Arrange area's regions, the regions scroll past a stationary playhead, as a tape would.

scrubbing Moving the pointer back and forth (in a scrubbing motion) while playing back an audio region to locate a specific section.

send An output on an audio channel that sends a controlled amount of a channel's sound through a bus to another audio channel strip.

sequencer A computer application that allows you to record both digital audio and MIDI data, and blend the sounds together in a software mixing console.

Shuffle A drag mode that causes a region to shuffle up to the region immediately to its left or right, depending on the Shuffle mode selected. This ensures that one region plays smoothly into the next with no drop in the track's audio.

SMPTE Society of Motion Picture and Television Engineers. These folks set up a synchronization system that divides time into hours, minutes, seconds, frames, and subframes.

software instrument The software counterpart to a hardware sampler or synthesizer module, or an acoustic sound source such as a drum kit or guitar. The sounds generated by software instruments are calculated by the computer CPU and played via the audio interface outputs. Often called *soft synths* or *soft samplers*.

solo A way to temporarily allow you to hear one or more selected tracks, events, or regions without hearing others that aren't soloed.

Solo tool A tool that enables you to listen to selected events or regions by themselves (click and hold the event or region to do so).

Standard MIDI file A common file type that almost any MIDI sequencer can read. In Logic Pro, you can export selected MIDI regions as Standard MIDI files.

step-input To record notes one step at a time in a MIDI region.

synthesizer A hardware or software device used to generate sounds. Logic Pro features several software synthesizers, including the EVOC 20 PolySynth, EFM1, ES E ES M, ES P, ES1, ES2, EVB3, EVD6, and EVP88.

SysEx System Exclusive data.

template An project file that is preconfigured with a set of Arrange area tracks designed for a specific purpose, such as mastering, 24-track recording, or surround mixing.

T

tempo The speed at which a piece of music is played, measured in beats per minute. You can create and edit tempo changes in the global Tempo track.

Text tool A tool for naming audio and MIDI regions.

time signature Two numerals separated by a slash that appear at the beginning of a project. Common time signatures are 4/4 and 2/4. The first number denotes the number of beats in a measure, or bar. The second number denotes a unit of time for each beat. With a 2/4 signature, each bar has two beats, and each beat is a quarter note long.

time stretch To change the length of an audio region without changing its pitch. You can do this in the Arrange area or Sample Editor.

Toolbar The top of the Arrange window features the Toolbar, which is used to access or hide certain onscreen areas, such as the Media or Lists area or the Inspector. It also contains a number of buttons for key functions. You may freely customize the Toolbar to meet your needs.

Tool menus Available in the local menu bar of a window, the Tool menus contain tools for editing, zooming, cropping, and otherwise manipulating items in the window.

track A row in the Arrange area that contains a collection of MIDI or audio regions that can be played back. Each track has a specified destination where the data will go.

track automation Used for programming control changes that are not necessarily tied to a specific region, such as a volume fade or a cutoff sweep. The track automation system allows you to quickly find and automate any plug-in parameter. It has its own recording modes, which function independently of Logic Pro's other recording features.

track list A list to the left of the Arrange area that displays the channel strips assigned to various tracks, as well as the track Mute, Solo, and other buttons.

Transform window An editor used to select and modify various aspects of MIDI events according to user-defined parameters.

Transport bar An area at the bottom of the Arrange window that holds buttons used to control Logic Pro's playback and recording functions. Several buttons (Record, Pause, Play, Stop, Rewind, Forward) work the same way as the control buttons on a cassette deck or recordable audio CD player.

V

velocity The speed at which a MIDI note is struck.

virtual instrument A software element that mimics a traditional hardware sound module.

W

WAV, WAVE The primary audio file format used by Windows-compatible computers. In Logic Pro, all recorded and bounced WAV files are in Broadcast Wave format.

waveform A visual representation of an audio signal.

zero crossing A point in an audio file where the waveform crosses the zero amplitude axis. If you cut an audio file at a zero crossing, there will be no click at the cut point.

Z

zoom An action that enlarges (zooms in on) or reduces (zooms out from) a viewing area in any window.

Zoom tool A tool that enables you to zoom in on any part of the display. Pressing Option-Control while selecting a part of the window section enlarges the area.

Index

Apple Certification
Fuel your mind.
Reach your potential.

Stand out from the crowd. Differentiate yourself and gain recognition for your expertise by earning Apple Certified Pro status to validate your Logic Pro 9 skills.

This book prepares you to earn Apple Certified Pro—Logic Pro 9 Level One. Level One certification attests to essential operational knowledge of the application. Level Two certification demonstrates mastery of advanced features and a deeper understanding of the application. Take it one step further and earn Master Pro certification in Logic Studio.

Three Steps to Certification

1   Choose your certification path.
    More info: training.apple.com/certification.

2   Select a location:

    Apple Authorized Training Centers (AATCs) offer all exams (Mac OS X, Pro Apps, iLife, iWork, and Xsan). AATC locations: training.apple.com/locations

    Prometric Testing Centers (1-888-275-3926) offer all Mac OS X exams, and the Final Cut Pro Level One exam. Prometric centers: www.prometric.com/apple

3   Register for and take your exam(s).

"Now when I go out to do corporate videos and I let them know that I'm certified, I get job after job after job."

—Chip McAllister, Final Cut Pro Editor and Winner of The Amazing Race 2004

Reasons to Become an Apple Certified Pro

- **Raise your earning potential.** Studies show that certified professionals can earn more than their non-certified peers.

- **Distinguish yourself from others in your industry.** Proven mastery of an application helps you stand out from the crowd.

- **Display your Apple Certification logo.** Each certification provides a logo to display on business cards, resumes and websites.

- **Publicize your Certifications.** Publish your certifications on the Apple Certified Professionals Registry to connect with schools, clients and employers.

Training Options

Apple's comprehensive curriculum addresses your needs, whether you're an IT or creative professional, educator, or service technician. Hands-on training is available through a worldwide network of Apple Authorized Training Centers (AATCs) or in a self-paced format through the Apple Training Series and Apple Pro Training Series. Learn more about Apple's curriculum and find an AATC near you at training.apple.com.

modwheelmood

Sunday Morning session taken from the album *Pearls to Pigs*

www.modwheelmood.com